First published in 1999 by
HORWOOD PUBLISHING LIMITED
International Publishers
Coll House, Westergate, Chichester, West Sussex, PO20 6QL
England

British Library Cataloguing in Publication Data
A catalogue record of this book is available from the British Library

ISBN 1-898563-56-X

Printed in Great Britain by Martins Printing Group, Bodmin, Cornwall

OBJECT-ORIENTED TECHNOLOGY AND COMPUTING SYSTEMS RE-ENGINEERING

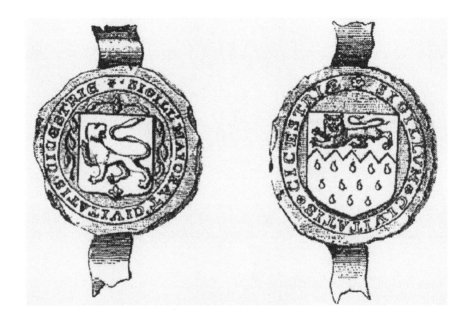

SICILLLUM MAIORAT CIVITATIS CICESTRIE
Mediaeval Seals of Mayors of the Roman and Georgian
city of Chichester in 1502 & 1530. The seals provided
derivative motifs for the Horwood Publishing colophon

Object-Oriented Technology and Computing Systems Re-Engineering

H. Zedan

and

A. Cau

both of
Software Technical Research Laboratory
De Montfort University
Leicester

Horwood Publishing
Chichester

About the Authors

Professor Hussein Zedan has been working for over a decade on formal specification and analysis of (distributed) real-time systems with the long-term aim of building a coherent set of conceptual frameworks and methods for the development and assessment of such systems. Central to this objective is the narrowing of the gap between the theoreticians and the practitioners by promoting and developing tools to assist the development of such systems. He had graduated from Cairo University in 1973 with a BSc in mathematics and added an MSc in 1977 by research on algebraic topology. He then came to England and gained his PhD at Bristol University for research on numerical computation. He is now the Technical Director of the Software Technology Research Laboratory in De Montfort University, Leicester.

Dr Antonio Cau graduated in computer science at Eindhoven University of Technology in Holland where he also obtained an MSc in 1989. In 1995 he obtained his PhD for research on the compositional refinement of reactive systems from Christia Albrechts University at Kiel in Germany. Coming to England, he worked as Research Associate in the Engineeering and Physical Sciences Researc Council on a project dealing with the compositional specification and verification of computing systems. He is now Research Fellow at De Montfort University, Leicester, working alongside Professor Zedan in the Software Technology Research Laboratory.

Table of Contents

Contents

Preface

There are many important and challenging issues in building software systems. Moreover, the complexity of such systems is continuously increasing. This, together with the sobering experience that the difficulty in building such systems grows much faster than their size, makes a disciplined, systematic and rigorous methodology essential for attaining a 'reasonable' level of dependability and trust in these systems. In response to this, an intense research activity has developed resulting in the production of several structured and formal development techniques that have been successfully applied in *forward* engineering such systems. For example, in the field of structured methods, we find SSDM, Yourdon, Jackson, CORE and HOOD whilst formal techniques include assertional methods, temporal logic, process algebra and automata.

Furthermore, object-oriented programming, over the past few years, has been recognised as the best way currently available for structuring software systems. It emphasises grouping together data and operation performed on them, encapsulating the whole behind a clean interface, and organising the resulting entities in a hierarchy based on specialisation in functionalities. In this way, it provides an excellent support for the construction of large scale systems, which can be built cheaply out of reusable components and which can be adapted easily to changing requirements.

To date, object technology has largely been a field of practitioners, who were driven by an intuitive understanding of the important concepts, arising out of the experience of building actual systems. There has been relatively little effort to develop formal theories about these concepts. However, in order for the field to mature, a more formal understanding of the basic concepts is necessary, forming a solid foundation for refinement and further development.

In addition, there exist many software components that are still in use and are in a *legacy* state. With the advent of new architectures, the need to introduce new functionalities and the improvement in design techniques, there is a strong need for *efficient* and *cost-effective* techniques to 're-engineer' these components maintaining its continuity of use. The process of re-engineering a system often requires the construction of a higher level abstraction of the system, a process known as *reverse engineering* ; and the development of a new system starting from its higher level of requirement specification (i.e. *forward engineering*). Recognising the functionality of an existing code is often seen as being the most difficult aspect of the process of re-engineering. To successfully re-engineer a system, we need to identify design decisions, intended use and domain specific details.

In the area of forward engineering, both formal techniques and structured methodologies have been applied. The use of the former in industry is not as widespread as the later but, where they have been applied, the evidence is somewhat encouraging. Recently there have been a healthy activity in integrating both techniques (for example, Yourdon with Z and SSDM with Z) as a means of overcoming some of the limitations of using formal methods generally by industry.

In the domain of reverse engineering, formal methods have also been put forward as a means to extract high level specification of existing software. In practice, these techniques have not been very successful and have hardly gained any support by industry.

This book presents the latest development in Object Technology and their impact in system re-engineering. It is the Proceedings of the Colloquium on Object Technology and System Re-engineering (COTSR) which was held at Christ Church, Oxford University, 6-8 April 1998. The aim of the COTSR is to be a forum that covers all aspects of research and development on object-technology, reuse and system re-engineering.

March 1999   Hussein Zedan
Antonio Cau

1

Toward an Object-Oriented
Design Methodology for Hybrid Systems

Viktor Friesen, André Nordwig

Technische Universität Berlin, FB 13, Sekr. FR 5-6,
Franklinstraße 28/29, D-10587 Berlin, Germany,
{friesen,nordwig}@cs.tu-berlin.de

Matthias Weber

Daimler-Benz AG, Research and Technology,
Alt-Moabit 96a, D-10559 Berlin, Germany,
Weber@DBAG.Bln.DaimlerBenz.Com

Abstract: In this paper, we present an object-oriented approach to the design of hybrid systems using UML^h, a variant of UML for hybrid systems. We introduce the main concepts of UML^h, describe a support tool, and look at their application for the design of a steam-boiler system.

1.1 INTRODUCTION

Hybrid systems are networks of components with discrete and continuous behavior. Typical examples of hybrid systems are physical processes along with their discrete controllers. As such systems are often involved in safety-critical applications, their analysis plays an important role in current research. Three major analysis strategies can be identified: verification, testing, and simulation. Recently, numerous formalisms have been developed for the precise specification of the behavior of hybrid systems; typical examples are Hybrid Automata [2], Extended Duration Calculus [6], and Hybrid CSP [12]. Most of these formalisms are designed to support formal verification. But there is a fundamental problem with the formal verification of hybrid systems: the majority of such systems are not analytically tractable, only for some special types of (in)equation systems do there exist closed solutions and are algorithms known specifying how these solutions can be found. Hence, formal verification can succeed only for a few special types of problems. On the other hand, systematic testing of a hybrid system using physical prototypes or even a real environment is very expensive. Moreover, errors found during unit or integration testing are very expensive to fix. In the case of safety-critical systems, the resources needed for (regression) testing may account for more than 2/3 of the overall development budget. Simulation is therefore an essential analysis method for hybrid systems, especially if it can help to identify errors at an early stage.

The complexity of applications involving hybrid systems continues to grow rapidly. Powerful structuring means are therefore needed to describe such systems. This is one of the reasons why recently proposed simulation languages like Omola [3], Dymola [7], Smile [13], or Modelica [8] all incorporate object-oriented structuring concepts. Another advantage of the object-oriented paradigm is the adequacy of modeling physical components as objects, which leads to model components that are more reusable. The software engineering group at the TU Berlin has proposed an integrated approach to the development of object-oriented simulations of hybrid systems [4]. The main idea behind this approach is to adapt the conventional software-development process to the simulation development. Here we distinguish three main activities: design, model specification, and implementation (Fig. 1.1). The results of these activities are a set of structure diagrams, a precise and complete description of the behavioral model (ZimOO specification), and a model in an executable simulation language (Smile model description), respectively. For the last two phases, we use the object-oriented specification language ZimOO [9] and the simulation language Smile [13]. The interplay between these last two development phases was described in [4].

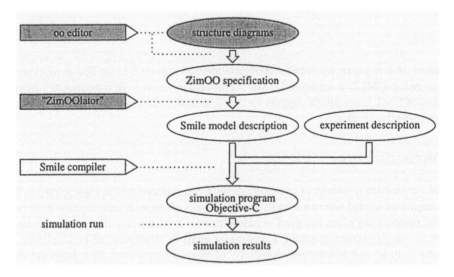

Figure 1.1: Structure of object-oriented simulation development

In this paper, we concentrate on the first phase. We describe an object-oriented notation and an accompanying methodology for the design of hybrid systems, which are based on UML (*U*nified *M*odeling *L*anguage [15]). This notation is called *UML^h(hybrid UML)*. UML is becoming a quasi standard in OOD of discrete systems. It integrates many popular notations of OOD, including class diagrams, use-case diagrams, collaboration diagrams, and statecharts. UML^h is still limited to class diagrams, but it is planned to extend it, adapting and integrating other UML concepts for hybrid systems.

So far, little research has been done on the object-oriented design of hybrid systems, the only relevant work, to our knowledge, being the OHMS approach (*O*bject-oriented *M*ethodology for *H*ybrid *S*ystems) [16]. There are two main differences between OHMS and UML^h. The first is that OHMS uses hybrid automata as a target language. This is a well-known formalism for hybrid-systems specification, but it is not object-oriented. This is not surprising because the main purpose of OHMS is to verify rather than simulate hybrid systems, and a powerful tool (HyTeX) is available for the symbolic verification of linear hybrid automata. As a target language for UML^h we are here using ZimOO, an object-oriented specification language, which was used as a basis for the development of UML^h. However, UML^h could, in principle, also be used in combination with other object-oriented languages for hybrid system modeling. Thus, the full power of object-oriented simulation languages can be exploited in the third development phase. The second difference between the two approaches is related to the class diagrams. OHMS provides only one general notation for a class. It can then be substituted by a hybrid automaton to describe continuous or hybrid behavior, or by a conventional automaton (a finite state machine) when the object represents purely discrete behavior. As different specification means are needed to describe discrete or continuous behavior (a method is really something quite different from a differential equation), we are convinced that — even at the design level — different notations are needed for discrete and continuous classes. UML^h therefore provides notations for three different kinds of classes: discrete, continuous, and hybrid[1].

The paper is organized as follows. In Section 1.2, we introduce the UML^h notation, explaining in particular the different kinds of classes and the relations between them. Section 1.3 introduces the UML^h methodology. A graphical editor for UML^h is described in Section 1.4. In Section, 1.5 we demonstrate the applicability of the proposed approach by designing a small section of a steam-boiler system [1]. Some concluding remarks are given in Section 1.6.

1.2 NOTATION

Object-oriented design languages and methods are becoming increasingly important. They prove very helpful in managing the high complexity of the software-development process. Although practically every OOD book contains numerous descriptive examples urging the reader to view the real world as a collection of objects, a closer look at conventional OOD notations reveals that, while they are very well suited for object-oriented software development, they are only of limited suitability for the development of technical systems with discrete behavior, and they are completely inadequate when dealing with physical systems exhibiting continuous behavior. The reason for this deficiency is quite simple: the object

---

[1]UML^h also supports so-called *abstract* classes, which are a generalization of the three "concrete" kinds of classes. This notion will be explained later.

descriptions are based on two key concepts — *attributes* describing the state of the object, and *methods (operations)* allowing this state to to be updated at certain discrete points in time. It is obvious that neither the continuous behavior of physical components nor the "continuous communication" between such components can be properly described using these concepts.

At the beginning of our project, there was no suitable graphical notation for hybrid systems. A new notation, UML^h, was therefore developed. As mentioned above, this notation is based on the Unified Modeling Language (UML) [15], thus ensuring compatibility with well-known methods. The requirements for such a notation were obtained by abstraction from specification languages for hybrid systems. The results of this analysis are the language concepts discussed in the following subsections.

1.2.1   Classes

To begin with, we should point out some semantic differences between conventional discrete artifacts and hybrid ones. This is important because we use a taxonomy similar to that of discrete models.

As in conventional object-oriented models, the *class* is the key concept of UML^h. A class defines the structure and behavior of a set of *objects*. In hybrid systems, both are found: discrete objects and objects characterized by continuous behavior. We therefore distinguish between discrete, continuous, and hybrid classes. The latter have a special semantics; they model hybrid objects, which serve to combine discrete and continuous objects. Fig. 1.2 shows the graphical representations of these classes.

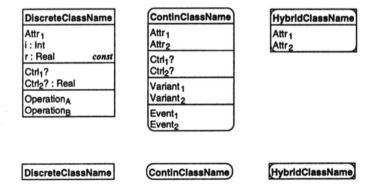

Figure 1.2: Notation of classes (top: expanded, bottom: collapsed)

Nontrivial classes may have large extensions, so it is useful to give a collapsed representation as shown at the bottom of Fig. 1.2.

Discrete classes

can be used to model discrete behavior, which is typically found in controllers. They are represented by rectangles, including a *name* and sets of *attributes*, *control variables*, and *operations*. *Names* are used to identify the classes throughout the model; they have a global scope.

The set of *attributes* together with their appropriate types defines the state space of the class. Each attribute may be complemented by an *extension* **const** or **state**, indicating whether the attribute's value is constant or not. Owing to the communication mechanism between objects, which is discussed later, there is no need for read permissions. Thus, all system objects have read access to the attributes.

The *control variables* are part of the class interface. They provide ports that are used for an asynchronous exchange of values between objects. The receiving "inner" discrete object has only read access to the control variables. Their values are changed by other "outer" objects. Control variables are used for modeling sensoric coupling between continuous and discrete components. It is important to separate control variables from state variables, otherwise external events could potentially violate the class invariant. Control variables are decorated by the suffix "?"; this is influenced by Z and ZimOO, which is based on Z notations. But there is an important semantic difference. As discussed below, there is no need to provide parameters for operations of discrete classes. Instead, the control variables are implicit parameters for all operations of the object. Moreover, as explained below, control variables serve to trigger operations.

Operations change the state of a discrete object by changing the values of its state variables. In our approach, discrete objects are independent parallel components that can be externally controlled by *control variables* only, operations are therefore called from the object itself. As soon as the precondition of an operation is met, it is executed immediately. Obviously, such preconditions depend essentially on the values of the control variables.

Continuous classes

can be used to model components with continuous behavior. The rounded corners of their shapes illustrate the smooth state trajectory. A continuous class is described by a (global) *name* and sets of *attributes*, *control variables*, *variants*, and (internal) *events*.

In continuous classes, *attributes* and *control variables* play the same sort of role as in discrete classes. The attributes define the state space of the class, the control variables being interpreted as ports which can be used to pass information to a continuous object in order to influence its behavior. Thus, control variables can be viewed here as interfaces to actuators.

Variants can be viewed as higher-level states of a continuous class. They should be used to describe a finite partitioning of the set of valuations of the attributes and the control variables. An example of such a partition are the three different submodels (ice, liquid, steam) for water, depending on the temperature.

It is often necessary to model jumps (discontinuities) in the otherwise continuous trajectories of state variables. Thus, *events*, which may effect such jumps, are also provided in the last section of the continuous class shape.

Hybrid classes

are used for coupling discrete and continuous classes. Hybrid objects link control variables to their associated attributes. This requires a referencing scheme for all the objects involved. These object references appear as attributes of hybrid classes.

A hybrid class is represented by a mixed box shape symbolizing its "hybrid" character.

Abstract classes

are intended to support the early stages of design. They are used for structuring the overall system in manageable components. Their introduction can be motivated as follows.

If a system has to be decomposed, there is often uncertainty about the proper classification of the identified artifacts. As a rule, an immediate classification at this stage is impossible because of the lack of knowledge about the nature of associated components. Thus, the identified components are modeled as *abstract classes*. Their only property is a unique *name*.

In later design phases, depending on the specific context, all abstract classes are replaced by one of the three class types mentioned above. The system model is therefore in a consistent valid state throughout the design process.

The diagram below shows the notation of abstract classes. The broken corners indicate the temporary nature of this nonconcrete kind of class.

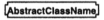

1.2.2 Relations

Relations are used to model the cooperation between identified components. The current version of UML^h supports three kinds of relations: association, inheritance, and aggregation.

Associations

are used to substructure the hybrid system at an early stage. First, a relation between classes can be identified using a very general name. Then, depending on its specific context, this will be implemented as inheritance or aggregation in later design phases. In UML^h, then, associations are temporary design artifacts.

As in conventional object-oriented models, they are represented by a line drawn between the relevant classes. Decorations like cardinalities or names specify their semantics. Currently, only binary associations are used. Fig. 1.3 gives an example in which five valves cooperate with one controller.

Figure 1.3: Association

Inheritance

is used to structure the model hierarchically as in conventional object-oriented models. This kind of relation is illustrated by a long hollow-tipped arrow pointing from the subclass to the superclass (Fig. 1.4).

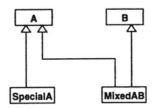

Figure 1.4: Inheritance

It is useful to allow multiple inheritance because e.g. physical properties encapsulated by continuous classes could be reused by inheritance without referencing separate objects to create a new class behavior. Owing to the different semantics of the classes introduced above, only classes of the same kind can have inheritance relations. Because of their abstract nature, only abstract classes can be used in inheritance relations with all other classes.

Aggregation

is used to model containment relations between objects. Though using the same notation (Fig. 1.5) as conventional object-oriented design notations, this relation has a different quality in UML[h]because there is no communication in the sense of operation calls. Aggregation is used instead to symbolize the coupling between corresponding control variables and attributes of the classes involved.

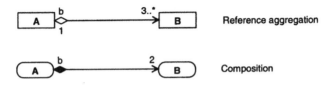

Figure 1.5: Aggregation

In this context, it is necessary to allow both kind of aggregations, i.e. reference aggregation and composition. While discrete and hybrid objects use reference aggregation, continuous classes use composition instead.

1.3 SOME INITIAL ELEMENTS OF A DESIGN METHODOLOGY

Some elementary design rules have been developed based on the experience gained while conducting several case studies. Despite the fact that there is no prescribed order of application, the rules are discussed in an order that is typical for their application.

1.3.1 Refinement by top-down decomposition

First, the system is described by a single abstract class (*root*). Starting with this initial model, the environment of this class is modeled by abstract classes, too. The relations between the identified classes are modeled as associations. A recursive application of this rule terminates at elementary components spanning a tree (Fig. 1.6).

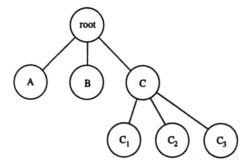

Figure 1.6: Result of substructuring

This rule reflects a typical top-down technique from software engineering: developed structures are refined in a stepwise manner from top to bottom.

1.3.2 Refinement by classification

Since the leaves of the above-developed tree structure cover relatively simple behavior only, they can be specialized according to their characteristics (continuous or discrete). Their associations can also be refined to aggregation or inheritance. By this procedure (which is directed bottom-up), the characteristics of many upper-level components are completely determined by those of lower level ones (Fig. 1.7).

As not all combinations of classes are valid in each relation, this stepwise refinement classifies adjacent classes, too. The following tables specify the valid pairs for both kinds of concrete relations.

"↓ inherits →"	A	H	D	C
Abstract	x	*	*	*
Hybrid	*	x	−	−
Discrete	*	−	x	−
Continuous	*	−	−	x

"↓ aggregates →"	A	H	D	C
Abstract	x	*	+	+
Hybrid	x	x	x	x
Discrete	*	−	x	−
Continuous	*	−	−	x

The symbol "x" denotes all normal valid pairs. Those which enforce further changes are marked with "*". For instance, a hybrid class can inherit from an abstract one. This

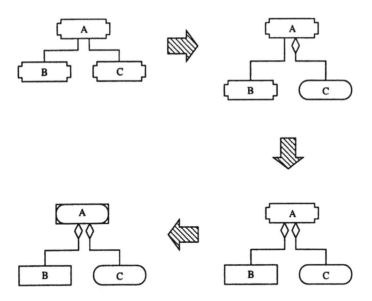

Figure 1.7: Successive-classification procedure

implies that the abstract class will be refined to a hybrid one in later phases. The sign "+" has the same semantics, but there are different possibilities for change, e.g. an abstract class A that aggregates a continuous class B could later be refined to a hybrid or to a continuous class. "−" denotes impossible relations.

1.3.3 Refinement by reuse

The rules discussed above produce a tree-structured model. But one important benefit of object-oriented modeling lies in the possibility it offers of reusing some of the submodels. With the help of the introduced development steps, new subsystems can be developed by reusing existing ones. Frequently used components can be collected in domain-specific libraries. Thus, the goal of each refinement step is to model minimal and universal classes that ideally describe one property of the sub-system.

The single-tree structure generated by the other rules is broken by application of this rule. Since it is possible to identify partial trees in the new structure, there are no restrictions of application of the other rules.

1.3.4 Refinement by "objectification"

Especially in early design phases, relations in hybrid systems are modeled as associations. These are particularly useful between discrete and continuous classes. But there is no possibility to specialize such a relation. This relation therefore has to be "objectified" as a hybrid class aggregating both of the classes involved. For instance, Fig. 1.8 refines the example from Fig. 1.3.

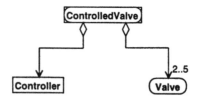

Figure 1.8: Objectified association

1.4 TOOL SUPPORT

To verify the usability of such a notation, it is necessary to provide tools that implement it. A graphical UML[h] editor has therefore been developed by the Software Engineering group at the TU Berlin. Its development follows the object-oriented paradigm. Starting with the identification of basic requirements for the functionalities in the problem domain, we considered the requirements for the application's graphical user interface. Then, the components of the editor were identified and designed. It is worth mentioning that a systematic approach was used here. Beginning with the design of the metamodel, the other components (view concept, controller concept, data management, and advanced functionalities) were developed on a stepwise basis.

Fig. 1.9 shows a screendump of the interface. It depicts the process of refining an association between an abstract class *SteamVessel* and a continuous class *VesselThermDyn* by an aggregation using popup control. This release of the tool supports TeX-export functionalities. Complex expressions can thus be used to describe textual elements, which is very useful in technical and physical applications (e.g. "\real" means "$\mathbb{R}$"). Some frequently used ones have already been translated into an analog representation (e.g. "\pi" is visualized as "π"). Another useful feature is the support for subscripts and indices.

To allow coupling with hybrid specification languages like ZimOO, there is also an export function. This coupling requires advanced features in the editor. For instance, it must be possible to set up constraints for attributes introduced earlier. These ZimOO-specific features were encapsulated in separate popup windows. Another export filter implements the conversion of the runtime metamodel to postscript. To illustrate the tools functionality, all the Figures in this paper and the ZimOO specifications in the next section were produced using it.

Through the introduction of conventional object-oriented classes in the metamodel. it was possible to document the whole development process using the tool itself[2]. This procedure provided a lot of hints for the tool's design. The development process can therefore be seen as an instance of bootstrapping.

To ensure portability and further support, the tool was implemented in Java using the Java Development Kit 1.1 [14]. This decision involves a lot of features. For example, an automated documentation via `javadoc` can be used which produces a hypertext glossary. Furthermore, Java comes with automatic memory management. There is thus no need to explicitly implement it. The lack of performance of the Java virtual machine was made up for by elaborate visualization algorithms.

---

[2]In other words, we have swallowed our own medicine.

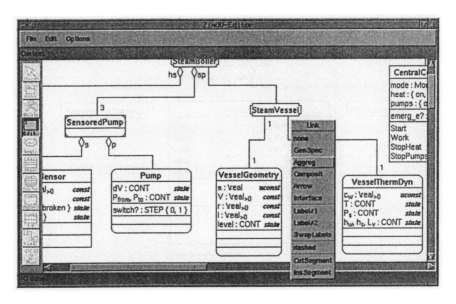

Figure 1.9: Screenshot

1.5 AN EXAMPLE

To demonstrate the applicability of our method, we used UML^h to develop part of the steam-boiler system, a well-known benchmark in the area of real-time systems [1]. This example has already been dealt with in some of our previous papers. In [5], correct control of the steam-boiler system was developed based on the given parameters of the environment. In [10], we showed how these parameters can be determined by simulation (here we already used a loose notation for object-oriented design). In this section, we show how UML^h supports the design of hybrid systems and the transition from design to a formal specification.

At the highest level of abstraction, a steam-boiler system consists of three components: the steam boiler itself, the heat source, and the control unit. We know that the control unit has to be a discrete class, but the three other classes are still abstract.

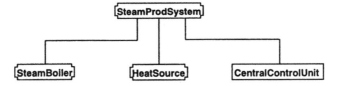

In the next design step, we decided to model the heat source by a continuous class and fix its attributes and model variants (Fig. 1.10). The constants $grad_{on}$ and $grad_{off}$ denote the increase and decrease of the heat power dQ, min and max denoting the minimum and maximum heat power, respectively. The control variables $mode?$ and $switch?$ can be viewed as instructions to the heat source; depending on their values, it switches to one of the variants $High$, Low, or Off. In the same design step, we decided that the central controller should contain a special heat controller (Fig. 1.10).

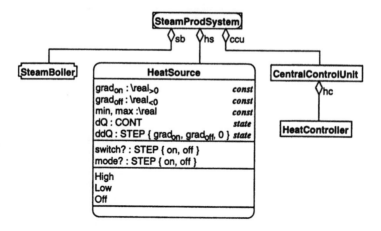

Figure 1.10: Refinement of the heater subsystem

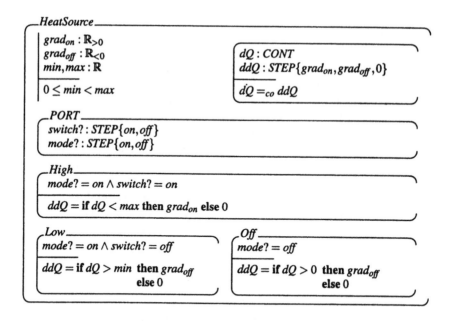

Figure 1.11: ZimOO specification of the heat source

In order to complete the design of the heat source, we show its ZimOO specification (Fig. 1.11) which is automatically generated from the UML[h] description shown in Fig. 1.10, together with some additional information concerning the class behavior (i.e. the precise specification of behavior equations). The differential equation $\dot{Q} =_{co} ddQ$ states that ddQ is the gradient of dQ ($=_{co}$ means that the differential equation holds whenever *ddQ* is continuous). The ZimOO specification describes in detail the relation between the control variables and the model variants. If *mode?* and *switch?* are both *on*, the system tries to supply as much heat power as possible, i.e. *max*. When *mode?* is *on* and *switch?* is *off*, the power supply decreases to *min*. *mode?* = *off* means that no heat power is needed at all.

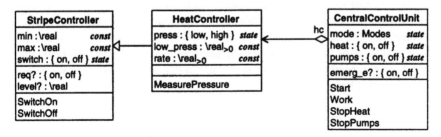

Figure 1.12: Model of the *HeatController*

Once the heat source has been completely specified, we can turn our attention to the heat controller. We model it as a child of a *StripeController* (Fig. 1.12), which tries to keep the value *level?* between *min* and *max*: if *req?* = *on*, it sets the state variable *switch* to *on* or *off* when the control variable *level?* reaches the limits *min* or *max*, respectively.

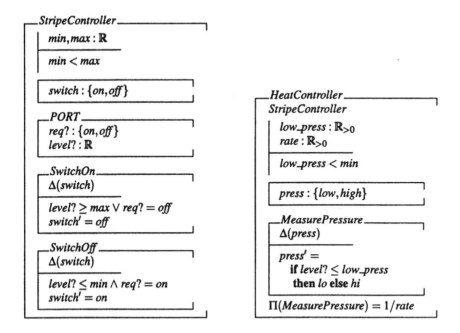

Figure 1.13: ZimOO specification of *StripeController* and *HeatController*

HeatController enriches this class by the operation *MeasurePress*, which computes a qualitative value (*press*) for the pressure inside the steam boiler. The constant *rate* indicates the frequency of the invocations of *MeasurePressure*. Thus, in addition to controlling the heat source, *HeatController* performs some measurements for the central control unit. Fig. 1.13 shows the ZimOO specifications of *StripeController* and *HeatController*.

Now we can specify in ZimOO the part of the steam-boiler system developed here. The ZimOO class *SteamProdSystem* is a ZimOO refinement of the UML^h diagram from Fig. 1.10. The actuator ⤳ connects the variable *heat* of the central control unit (not refined here) to the control variable *mode*? of the heat source. Similarly, *switch* of the heat controller is connected to *switch*? of the heat source. The control variable *level*? of the heat controller measures the pressure of the steam-boiler vessel (*sb.ve*), which owing to lack of space is not further specified here.

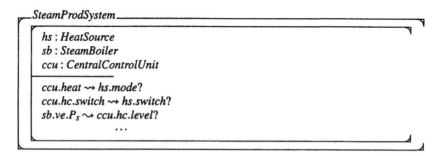

For the sake of completeness, we add the following diagram showing the complete class structure of the entire system.

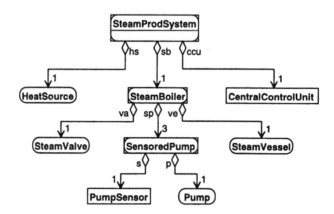

1.6   CONCLUSIONS

In this paper, we presented an object-oriented approach to the design of hybrid systems using the UML^h notation, a variant of UML for hybrid systems. Though UML^h is still under development, we have demonstrated that it can already be used to design hybrid systems such as the steam-boiler benchmark. Further work on UML^h and its tool support will include: various extensions to its class diagrams, hybrid statecharts, and collaboration diagrams for hybrid systems.

1.7 REFERENCES

[1] J.-R. Abrial, E. Börger, and H. Langmaack, editors. Formal Methods for Industrial Applications: Specifying and Programming the Steam Boiler Control, volume 1165 of LNCS. Springer-Verlag, 1996.

[2] R. Alur, C. Courcoubetis, T. A. Henzinger, and P.-H. Ho. Hybrid automata: An algorithmic approach to the specification and verification of hybrid systems. In Grossman et al. [11], pp. 209–229.

[3] M. Andersson. Object-Oriented Modelling and Simulation of Hybrid Systems. PhD thesis, Lund Institute of Technology, Denmark, December 1994.

[4] M. Biersack, V. Friesen, S. Jähnichen, M. Klose, and M. Simons. Towards an architecture for simulation environments. In Proceedings of the Summer Computer Simulation Conference. The Society for Computer Simulation (SCSC'95), 1995.

[5] R. Büssow and M. Weber. A steam-boiler control specification with Statecharts and Z. In Abrial et al. [1], pp. 109–128.

[6] Z. Chaochen, A. P. Ravn, and M. R. Hansen. An extended duration calculus for hybrid real-time systems. In Grossman et al. [11], pp. 36–59.

[7] H. Elmqvist, F. E. Cellier, and M. Otter. Object-oriented modeling of hybrid systems. In ESS'93, European Simulation Symposium, Delft, October 25-28 1993.

[8] H. Elmqvist and S. E. Mattsson. Modelica — The next generation modeling language: An international design effort. In Proceedings of the 1st World Congress on System Simulation (WCSS'97), Singapore, August 1997.

[9] V. Friesen. An exercise in hybrid system specification using an extension of Z. In A. Bouajjani and O. Maler, editors, Second European Workshop on Real-Time and Hybrid Systems, pp. 311–316, 1995.

[10] V. Friesen, S. Jähnichen, and M. Weber. Specification of software controlling a discrete-continuous environment. In 19th International Conference on Software Engineering (ICSE-19). IEEE Computer Society, 1997.

[11] R. Grossman, A. Nerode, H. Rischel, and A. Ravn, editors. Hybrid Systems, volume 736 of LNCS. Springer-Verlag, 1993.

[12] He Jifeng. From CSP to hybrid systems. In A. W. Roscoe, editor, A Classical Mind, Essays in Honour of C. A. R. Hoare, pp. 171–189. Prentice Hall, 1994.

[13] M. Kloas, V. Friesen, and M. Simons. Smile — A simulation environment for energy systems. In A. Sydow, editor, Proceedings of the 5th International IMACS-Symposium on Systems Analysis and Simulation (SAS'95), pp. 503–506. Gordon and Breach Publishers, 1995.

[14] D. Kramer. JDK 1.1.1 Documentation. Sun Microsystems, Inc., 1997.

[15] Rational. Unified Modeling Language, 13. January 1997. Version 1.0.

[16] D. Sinclair. Using an object-oriented methodology to bring a hybrid system from initial concept to formal definition. In O. Maler, editor, Hybrid and Real-Time Systems (HART'97), volume 1201 of LNCS, pp. 186–198. Springer-Verlag, 1997.

2

Design Patterns and their Role in Formal Object-oriented Development

Kevin Lano, Stephen Goldsack

Dept. of Computing, Imperial College
180 Queens Gate
London SW7 2BZ
UK

Abstract: This paper describes how object-oriented design patterns can be used within a formal development process, and how the structure of formal requirements specifications, as expressed in their invariant properties, may serve to suggest suitable patterns to be used in their design and implementation.

An example of a simple real-time system is used to illustrate the approach.

2.1 OBJECT-ORIENTED DESIGN PATTERNS

Design patterns are characteristic structures of classes (or of the objects which are their instances) which can be reused to achieve particular design goals in an elegant manner. For example, the "State" design pattern discussed in Section 2.2.3 below, replaces local attributes (instance variables) of a class that record its state (in the sense of a finite state machine) and conditional statements in the methods selecting operations according to the state, by an object which provides polymorphic functionality in place of the conditionals. If design patterns are to be used in structuring specifications in formal object-oriented languages and methods, such as VDM^{++} [4], the conditions under which their use leads to a functionally-correct refinement step need to be identified. In this paper VDM^{++} is used to illustrate the ideas. A short summary of the notation is given in the appendix.

2.2   OBJECT STATE ATTRIBUTES AND INVARIANTS

We have recently shown (see [7], and [8]) how structural transformations may be used as a form of refinement in developing designs for systems initially specified as monolithic objects. The approach is illustrated in Figure 2.1.

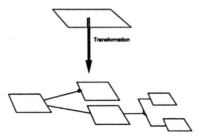

Figure 2.1: Design development by class transformation

In the course of the transformation, which may be carried out in stages, the state variables of the initial class become spread amongst the objects forming the derived system. Any invariants which hold over the data in the initial class must be observed also in the totality of the derived classes; each object encapsulating part of the data must ensure the holding at all times of those parts of the invariant which relate to the data it holds. Thus the invariant will be decomposed into terms to be maintained by the separate classes. For this reason the logical structure of the invariant plays an important role in determining the appropriate system design.

It should be noted that, in referring to the invariant properties of a system, we include essentially all the system requirements, which may be expressed as predicates, defining properties which must hold "always". In a real-time system we can consider as invariants at least the following:

1. Traditional data invariants, such as appear in descriptions of abstract data types. Also loop invariants in Hoare's logic of programming.

2. Physical laws relating physical variables. Eg. relations between variables expressed as differential equations. Particularly important invariants in real time systems are the conservation laws for energy and momentum.

3. Events and their consequences. Whenever a particular event occurs, the system must respond in a specified way. Events may be external signals, or may be the onset of some desirable or undesirable (alarm) condition. Responses to events are expressed using the notation:

   whenever *condition* **also [from** δ**]** $==>$ *new_condition*

   where the event is any state change involving *condition* becoming true. The response (making *new_condition* true) must be completed within δ time units of the event.

4. Synchronisation rules.

In the following sections we show how an invariant structure can relate to the appropriate object design structures, and how design patterns can be justified by applying the approach. We then illustrate the design process with an example of a simple real-time system.

2.2.1 Conjunction in the invariant

Consider first a class describing a system with two state variables, and an invariant which is a conjunction of terms. This is illustrated as class *Example*1 in Figure 2.2.

```
class Example1                          class Example1b
instance variables                      instance variables
  X  :  X_type;                           my_X  :  • X_class;
  Y  :  Y_type;                           my_Y  :  • Y_class;
  ...                                     ...
init objectstate == ...                 init objectstate ==
inv objectstate ==                              (my_X := X_class!new;
  inv_x(X) ∧ inv_y(Y) ∧ inv_xy(X,Y)             my_Y := Y_class!new)
methods                                 methods
  request()  ==                           request()  ==
         [pre...                                (my_X!request();
            post ....]                           my_Y!request();
end Example1                                     ...)
                                        auxilliary reasoning
                                        inv objectstate ==
                                                inv_xy(my_X.X, my_Y.Y)
                                        end Example1b
```

Figure 2.2: Transformation of a class with a conjunctive invariant.

Every invariant which is expressed as a predicate over the state variables may be transformed in this way. The terms of the conjunctive normal form are collected into those depending on X, those depending on Y and those relating X and Y. Any or all of the terms may be empty, and if the terms relating X and Y are complex, then this transformation would be an inappropriate design. In the transformation, this class is replaced by *Example*1b in which the state variables of *Example*1 are replaced by references to instances of container classes, holding respectively values of type X_type and Y_type. Typically such links represent client/server relationships and would be represented as associations in OMT or UML. Those terms of the invariant which refer only to X must form the invariant of the X instance stored in the X_class instance. The code for this is not shown here, but it is called my_X. It must remain the role of the client class *Example*1b to maintain the appropriate relationship defined by $inv_{xy}(X,Y)$. Of course, this can be generalised to situations with more than two instance variables.

The methods of *Example*1 now become split, and those parts which act on X and maintain $inv_x(X)$ become methods of the dependent class, and are called from the client. The treatment of this splitting is given in more detail in [7].

To summarise, any system which is represented as a collection of classes related by

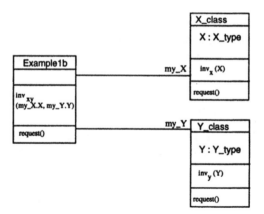

Figure 2.3: A simple design supporting conjunction of the invariant terms

association has an overall invariant which is the conjunction of the partial invariants maintained by each element of the association. Figure 2.3 illustrates this decomposition. Though it is not listed as a design pattern in the book by Gamma et al [6] it must be the commonest of all the possible designs in practice.

2.2.2 Disjunction in the invariant

Suppose we have a system which can be in a number of different states, described, for example, by a statechart. The current state is recorded by the value of an instance variable *currentstate* : *CState* (where *CState* is an enumerated type). The system may have additional state variables, some which are manipulated by the system in any of its states, while others are changed only in certain states. The requirements will specify constraints on the permitted values of these variables. The invariant to be preserved will be a union of terms relevant to the current state, thus:

$$currentstate \ = \ < state1 > \ \wedge \ inv1 \ \vee$$
$$currentstate \ = \ < state2 > \ \wedge \ inv2$$

or equivalently:

cases *currentstate* :
$$< state1 > \ \rightarrow \ inv1,$$
$$< state2 > \ \rightarrow \ inv2$$

Typically the methods of the object must also use conditional statements (if or case statements) using the *currentstate* variable to select the operations to be performed when the method is invoked. The code steps involved in the branch taken when the system is in some particular state must preserve the partial invariant over the data it manipulates when in that state. The class *Example2* shown in Figure 2.4 illustrates the situation. This is transformed to *Example2b* by introducing an object *stateobj* of class *State*. *State* has subtypes *ConcreteState1*, etc to represent each of the elements of *Cstate*.

```
class Example2                                    class Example2b
types                                             instance variables
  CState = < state1 > | < state2 > | ...            stateobj :  @State;
instance variables                                  store :  X_type;
  currentstate :  CState;                            ...
  store :  X_type;                                 init objectstate ==
  ...;                                               (stateobj := ConcreteState1!new;
init objectstate ==                                  store := ...)
  (currentstate := < state1 >;                   methods
   store := ....; )                                setstate(S :  CState) ==
inv objectstate ==                                   cases S :
        cases  currentstate :                          < state1 >  →
          < state1 >  →   inv1,                            stateobj := ConcreteState1!new,
          < state2 >  →   inv2                          < state2 >  →
methods                                                    stateobj := ConcreteState2!new
  request() ==                                          ...;
    cases  currentstate :
      < state1 >  →   Code1,                      request() ==
      < state2 >  →   Code2,                          stateobj!handle()
      ...
                                                  end Example2b
```

Figure 2.4: Transformation of a class with a disjunctive invariant

Note that there is a design choice here. In the form given, a new instance of the appropriate subclass is formed at each new change of state. The new state is then re-initialised. An alternative is to store a set of references to subclasses to be created (and so initialised) once, and allocated as the value for *stateobj* by assignment, each time a state change is requested. This preserves the local state of the sub-class object at the next entry.

The transformed structure is illustrated in Figure 2.5.

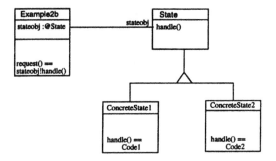

Figure 2.5: OMT class diagram, illustrating *Example2b*

2.2.3 The state pattern

The design we have developed in the above is exactly the "State" pattern [6] (pp 305–313) which replaces state variables by new subordinate objects and implements the state-dependent behaviour of the original object by polymorphism. The aim is to avoid excessive case-considerations within the method definitions of the object, and to factor out state-independent functionality. It is similar in some respects to the *AbstractFactory* design pattern (ibid pp 87–95), but involves more general behaviour than object creation. In [7] we have shown how to derive the "Abstract Factory" pattern.

In these developments, the attribute *currentstate* in *Example2* has been replaced in *Example2b* by *stateobj* which holds a reference to an object of class *State*, an abstract class with concrete subclasses whose state variables correspond to the possible values of *currentstate* in *Example2*. Other attributes of *Example2* remain in *Example2b*. The method *handle* has definition *Code1* in *ConcreteState1* and *Code2* in *ConcreteState2* and in other subclasses of *State* representing concrete states.

Transitions from one state to another are implemented in *Example2b* by object deletion and creation: *currentstate* := < *statei* > becomes *setstate*(< *statei* >) in *Example2b*, that is:

     stateobj := *ConcreteStatei!new*

currentstate is interpreted by the term

    if *stateobj* ∈ $\overline{ConcreteState1}$
    then < *state1* >
    else
      if ...

where $\overline{C}$ represents the set of existing objects of a class *C*. Other attributes *att* in *Example2* are interpreted by *att* in *Example2b* if *att* is not mentioned in *Code1* or *Code2*. Attributes *att* used in either of these codes need to be moved into *State* and are interpreted by *stateobj.att*. @*Example2* is interpreted by @*Example2b* and $\overline{Example2}$ by $\overline{Example2b}$. Similarly for the creation and deletion actions of these classes.

2.3 CONTROL SYSTEM EXAMPLE

This case study concerns a simple transfer tank (Figure 2.6) involving a valve to feed fluid into the tank, an exit valve (assumed always open here), a relief valve, a stirrer, and a set of level sensors (or a continuous level measure) for detecting the points at where agitation should start and stop, and when the tank has become full.   We can consider that there

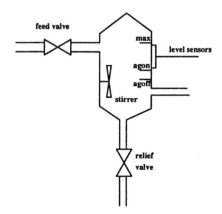

Figure 2.6: Transfer Tank Components

are two main states: the state of *normal* operation where the level of fluid in the tank is below the *max* level, and the state *overfull* where the level is above *max*. The former state can be subdivided into the states where the agitator is either on or off called *agitating* and *not_agitating* respectively (Figure 2.7).

This system is described in terms of the following variables and invariants:

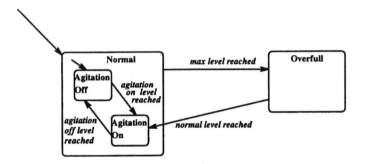

Figure 2.7: Transfer Tank States

1. A continuous variable, *level*, giving the level of the fluid in the tank. Note that this is not directly under the control of the system, but may be sampled at any time to determine its current value.

2. Variables *feedvalvestate* and *reliefvalvestate* of type *devicestate* = < *on* > | < *off* >. These represent the states of external devices, which can be controlled by the system.

3. A variable *agitator* also of type *devicestate*.

4. Constant levels *max_level*, *agitation_on_level* and *agitation_off_level*:

   $$agitation\_off\_level \; < \; agitation\_on\_level \; < \; max\_level$$

The abstract requirements of the control system are therefore as follows:

1. *mainstate* = < *normal* > ∧ *level* < *max* ∧ *feedvalvestate* = < *on* > ∧ *reliefvalvestate* = < *off* > ∨

2. *mainstate* = < *overfull* > ∧ *level* ≥ *max* ∧ *feedvalvestate* = < *off* > ∧ *reliefvalvestate* = < *on* > ∨

3. *agitationstate* = < *agitating* > ∧ *agitator* = < *on* > ∧ *mainstate* = < *normal* > ∨

4. *agitationstate* = < *not_agitating* > ∧ *agitator* = < *off* > ∧ *mainstate* = < *normal* >

These are static requirements, specifying the allowed system states. The dynamic requirements, describing how the system will change with time, are:

1. when the level passes the *agitation_on* level going up, switch the agitator on, within time deadline δ_1;

2. when the level passes the *max* level going up, close the feed valve and open the relief valve, within time deadline δ_2;

3. when the level passes 0.9 ∗ *max* going down, open the feed valve and close the relief valve, within time deadline δ_3.

4. when the level passes the *agitation_off* level going down, switch the agitator off, within time deadline δ_4.

In Figure 2.8 the static requirements are expressed as normal invariants of the tank high level controller (HLC) while the dynamic conditions are given using whenever clauses.

Global types, constants and functions which must be known to more than one class are defined in a class *SystemTypes* and inherited into all classes which share them. This class can have no variables or items with state.

class *SystemTypes*
constants
      max_level,
      agitation_on_level,
      agitation_off_level : *Real*
               – constant values to be defined
types
      devicestate = < *on* > | < *off* >;
      mainstate = < *normal* > | < *overfull* >;
      agitationstate = < *agitating* > | < *not_agitating* >
end *SystemTypes*

The guidelines above show that this specification can be refined into a structure with the *normal* and *overfull* states as in the State pattern, and with 4 'request' events corresponding to the transitions of Figure 2.7. However, we can simplify the problem by applying an initial transformation on the statechart to *generalise* these events [11, 1] to reduce the set of events that the controller needs to deal with. The *agitation_on_reached* and *agitation_off_reached* events can be combined into a *agitation_level_change* event, and the *max_level_reached* and *normal_level_reached* events combined into a *max_level_change* event (Figure 2.9).

Using a technique such as procedural controller synthesis [13] we obtain a controller design of the form:

```
class TTController
  is subclass of SystemTypes
instance variables
  currentstate :  mainstate;
  agitstate :  agitationstate;
  feedvalve :  • FeedValve;
  reliefvalve :  • ReliefValve;
  agitator :  • Agitator
inv objectstate  ==  /*   Four clauses of static requirements  */
init objectstate  ==  ...
methods
  max_level_change()  ==
     cases currentstate :
       < normal >   →
          (feedvalve!close();
           reliefvalve!open();
           currentstate  :=  < overfull >),
       < overfull >   →
          (feedvalve!open();
```

class *TankHLC* **is subclass of** *SystemTypes*
instance variables
      current_mainstate : mainstate;
      current_agitation_state : agitationstate;
time variables
      input *level : Real*;
      feedvalve, reliefvalve : devicestate;
      agitator : devicestate
init objectstate ==
      (*current_mainstate* $:= <normal>$;
      feedvalve $:= <on>$;
      reliefvalve $:= <off>$;
      current_agitationstate $:= <not\_agitating>$)
assumptions /* At time 0 the level is 0: */
      $t = 0 \Rightarrow level(t) = 0$
inv objectstate ==
cases *current_mainstate*:
      $<normal> \rightarrow$
         feedvalve $= <on> \wedge$ *reliefvalve* $= <off> \wedge$
         cases *current_agitation_state*:
            $<agitating> \rightarrow agitator = <on>$,
            $<not\_agitating> \rightarrow agitator = <off>$
         end,
      $<overfull> \rightarrow$
         feedvalve $= <off> \wedge$ *reliefvalve* $= <on>$
end
effects
      mainstate $= <normal> \wedge$
      current_agitationstate $= <not\_agitating> \Rightarrow$
         whenever *level* $> agitation\_on\_level$
         also from $\delta_1 ==>$ *current_agitation_state* $= <agitating>$;

      mainstate $= <normal> \Rightarrow$
         whenever *level* $> max\_level$
         also from $\delta_2 ==>$ *mainstate* $= <overfull>$;

      mainstate $= <overfull> \Rightarrow$
         whenever *level* $< 0.9 * max\_level$
         also from $\delta_3 ==>$ *mainstate* $= <normal>$

      mainstate $= <normal> \wedge$ *current_agitation_state* $= <agitating> \Rightarrow$
         whenever *level* $< agitation\_off\_level$
         also from $\delta_4 ==>$ *current_agitation_state* $= <not\_agitating>$
end *TankHLC*

Figure 2.8: High level system specification for Transfer Tank Controller

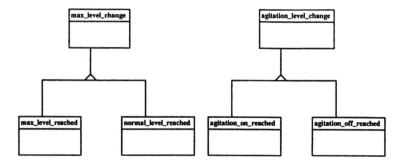

Figure 2.9: Event Generalisation

> *reliefvalve!close*();
> *currentstate* := < *normal* >);

agitation_level_change() ==
    cases *currentstate* :
      < *normal* >   →
        (cases *agitstate* :
          < *agitating* >   →
            (*agitator!switch_off*();
            agitstate := < *not_agitating* >),
          < *not_agitating* >   →
            (*agitator!switch_on*();
            agitstate := < *agitating* >)),
      < *overfull* >   → skip
end *TTController*

The disjunction transformation can now be applied, and the nested **cases** expression in the *normal* state invariant suggests an iteration of this pattern, with the *Normal* class playing the role of a further *State* class and being used as an abstract parent of further subclasses *Agitating* and *Not_agitating*. This is illustrated in Figure 2.10.

    Applying the disjunction transformation once, to *Cstate* as *mainstate*, we get a client class *TransferTankHLC* (playing the role of *Example2b*):

```
class TransferTankHLC
  is subclass of SystemTypes
instance variables
  stateobj : • TransferTank;
  normalstate : • TransferTank;
  overfullstate : • TransferTank
init objectstate ==
  (normalstate := Normal!new;
   overfullstate := Overfull!new;
   stateobj := normalstate)
methods
  swapstate() ==
      if stateobj = overfullstate
```

```
       then stateobj := normalstate
       else stateobj := overfullstate;

  max_level_change()  ==
        (stateobj!max_level_change();
         swapstate());

  agitation_level_change()  ==
        stateobj!agitation_level_change()
end TransferTankHLC
```

Note that this uses the alternative technique for state changing. In their states the subclasses access the external devices, and it would not be helpful to match the method calls to the external hardware afresh on each entry to a state.

Subclasses *Normal* and *Overfull* of *TransferTank* (which plays the role of *State* in Figure 2.4) are then defined.

```
class TransferTank
  is subclass of SystemTypes
instance variables
  feedvalve : • FeedValve;
  reliefvalve : • ReliefValve
init objectstate ==
  (feedvalve := FeedValve!new;
   reliefvalve := ReliefValve!new)
methods
  max_level_change()
       is subclass responsibility;

  agitation_level_change()
       is subclass responsibility
end TransferTank
```

We assume that the classes representing device interfaces, *FeedValve*, *ReliefValve* and *Stirrer*, possess a unique instance at all times, and simply return this as the result of the *new* method.

Normal has the form:

```
class Normal
  is subclass of TransferTank
instance variables
  agitstate : agitationstate;
  agitator : • Stirrer
init objectstate == ...
methods
  max_level_change()  ==
        (feedvalve!close();
         reliefvalve!open());

  agitation_level_change()  ==
        cases agitstate :
```

```
          < agitating >   →
              (agitator!switch_off();
               agitstate  :=  < not_agitating >),
          < not_agitating >   →
              (agitator!switch_on();
               agitstate  :=  < agitating >)
end Normal
```

This class has invariant based on the last two cases of the static requirements of Section 2.3.

Overfull is the class:

```
class Overfull
  is subclass of TransferTank
methods
  max_level_change()  ==
      (feedvalve!open();
       reliefvalve!close());

  agitation_level_change()  ==  skip
end Overfull
```

We now recognise that the transformation can be applied again, with *Normal* playing the role of *Example2*, and *agitationstate* the role of *Cstate*, so we obtain (as the *Example2b* class):

```
class NormalHLC
  is subclass of TransferTank
instance variables
  stateobj :  • Normal;
  agitatingstate :  • Normal;
  notagitatingstate :  • Normal
init objectstate ==
  (agitatingstate  :=  Agitating!new;
   notagitatingstate  :=  NotAgitating!new;
   stateobj  :=  notagitatingstate)
methods
  swapstate()  ==
      if stateobj  =  agitatingstate
      then stateobj  :=  notagitatingstate
      else stateobj  :=  agitatingstate;

  agitation_level_change()  ==
      (stateobj!agitation_level_change();
       swapstate())
end NormalHLC
```

NormalHLC replaces *Normal* as a subclass of *TransferTank*, and we define a new version of *Normal* which plays the role of *State* in this second transformation:

```
class Normal
instance variables
```

```
  agitator :  • Stirrer
init objectstate ==
  agitator  :=  Stirrer!new
methods
  agitation_level_change()
      is subclass responsibility
end Normal

class Agitating
  is subclass of Normal
methods
  agitation_level_change()  ==
              agitator!switch_off()
end Agitating

class NotAgitating
  is subclass of Normal
methods
  agitation_level_change()  ==
              agitator!switch_on()
end NotAgitating
```

2.4 SOME FURTHER "STANDARD" DESIGN STRUCTURES

2.4.1 A sampling interface

In most real-time control systems certain of the values used and manipulated by the controller are actually external to the software. We need to introduce some form of "hardware wrapper" to make the external abstractions accessible to the specified software. The quantities in question may be inputs or outputs; they may be continuous variables, eg. forces, velocities, or in the present case the fluid level which is an input. But there may also be discrete quantities, like on/off states of valves, switches and so on. In the present example, the output states of the feed valve and relief valve and of the agitator are typical of discrete outputs.

Consider first the fluid level. Such continuous variables can be represented only approximately in a computer. The continuous magnitude must be converted to a digital representation, and stored in a digital register. Special purpose hardware for this is usually called an analogue/digital converter. It is external to the computer, but an interface enables the value stored in its register to be read, and the precision is usually sufficient to make the approximation involved in rounding the continuous value to the nearest bit fully adequate. However, the continuous variation with the passage of *time* can only be approximated by polling the value at discrete times, replacing the continuous function by a step function. This is achieved by introducing two new classes. The first is a *Sensor* which provides the software interface to the D/A converter. The second is a *Sampler* which reads the value periodically and transfers the result to the program. This is usually called "polling". The effect of the polling in the present problem is defined by the **whenever** clauses. Because the value is being obtained only periodically, the instant at which an event occurs such as the level reaching the *max_level* value can be determined only within a precision of a cycle of the polling. It is an obligation of the designer to show that this is sufficiently precise for the purpose.

In Figure 2.10 we show the completed design in which the classes *Sampler* and *Sensor* have been added, in a way which may be considered a simple design pattern for implementing an interface of this kind.

Polling is generated by periodically executed code in one of the classes, which is continuously active. Designs are possible with this code in the sampler which periodically obtains the value and sends it to the controller or in the controller itself which periodically requests a sample from the sampler. Here we have chosen to present the first option.

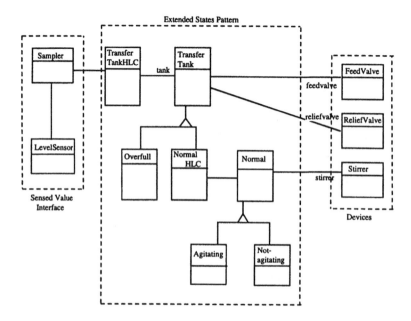

Figure 2.10: Final Design Structure of System

Figure 2.11 is the outline of a sampler which implements the four **whenever** statements in the specification. It uses the periodic thread to specify that the *sample* method is called regularly with the desired frequency.

2.4.2　The switched states in the output

The outputs in this problem are the device states, $< on >$ and $< off >$, of the valves and stirrer. Referring to Figure 2.10 one might feel that these are simple associations covered by the discussion in Section 2.2.1. However, the invariants of the devices are not handled by the devices themselves. They are of the form:

cases *mainstate* :
$$< normal > \rightarrow reliefvalvestate = < off > \wedge feedvalvestate = < on >$$
$$< overfull > \rightarrow reliefvalvestate = < on > \wedge feedvalvestate = < off >$$

```
class Sampler is subclass of SystemTypes
instance variables
   controller :  • TransferTankHLC ;
   levelsensor :  • LevelSensor ;
   oldlevel :  Real;
init objectstate ==
   (controller  :=  TransferTankHLC!new;
    levelsensor  :=  LevelSensor!new;
    oldlevel  :=  levelsensor!get_reading())
methods
   sample()  ==
      (dcl lev :  R  :=  levelsensor!get_reading();
          if   oldlevel  ≤  agitation_on_level ∧ lev  >  agitation_on_level
                      then    controller!agitation_level_change()
      elsif   oldlevel  ≤  max_level ∧   lev  >  max_level
                      then    controller!max_level_change()
      elsif   oldlevel  ≥  0.9 ∗ max_level ∧ lev  <  0.9 ∗ max_level
                      then    controller!max_level_change()
      elsif   oldlevel  ≥  agitation_off_level ∧ lev  <  agitation_off_level
                      then    controller!agitation_level_change();
          oldlevel  :=  lev)

thread
   periodic(τ) (sample)
end Sampler
```

Figure 2.11: The sampler class

This is obtained by switching the device state as part of the state change of the main-state. This seems to be a sufficiently regular situation to deserve recognition as a real-time pattern.

2.5   VERIFICATION

We can prove the real-time properties of the refinement, provided the response requirements expressed by the *whenever* assertions are met. This requires suitable constraints on the sampling period τ and on the computation times of the system.

1. To detect events by polling with periodicity τ and with a sampling method m, with a deadline D, is a correct step provided the condition being polled can be shown to remain true once it becomes true for at least a time $t_C > \tau + D$, and to remain false for at least t_C once it becomes false – this is needed to ensure that no events are missed.

2. The execution time of the sampling method must also satisfy:

$$duration(m) \leq D \leq \tau$$

3. In order that the whenever constraints are met, we need

$$D+\tau < \delta_1, D+\tau < \delta_2, etc.$$

2.6 CONCLUSION

This paper has illustrated how design patterns can be used in a formal development process, the design being formed by structural transformations, the choice of patterns being guided by the logical structure of the requirements statement, treated as an invariant.

The example used is rather simple, as the classes involved in the various states have no instance variables, really only performing actions at the time when they become active, when the system "enters" the state. Applications of the ideas to the re-engineering of large batch processing legacy systems are presented in [10]. Other transformations for Syntropy and UML are described in [11].

2.7 REFERENCES

[1] M. Awad, M. Kuusela and J. Ziegler. Object-oriented Technology for Real-time Systems. Prentice Hall, 1996.

[2] S. Cook and J. Daniels. Designing Object Systems: Object-Oriented Modelling with Syntropy. Prentice Hall, Sept 1994.

[3] E. Dürr and N. Plat. VDM^{++} Language Reference Manual. Afrodite document AFRO/CG/ED/LRM/V10. Can be obtained from http://www.ifad.dk.

[4] E. Dürr and E. Dusink. The role of VDM^{++} in the development of a real-time tracking and tracing system. In J Woodcock and P Larsen, editors, FME '93, Lecture Notes in Computer Science. Springer-Verlag, 1993.

[5] J. Fiadeiro and T. Maibaum. Describing, Structuring and Implementing Objects, in de Bakker et al., Foundations of Object Oriented languages, LNCS 489, Springer-Verlag, 1991.

[6] E. Gamma, R. Helm, R. Johnson and J. Vlissides. Design Patterns: Elements of Reusable Object-oriented Software. Addison-Wesley, 1994.

[7] S. Goldsack, K. Lano and E. Dürr. Annealing, Object Decomposition and Design Patterns. TOOLS Pacific 1996. Melbourne November 1996.

[8] S. Goldsack, K. Lano and E. Dürr. Invariants as Design Templates in Object-based Systems, Workshop on Foundations of component-based systems, Zurich, September 1997.

[9] S. Goldsack and E. Dürr. Concurrency and Real-time in VDM^{++} Chapter 6, pp. 86–112 in Formal Methods and Object Technology, S.J. Goldsack and S.J.H. Kent (Eds). ISBN3-540-19977-2 Springer Verlag 1996.

[10] K. Lano and N. Malik. Reengineering Legacy Applications using Design Patterns, STEP 97, IEEE Press, 1997.

[11] K. Lano and J. Bicarregui. Refinement through Pictures: Formalising Syntropy Refinement Concepts, 1st BCS/FACS workshop on "Making Object Oriented Methods More Rigorous", Imperial College, 1997.

[12] K. Lano. Logical Specification of Reactive and Real-Time Systems, to appear in Journal of Logic and Computation, 1998.

[13] A. Sanchez. Formal Specification and Synthesis of Procedural Controllers for Process Systems, Springer-Verlag. Lecture Notes in Control and Information Sciences, vol. 212. 1996.

THE ESSENCE OF VDM^{++}

Full details of VDM^{++} can be found in the language reference manual [3].

VDM^{++} adds the familiar concepts of classes and objects to standard VDM. The class becomes the module for structuring VDM specifications. Real-time elements, such as a variable *now* representing the current time, and specifications of time bounds for method executions and event responses, are also added to VDM-SL. A semantics for VDM^{++} in Real-Time Action Logic is given in [12].

Types, functions, values and instance variables use familiar VDM_SL notations. Almost all notations allowed in VDM_SL are allowed also in VDM^{++}. Instance variables are extended to include reference types, written with a prefix @. Thus *myobj* : @*ClassName* declares an item, *myobj*, which stores a pointer to some object of class *ClassName*.

As in VDM_SL, state variables may be associated with initialisation statements and with invariant specifications.

Methods are closely modelled on VDM operations, and may be given procedural definitions or be defined more abstractly with pre and post conditions. A procedurally defined method may have statements executed in loops or sequences in a way close to familiar programming notations, but one or more of the statements may be abstractly defined as a *specification statement* written

$$[\textbf{ext} \ < external \ clauses >$$
$$\textbf{pre} \ < pre \ conditions >$$
$$\textbf{post} \ < post \ conditions > \ ]$$

A method which is abstractly specified is identical to a procedural method having just one statement, presented as a specification statement.

To support concurrency a class may define a *thread* part delimited with the key word **thread** and the execution of its methods may be controlled by synchronisation rules in a part introduced by the keyword **sync**. For real-time specifications keywords **now** and $\overleftarrow{\textbf{now}}$ in the postcondition of a method defined by a specification statement give access to times (on a system clock) of the start event and the completion event of the method while a **whenever** expression enables events and their consequences to be described. Details of most of these features are given in a chapter of the book [9].

The language is supported by a toolset, known as the Venus toolset, developed in collaboration between the industrial partners Verilog, IFAD and CAP. Information about Venus, including the syntax for VDM^{++} can be accessed on the World Wide Web at the address: http://www.ifad.dk/products/venus.

3

Devising Coexistence Strategies for Objects with Legacy Systems

Gerardo Canfora, Aniello Cimitile, Andrea De Lucia

Facoltà di Ingegneria - Università del Sannio
Palazzo Bosco Lucarelli,
Piazza Roma - 82100
Benevento, Italy
canfora@ingbn.unisa.it, cimitile@unina.it, delucia@ingbn.unisa.it

Giuseppe A. Di Lucca

Dipartimento di Informatica e Sistemistica - Università di Napoli "Federico II"
Via Claudio, 21 - 80125
Naples, Italy
dilucca@unina.it

Abstract: The research described in this paper addresses the coexistence of systems, i.e. the problem of running in the same environment products from different families achieving a defined level of integration. In particular, we deal with the coexistence of legacy systems and new systems, which is a preliminary step for many migration and replacement strategies. The paper surveys possible approaches and methods, discusses the relative applicability and level of automation, and outlines the major limitations and risks. The focus is on the constraints to impose on a new system to make the coexistence with a legacy system technically feasible and economically convenient. These constraints depend on the extensiveness of the changes that can be made on the legacy code: the more extensively the legacy code can be reengineered the less constraints are to be imposed on the new system. We discuss the constraints in the case that reengineering is reduced at a minimum; the legacy code is changed to the extent that is necessary to trap and redirect/propagate data accesses. Finally, the paper briefly analyses the key factors which affect the reengineering of the legacy system and, consequently, contribute to fixing the constraints.

3.1 INTRODUCTION

Legacy systems and new systems must often cooperate to accomplish the strategic mission of an organisation and to achieve its key objectives. This is a particular aspect of the coexistence problem which arises every time that software products from different families have to run in the same hardware/software environment with a defined level of integration.

There are a number of circumstances in which the coexistence assumes a relevant role; most of these scenarios belong to one of the two following cases:

- the coexistence of two (sub)systems developed independently, possibly in different times and using heterogeneous approaches, technologies, and tools;

- the coexistence within the same software system of parts which exploit different technological solutions.

The first scenario arises when an organisation decides to widen its software portfolio with a new system, possibly developed exploiting modern methods and up-to-date technologies, and the new system requires the resources (data and functions) defined by one or more other systems in the organisation's portfolio. The second case is frequent in incremental migration strategies which entail the replacement of selected parts of the legacy systems with newly developed components that take up the functions of the old code (a notable example is the chicken little approach proposed by Brodie and Stonebraker [4]). Our focus is on the second scenario and in particular on the coexistence problems which derive from migrating to object-oriented technology.

The interactions between software systems assume essentially two different forms:

- functional interactions, which entail that the functions of one system are accessed from the outside;

- data interactions, which derive from the fact that systems share a (partial) view of their data models.

The coexistence of legacy and new systems that exhibit only functional interactions requires that the legacy code is reworked to make its components accessible from the outside. A recommended solution consists of encapsulating the legacy code in a wrapper which exports the desired resources. This approach is particularly promising when the new system is object-oriented, as encapsulation may be easily achieved by building an object wrapper which offers all the functions of the legacy system as if through the interface of an object. Briefly, an object wrapper is a sort of coarse-grained object where the methods are the relevant functions of the system, or system's component, encapsulated; the main advantage is that the encapsulated system and the new objects may interact by message passing. Wrapping has shown promise as a way to give existing systems a new lease of life at a reduced cost and with low risks [2]. However, as with any other solution in the arena of legacy systems, wrapping presents costs and risks that have to be carefully evaluated to choose the best suited approach for any specific legacy system [14].

The focus of this paper is on the coexistence of systems which interact through data, and particularly on the case that a legacy system and a new object-oriented system access and modify, in addition to their own persistent data, a common set of persistent data. This case of coexistence may be addressed by wrapping too. However, risks are higher as there are real data integrity issues to be taken into account.

In this paper we discuss the constraints to impose on a new system to make the coexistence with a legacy system technically feasible and economically convenient. These constraints depend on the extensiveness of the changes that can be made on the legacy code: the more extensively the legacy code can be reengineered the less constraints are to be imposed on the new system. We discuss the constraints in the case that reengineering is reduced at a minimum, i.e. the legacy code is changed to the extent that is necessary to trap and redirect/propagate data accesses.

The reminder of this paper is organised as follows. Section 3.2 gives background information on the ERCOLE project, in which the particular work described in this paper is framed, and defines the problem being addressed. Section 3.3 discusses coexistence strategies for systems which exhibit data interactions, while section 3.4 illustrates the data integrity problem. The constraints are discussed in section 3.5. Finally, section 3.6 summarises the work done and gives some concluding remarks.

3.2   THE ERCOLE PROJECT: BACKGROUND INFORMATION AND GOALS

The ERCOLE (Encapsulation, Reengineering and Coexistence of Object with Legacy) project is concerned with the migration of legacy systems toward object-oriented platforms [7]. It is jointly carried on by CORINTO (Consorzio di Ricerca Nazionale per Tecnologia ad Oggetti) - a research consortium which includes IBM, Apple and SELFIN - and the Faculty of Engineering of the University of Sannio.

The ERCOLE project aims to provide a migration strategy and the supporting technology. It confronts two major issues:

- migrating a legacy system has its own costs and risks. In order to convince software managers that a migration program is a valuable approach to solving the problems of legacy systems, costs and risks are to be reduced at a minimum and techniques and tools have to be defined to plan and control them;

- very large companies around the world face the problems of their legacy systems by establishing permanent structures whose specific mission is the management of a single system or a group of systems, depending on size. However, these permanent, specialised structures entail very high costs that are often not affordable by small/medium enterprises, with a consequent erosion of competition.

The first issue is addressed by developing an incremental migration strategy: selected parts of the legacy system are replaced by newly developed components that take up the functions of the old code. Replacement happens based on a global schedule and this permits planning and control of costs and risks. The second issue is addressed by defining a coexistence framework which facilitates the cooperation of legacy systems and new systems. In this way, small/medium enterprises which have acquired, or developed in house, additional components to customise/expand the functionality of a packaged system, may replace the base package without having to re-develop the custom components.

We are using the IBM family of products ACG (Applicazioni Contabili Gestionali) as a target to experiment and assess the migration strategy and the coexistence framework. ACG is a modular accountancy package written in RPG on the IBM AS/400 machine using the native OS/400 relational database. It consists of a set of components that can be combined in different configurations to address a number of problems. In addition to the modules released by IBM, numerous additional components have been produced by IBM's solution providers (most of the times small/medium software houses) to provide answers to the needs of particular customers.

IBM is currently developing a new object-oriented version of the package. This uses a persistence framework to manage persistent objects, and in particular to store the object attributes into a relational database. The framework allows developers to define the correspondence schema that maps the object attributes onto the relational table fields. Once this correspondence has been defined, the developer accesses persistent data in an object-oriented fashion and the framework translates the accesses to the object attributes into accesses to the corresponding table fields.

The introduction on the marketplace of this new version of the package will be successful only if it will be accompanied by a method and a technology that support: the coexistence of components of the old ACG package with components of the new object-oriented version; the coexistence of the new package version with custom components developed for the original ACG package, and; the migration of these custom components toward the new object-oriented architecture. The ERCOLE project aims exactly on these points.

ACG is one of the most widespread software packages among Italian small/medium enterprises and peripheral government organisations; at present there are 40.000 IBM AS/400 installations and 25.000 ACG licences in Italy (data taken from [1]). Therefore, the ERCOLE project is expected to have a significant economic impact on the Italian software industry.

3.3 COEXISTENCE STRATEGIES FOR SYSTEMS THAT EXHIBIT DATA INTERACTIONS

The coexistence of a legacy system with new object-oriented systems requires that the legacy code is encapsulated in an object wrapper which makes accessible from the outside the functions of the legacy code through the interface of an object. This has its costs and risks and an error in the selection of the approaches and technologies used to build the object wrapper may determine the failure of a coexistence project. Risks are particularly high when the legacy system and the new object-oriented system exhibit data interactions, as the consistency and coherence of the shared data must be ensured. The key design choice is concerned with retaining (possibly unchanged) both the native database of the legacy system and the database of the new object-oriented system or, on the contrary, integrating the data and eliminating one of the two databases. There are four possible approaches [8]:

- duplicating the common data and keeping the two copies synchronised. Synchronisation may be achieved with several different technological solutions which range from writing batch jobs (whenever this is compatible with the system mission) to using the triggering mechanisms of the underlying database management systems;

- maintaining a single copy of the common data in the database of the legacy system. Common data are copied on the attributes of the new objects on demand by sending a message to the object wrapper. Updating of the common data with the values of the attributes of an object also requires that a message is sent to the object wrapper;

- migrating the data of the legacy system to the new objects. The options are migrating only the common data - in this case the legacy system will retain its native database - or migrating all the data and eliminating the native database of the legacy system. Realisation may entail the direct access of the legacy system to the database management system on which the persistence framework is built; the access to the database through the mediation of the persistence framework; the access to the database through messages to the objects of the new system;

- deriving an object model by reverse engineering the legacy system and integrating it into the object model of the new system. This essentially requires that relevant pieces of the native database of the legacy system are individually wrapped using chunks of legacy code as methods [6].

Regardless of the approach adopted, practical implementation must ensure the consistency and coherence of common data: each change made by one of the two systems must not compromise the ability of the other system to correctly retrieve and treat the common data. This is the data integrity problem which requires that constraints are imposed on the data models of the two systems which have to coexist.

3.4   THE DATA INTEGRITY PROBLEM

Legacy systems access persistent data in terms of I/O operations on flat files or through accesses to the tables of a relational database, as in the case of ACG. New object-oriented systems manipulate persistent data in the form of attributes of (persistent) objects which are possibly mapped on a relational database by means of a persistence framework. The data integrity problem consists of devising a minimal set of constraints to impose on the two systems which have to coexist to ensure the consistency and coherence of the common data. Whilst the constraints could be imposed on either the legacy system or the new system, the constraints imposed on the legacy system would entail reengineering of the procedural code and the native database. The high costs and risks associated with the reengineering of a legacy database has motivated our choice to devise the constraints with reference to the object-oriented system's data model. Therefore, the data integrity problem we deal with consists of devising the constraints that the object-oriented system's data model has to respect to make sure that: a modification to a file (or table of a relational database) made by the legacy system does not affect the correct behaviour of the new object-oriented system, and; a modification of the state of a persistent object does not affect the correct behaviour of the legacy system.

The constraints depend on how extensively the legacy system can be reengineered. Indeed, the constraints are not due to the need for mapping the legacy database on the object-oriented system's data model: migrating a relational database to an object model without reusing the associated programs does not require constraints as the relational paradigm is a subset of the object-oriented paradigm [10]. The need for imposing constraints derives from the choice to reusing the procedural code. Also in this case, a trade-off exists between the extensiveness of reengineering and the constraints: the more extensively the legacy system may be reengineered the less constraints are to be imposed on the data model of the new object-oriented system.

At one end of the reengineering spectrum is the case that the legacy database is completely restructured, which reduces the constraints at a minimum. In this case the procedural code cannot be reused in its original form but it must be extensively reengineered. This may require that the legacy programs are sliced with respect to the I/O statements [5, 11] and the slices are then recombined in a different way to build semantically-equivalent programs [9] that work correctly with the new structure of the database.

At the other end of the spectrum is the case that the legacy system remains basically unchanged; code is modified to the extent needed to trap the I/O statements and redirect or propagate them according to the coexistence strategy adopted. The correspondence between the two views of the common data is maintained by a schema mapper which may range from a simple table to a complex middle-ware (see figure 3.1).

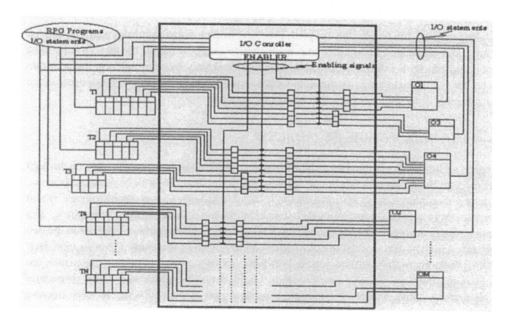

Figure 3.1: The schema mapper

We discuss the constraints in the second scenario. The ERCOLE project investigated the scenario of minimal reengineering because of the large number of ACG's customisations produced by IBM's solution providers to satisfy the needs of particular customers. The consequence is that the extensiveness and kind of the reengineering on the legacy code depends on the particular installation and costs and risks are very often not affordable by the solutions providers.

3.4.1   Minimal reengineering and the need for constraints on the object model

The coexistence problem we deal with can be summarised as follows: a legacy system and a new object-oriented system share a common set of persistent data. The perspective of the legacy system is that the common data are contained into N relational tables, while the new system assumes that the common data are contained in the attributes of M persistent objects. The content of each one of the N relational tables may be distributed on K persistent objects; similarly, the attributes of each one of the M persistent objects may be distributed on H relational tables. As an example, the content of the relational table T1 in figure 3.1 is distributed on two objects, O1 and O3, while the content of object O4 is distributed on the relational tables T2 and T3.

A modification made to a relational table by the legacy system (for example the updating of a row or the addition of a new row) entails a change in the state of the K persistent objects on which the table's content is mapped. The constraints have to ensure that the new state of these K objects is consistent, i.e. the new object-oriented system preserves its correct behaviour regardless of the fact that the state of some object has been (re-)defined by an external system.

Similarly, a change of the state of a persistent object entails the modification on the content of the H tables on which the object's attributes are mapped. In this case the constraints have to ensure that the access made by the legacy system to one of these H tables returns a piece of data which is consistent as far as the expectations of the legacy system are concerned, thus preserving its correct behaviour.

3.5   THE CONSTRAINTS IN THE SCENARIO OF MINIMAL REENGINEER-ING

This section discusses the constraints that allow an object-oriented system to coexist with a legacy system. These constraints can be used either to guide the development of a new system or to verify whether or not an object-oriented system can coexist with a legacy system in the scenario of minimal reengineering described in section 3.4. The constraints also affect the complexity of the schema mapper.

A relational data model derived from an object-oriented data model tends to be in the third normal form, and it surely satisfies the second normal form [3, 12]. This is because well designed objects corresponds to distinguishable elements in the application domain. Distinguishable objects are univocally identified by a key (a group of their attributes); in a relational data model this corresponds to the second normal form which entails that each table row has a unique primary key. The consequence is that mapping relational tables onto objects is easier if the relational model satisfies the second normal form. On the other hand, normal forms higher than the second normal form may compound this mapping.

The constraints affect only the tables and the objects which contain the data shared by the two systems; the fields of these tables may or may not coincide with the attributes of the objects. If they do not coincide, two cases are possible:

- the set of the object attributes is a subset of the table fields, i.e. the new data model loses part of the data contained in the database of legacy system;

- the set of all the table fields is a subset of the object attributes, i.e. the new data model contains new data which are not treated by the legacy system.

In the first case the set of the object attributes must include all the mandatory fields (In most relational databases mandatory fields are syntactically identified by the option "NOT NULL".) of the tables. This constraint is to ensure the integrity and consistency of the legacy system's data when the common data are updated by the new system. Similarly, in the second case the object attributes without a corresponding field in the tables must not be mandatory. Non mandatory fields (attributes) can be lost (added) provided that the schema mapper will produce the null value when the corresponding tables (objects) are updates by the new (legacy) system.

Further constraints depend on the mapping of tables onto objects. Three basic cases have been identified as shown in figure 3.2: (i) mapping one table onto one object; (ii) mapping one table onto more than one object; (iii) mapping more than one table onto one object. These cases can be generalised to the case of mapping a set tables onto a set of objects. For each case three sub-cases are to be considered: (a) object attributes can be perfectly mapped onto table fields; (b) the new objects lose fields contained in the tables; (c) the new objects contain attributes which do not have corresponding table fields. Because the new object model must not lose mandatory fields and must not contain new mandatory attributes, sub-cases (b) and (c) can be reduced to sub-case (a) if we only consider mandatory table fields and mandatory object attributes. Next sections discuss the constraints concerning the three basic cases and their generalisation with respect to sub-case (a).

3.5.1   The schema of a table coincides with the structure of one object

This is the simplest case as the information contained in a row of the table can be perfectly mapped onto a single object. The schema mapper is a simple correspondence table which maps the fields of the table onto the object attributes.

3.5.2   The fields of a table are partitioned on the attributes of a set of objects

This case arises when the legacy system and the new system resolve aggregations and/or generalisations/specialisations in different ways. As an example, more than one element of the application domain may have been merged in the same table during the development of the legacy system, while in the object-oriented data model these elements correspond to different related objects.

Blaha, Premerlani, and Rumbaugh [3, 12] describe a set of rules to transform object associations into relations among tables of a relational database; these can be used to verify the correspondence between a table of the legacy database and the objects of the new model.

The constraints to be imposed on the new object-oriented system concern the way objects that include attributes corresponding to mandatory fields of the table are stored (of course, mandatory fields include the table key). Mandatory fields can be mapped on attributes of more than one object, although the key of a table in the second normal form

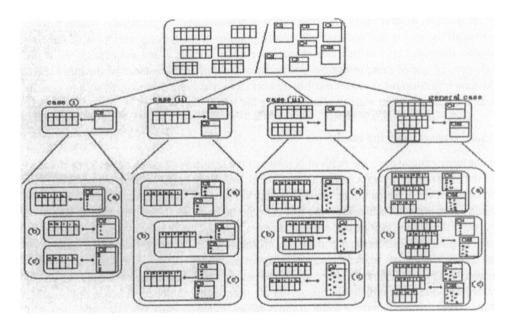

Figure 3.2: The basic cases for mapping tables onto objects

must correspond to the attributes of one object. The schema mapper must ensure that the legacy system accesses a row of the table only if all its mandatory fields have been instantiated. This means that if the new system stores a persistent object, the schema mapper will have to make the corresponding table row unavailable until the other objects which contain attributes corresponding to mandatory fields of the table have been stored. In the case of duplication of the databases the schema mapper can simply delay the writing of the table row until all its mandatory fields have been defined. It is worth stressing that the new system must necessarily define all the objects containing attributes that correspond to the mandatory fields of the table, although these can be stored at different times.

3.5.3   The fields of more than one table correspond to the attributes of one object

This can be considered as the dual of the previous case; again it arises when associations among elements of the application domain are resolved in different ways in the legacy system and in the new system. In this case the new object can be seen as a de-normalisation of the corresponding tables in the legacy system, or in general it results from merging related tables.

No constraints have to be imposed on the new system, as the schema mapper is always able to map any instance of the new object onto the rows of the corresponding tables. However, when the legacy system writes a row of one of these tables, the schema mapper has to make the corresponding object instance unavailable until all the mandatory attributes of the object have been instantiated, i.e., until all the rows containing fields corresponding to these attributes have been written by the legacy application.

It is worth to stress that the coexistence is possible only if the legacy system always writes all the tables that contain fields corresponding to mandatory attributes of the new object, although this can be made at different times. If this is not the case, i. e. if the existence of one of these rows does not necessarily imply the existence of the other rows, the new object-oriented model must be reworked to make the new system able to coexist with the legacy system without reengineering the latter.

3.5.4 Generalising the results

In the more general case, the fields of N tables of the legacy system can be perfectly mapped on the attributes of M objects in the new data model. With perfectly mapped we mean that no subset of the N tables can be mapped on any subset of the M objects. The considerations made in the previous subsections are still valid in this case: all the objects have to be stored by the new system before the schema mapper enables the legacy system to access the corresponding table rows and conversely, all the rows of the table have to be written by the legacy application before the schema mapper makes the corresponding object instances available. The constraint to be imposed on the new system is that it must always store all the M objects, although at different times. On the other hand, the coexistence is not possible if the legacy system can write some of the N tables, independently from the other tables; if this happens, the data model of the new system has to be changed and better adapted to the legacy database, if the legacy system has to be not reengineered.

3.6 CONCLUDING REMARKS

We have discussed the problems related to the coexistence of legacy systems with new object-oriented systems. This is a preliminary problem to be solved to implement any incremental migration/replacement strategy. The paper has surveyed approaches and methods, focusing on the constraints to impose on the new system to make the coexistence with a legacy system technically feasible and economically convenient. These constraints depend on the extensiveness of the changes that can be made on the legacy code: the more extensively the legacy code can be reengineered the less constraints are to be imposed on the new system. Constraints have been discussed assuming that reengineering is reduced at a minimum, i.e. the legacy code is changed to the extent that is necessary to trap and redirect/propagate data accesses.

Because the constraints depend on the extensiveness of the reengineering that can be made on the legacy system, and this is generally fixed on the basis of its costs and risks [13], it is valuable to discuss briefly the key factors which affect the reengineering effort. These may concern either the data model of the legacy system or its procedural code.

One of the most important factors related to the data model is the level of normalisation: extensive normalisation may take relational tables away from the entities in the real world. This is particular true for levels of normalisation higher than the second normal form. On the other hand, a good object-oriented data model should consist of objects which correspond to real world entities. The consequence is that highly normalised relational databases are more difficult to be mapped onto object-oriented data models; a preliminary de-normalisation process may be necessary to (re-)derive tables which correspond to real world entities (and hopefully to objects). With the current state of reverse engineering, such a de-normalisation process is not completely automated; human experts are needed, and this increases costs and risks.

The two main factors related with the procedural code are the deterioration and the decomposability. The deterioration is a measure of the decrease of the maintainability of a system (lack of analysability, modifiability, stability and testability) due to the maintenance operations the system has undergone in its life-cycle. It may concern either the code or the accompanying documentation. The decomposability is a measure of the identifiability and independence of the main components of a system. All systems can be considered as having three components: interfaces, domain functions, and data management services. The decomposability of a system indicates how well these components are reflected in its architecture. Decomposable systems are easier to be reengineered.

The effort for reengineering a legacy system to allow it to coexist with an object-oriented system in the presence of data interactions is generally acceptable if the legacy system is at least semi-decomposable with respect to the data management services.

3.7 ACKNOWLEDGEMENTS

The research described in this paper has been conducted with the financial support of COR-INTO (Consorzio di Ricerca Nazionale per la Tecnologia ad Oggetti) within the research project ERCOLE (Encapsulation, Reengineering and Coexistence of Object with Legacy). We would like to express our gratitude to Fabio Castiglioni and Silvia Petruzzelli for their contribution to the development of the work presented here. Patrizia Angelini, Michele De Leo, Maria Pia Dicuonzo, Patrizia Guerra, Maria Nella Palese, and Mary Tafuri have contributed to the implementation of a schema mapper as outlined in this paper.

3.8 REFERENCES

[1] P. Angelini. Il Mondo AS/400, Informatica Oggi & Unix, Gruppo Editoriale Jackson, no. 131, 1996, pp. 40–46.

[2] K. H. Bennett. Legacy Systems: Coping with Success, IEEE Software, vol. 12, no. 1, 1995, pp. 19–23.

[3] M. R. Blaha, W. J. Premerlani, and J. E. Rumbaugh. Relational Database Design Using an Object-Oriented Methodology, Communication of the ACM, vol. 31, no. 4, 1988, pp. 414–427.

[4] M. L. Brodie and M. Stonebraker. Migrating Legacy Systems - Gateways, Interfaces & the Incremental Approach, Morgan Kaufmann Publishers, Inc., San Francisco, CA, USA, 1995.

[5] G. Canfora, A. De Lucia, G. A. Di Lucca, and A. R. Fasolino. Slicing Large Programs to Isolate Reusable Functions, Proc. of the EUROMICRO Conference, Liverpool, UK, 1994, IEEE CS Press, pp. 140–147.

[6] A. Cimitile, A. De Lucia, G. A. Di Lucca, and A. R. Fasolino. Identifying Objects in Legacy Systems, Proc. of 5th International Workshop on Program Comprehension, Dearborn, MI, USA, 1997, IEEE CS Press, pp. 138–147.

[7] A. De Lucia, G.A. Di Lucca, A.R. Fasolino, P. Guerra, and S. Petruzzelli. Migrating Legacy Systems towards Object-Oriented Platforms, Proc. of International Conference on Software Maintenance, Bari, Italy, 1997, IEEE CS Press, pp. 122–129.

[8] I. Graham. Migrating to Object Technology, Addison Wesley, Reading, MA, USA, 1994.

[9] S. Horwitz, J. Prins, and T. Reps. Integrating Non-interfering Versions of Programs, ACM Transactions on Programming Languages and Systems, vol. 11, no. 3, 1989, pp. 345–387.

[10] J. Jahnke, W. Schafer, and A. Zundorf. A Design Environment for Migrating relational to Object Oriented Database Systems, Proc. of International Conference on Software Maintenance, Monterey, CA, USA, 1996, IEEE CS Press, pp. 163–170.

[11] F. Lanubile and G. Visaggio. Function Recovery based on Program Slicing, Proc. of the International Conference on Software Maintenance, Montreal, Quebec, Canada, 1993, IEEE CS Press, pp. 396–404.

[12] J. E. Rumbaugh, M. R. Blaha, and W. J. Premerlani. Object-Oriented Modelling and Design, Prentice Hall, Englewood Cliffs, NJ, USA, 1991.

[13] H. M. Sneed. Planning the Reengineering of Legacy Systems, IEEE Software, vol. 12, no. 1, 1995, pp. 24–34.

[14] H. M. Sneed. Reengineering or Wrapping: A Strategical Decision, Reverse Engineering Newsletter, Committee on Reverse Engineering, Technical Council on Software Engineering, IEEE CS Press, no. 13, 1996, pp. 1–2.

4

Object-Oriented Model for Expert Systems Implementation

F. Alonso Amo, J. L. Fuertes, L. Martínez, C. Montes, R. Navajo
Facultad de Informática - UPM
Campus de Montegancedo, s/n
Boadilla del Monte
28660 Madrid
Spain
Tel: (34-1) 336 7411
Fax: (34-1) 336 7412
E-mail: falonso@fi.upm.es

Abstract: To date expert systems have been routinely implemented using development tools, such as GURU, Crystal, ART-IM, etc. There are serious drawbacks to this type of implementation, apart from the fact that it produces inefficient expert systems. This has led us to develop an object-oriented Reusable Open Model for ES Implementation (ROMES) which overcomes the disadvantages of the above tools. This paper describes this model and its application to an expert system for the homeopathic treatment of glaucoma. It also compares development of this system using the GURU tool and the ROMES model, finding that efficiency was higher when the ROMES model was used.

4.1 INTRODUCTION

During the 1960s, computer power and the use of good heuristics (sound logical rules) were thought to be sufficient to solve any type of software problem. This was referred to as the paradigm of power. Later, with the birth of artificial intelligence and the construction of expert systems, such as MYCIN [16], developed to treat bacterial diseases, in the 1970s, it was found that problem solving depended on the amount of knowledge about the problem. This gave rise to the paradigm of knowledge, and the development of knowledge engineering as opposed to software engineering.

It became clear that the problems resolved by this branch of engineering had some (or all) of the following peculiarities, typical of poorly defined problems: poorly structured, subjective requirements, context dependent, conditions of uncertainty, as a result of data, information or knowledge incompleteness, inaccuracy or inconsistency.

Therefore, the traditional software engineering waterfall life cycle that addressed well-defined problems was of no use for developing this type of software. Neither was the prototyping life cycle nor Boehm's spiral model [6] well suited for solving this type of problems, as they had the drawback of not taking into account the time variable in software development. For example, in an application with non-structured information set in the field of software engineering, such as a business decision support system, the user seldom knows the requirements a priori. Therefore, analytical models need to be designed to get the information required. In this case, the spiral model sets out the development guidelines to be followed to produce the operational system within a given space of time using prototypes. However, when a knowledge-based system (KBS) is being developed, such as a medical expert system for automated disease diagnosis, system development may largely fit in with Boehm's spiral model at a given point in time, but the expert's knowledge of the disease increases with time, and this new knowledge must be inputted into the expert system at some point, giving rise to a new, albeit shorter, development cycle with similar characteristics to the preceding phase. The conical/spiral-type life cycle, designed by the authors and other colleagues [2, 3], is being used in academic and professional spheres (e.g., Madrid School of Computer Science) for the development of this type of knowledge engineering systems with excellent results.

4.2   FROM THE APPLICATION DOMAIN TO THE IMPLEMENTATION DOMAIN

An in-depth analysis of the conical/spiral model, shown in Figure 4.1, reveals that the KBS is initially modelled from the viewpoint of the user (from system requirements to knowledge conceptualisation), outputting the conceptual model of the KBS. The system is later approached from the viewpoint of the computer (from formalisation to validation and acceptance by the client), outputting the operational product. More formally, as Blum [5] pointed out, the development of KBS can be described as a series of transformations (T1, T2, T3) from task identification in the application domain to a software product that operates in the implementation domain (4.2). Figure 4.2 identifies two modelling activities: conceptual modelling, in the application domain, that models how the software is to respond to system specifications, and formal modelling, in the implementation domain, that starts once a conceptual model exists and models how the computer must respond to those specifications. The conceptual and formal models are different and, logically, one cannot be derived from the other.

The conceptual model determines validity and the formal model, correctness. It is essential to establish the correctness of a conceptual model, as formal models may uncover errors that invalidate the model. However, object orientation has become a powerful technique in largely bridging the gap (transformation T2) between conceptual and formal

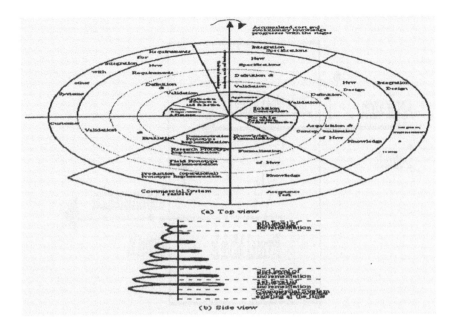

(a) Top view

(b) Side view

Figure 4.1: Spiral/Conical Model of KE System Life Cycle (IDEAL Methodology)

system modelling [4]. The concept diagram, which models system knowledge can be translated to the object-oriented class diagram, and the knowledge map, which sets out the steps for attaining a goal, is represented as an object intersection diagram, where the goal is the scenario.

Centring on the implementation domain, which is what we are concerned with here, we find that computer tools, such as GURU, Crystal, ART-IM, etc., have been used up to now to develop the implementation model. While these tools speed up expert system production, they have the following drawbacks:

- They are normally very large and are themselves complex systems, which means that their acquisition, evaluation and use require a major investment in terms of time, money and other resources;

- An expert system developed using any of these tools is bound to it, preventing generation of a tool-independent executable;

- When the ES is running, much of the tool is not being used and is wasting memory space, while the product is not very efficient; Documentation

- Each tool only addresses a particular problem, mainly because it does not cover all the techniques used in knowledge engineering. Scalability

The above considerations led us to define an object-oriented software development model, called ROMES (Reusable Open Model for Expert Systems), designed to enable rapid, extendible and efficient implementation of expert systems, preventing the problems described above and typical of current integrated development tools.here.

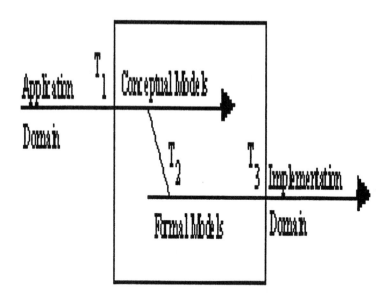

Figure 4.2:

4.3   REUSABLE OPEN MODEL FOR EXPERT SYSTEM IMPLEMENTATION (ROMES)

Expert system construction mainly implies the implementation of its three main parts:

- The knowledge base, with knowledge representation in the shape of data and methods;

- The inference engine, that applies the methods to infer new knowledge from the input knowledge;

- The user interface, providing for system-user and user-system communication, displaying, among other things, system knowledge and reasoning strategy.

where parts 1 and 2, particularly, are what distinguish an ES from a conventional software system. These elements are defined in the ROMES model by means of the classes DATUM, KNOWLEDGEBASE, RULE and USER_INTERFACE, as specified in the class diagram shown in Figure 4.3. The datum class, enabling definition of any data type, has an inheritance hierarchy with each specific data type (Type 1, Type 2, ... , Type n) used in the model, reciprocal relations of association of 1:n with the knowledgebase and rule classes (one datum may belong to one or more knowledgebases and rules and vice versa, one knowledgebase or rule has several data) and of 1:1 with the user_interface class (one datum is related with just one interface in the model). The knowledgebase and rule classes are associated to each other in a relation of 1:n (a knowledgebase has several rules and a rule can be a member of several classes) and they are associated with the user interface at 1:1 (a knowledgebase and a rule access a single interface). The user_interface class is related to the others at 1:n (it accesses several data, knowledgebases and rules).

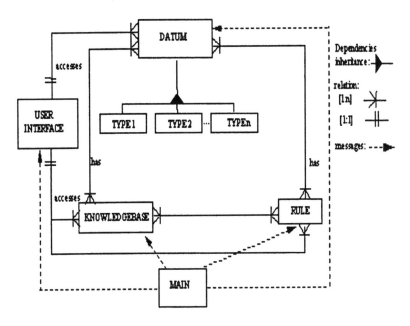

Figure 4.3: ROMES Class Diagram

MAIN is the main module, whose primary function is to instantiate objects from each class and start expert system execution, referring control to the user interface. Next, we describe the essential properties of each class defined in the model.

4.3.1   DATUM Class

The entire inference engine data structure is based on the class datum. All the data types used in the rules and for matching fact-base elements are created on this basis through inheritance. Matching is implemented in a special way (see Figure 4.4) based on the RETE algorithm [11]. The class datum has a series of mechanisms (methods) to notify the inference engine of changes occurring in the variables used in reasoning. Thus, if these mechanisms are to be operational, the variables used in the rules must be instances of the class datum or its derivatives. These instances must be named when they are created; this name is used to display their content to the user as a result of a knowledge-base query. The instances are created using the Datum constructor as *unknown* and will become *known* when the datum object takes a value during the inference process. This change is made by the method Modification which acts as a demon, firing as soon as the datum is changed and notifying the change to all the rules containing it and all the data belonging to these rules. To this end, each instance of the class datum will have a list of rules whose *antecedent* it influences, and the rules are notified, in the case of forward chaining, by the method AddressAntecedent when the value of the instance changes. Similarly, it will have a list of

rules whose *consequent* it affects, and the rules are notified by the method AddressConse-
quent. Furthermore, it will have another list including other instances that are notified by
the method AddressDatum when the value of the datum in question changes. This functionality is particularly useful for propagating the changes to the other objects and will be
used if a rule is to be fired when a given object, or any parts of it, has been changed.

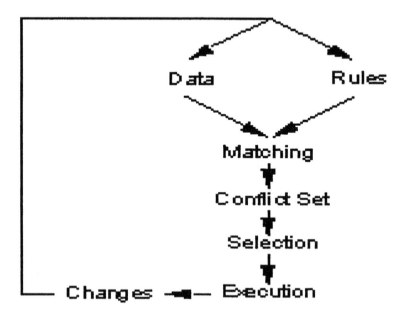

Figure 4.4: RETE Net

The class datum also incorporates other useful methods - like copy a datum, query
status, return its name, display its contents, etc. -, which will enable the user to develop an
expert system flexibly.

4.3.2   RULE Class

The class rule is the base class from which all the rules making up the expert system derive.
The chosen knowledge representation is based on production rules of the type if condition
then actions, because they offer the following benefits [8]:

- Modularity: Each rule defines a unit of knowledge whose meaning is independent of
  the other rules;

- Incrementability: As the rules are independent, new rules can easily be added to the
  knowledge base, thus incrementing system knowledge;

- Transparency: A rule-based system is well suited for tracing the rules that have been
  fired to attain the goal.

An embedded object-oriented methodology combined with the semantic richness of rule-based systems provides a powerful mechanism for knowledge-based system specification and development. An instance of the class rule is structured as follows:

- The *name* of the rule, which identifies the rule and is supplied by the RULE constructor;

- The *priority* of the rule (integer of 0 to 100; default = 50);

- The *maximum number* of times a rule may be fired during a query (default = 1);

- The *explanation*, a text that explains the reasons why a rule is used;

- The *criterion* for selection of the next rule to be fired in the conflict set.

Additionally, it will have a *list of antecedent variables*, which contains all the variables involved when evaluating the premise, and another *list of consequent variables*, which contains all the variables that undergo a change owing to a rule being fired. These variables must be instances derived from the class datum so that they inherit the above-mentioned mechanisms. The class has the methods AntecedentVariable and ConsequentVariable to record the variables in the above lists and construct the body of the rule using the Antecedent and Consequent methods. The rule is notified of a change in an antecedent variable during forward chaining or in a consequent variable during backward chaining. The class rule also includes other methods to check that the rule's antecedent is true, alter its priority, enter the rule into the conflict set, check whether one rule has a lower priority than another, explain the reasons for its use, etc.

4.3.3 KNOWLEDGEBASE Class

The class knowledgebase constitutes the framework for the construction of knowledge bases. All the knowledgebase instances needed to build the expert system derive from it. In the ROMES model, a knowledge base is composed of a goal and a list of rules, to which a series of parameters are applied to guide the reasoning towards the goal when the base is queried. An instance of the class knowledgebase is structured as follows:

- The *name* of the knowledge base, which is specified when an instance is created;

- The *goal*, which is the variable to be reached when querying the base;

- The *list of rules* making up the knowledge base;

- The *criterion* for selection which determines the next rule to be fired during a base query;

- The *type of chaining* to be used (forward, backward and mixed; default = mixed) [14], and

- The *reasoning* set out in the list of rules fired after a database query, enabling display of all of the explanations given by the rules.

The model implements a list of all the knowledge bases instantiated at any one time, such that when a query is made, a knowledge base name search is carried out using the class method GeneralQuery, and the goal search is started using the chaining type specified in the method at the beginning of the query or the default type. As a result of the search, the list of the rules that have been fired, which provides the reasoning strategy, will be produced by means of the class method GeneralExplanation and the system will display each of the explanations given for the rules fired under *reasoning*. The capability of explanation is one of the features of the model, and it is used to explain to the user the need for a given datum or how the conclusions have been reached, providing a perfect understanding of complex problems. The model defines two conflict sets for each knowledge base, one for forward chaining (rules whose antecedent is true at a given time during the query) and another for backward chaining (rules whose consequent assigns a value to the goal). It also provides for queries of other knowledge bases while a given base is being queried, for which purpose it will have a list of operational bases and an indicator (active, passive or waiting) of the status of each base. The expert system control module is located in the class knowledgebase by the Query method which searches for the goal using the goal specification, the next rule selection criterion and by settling conflict sets. During the reasoning process, it is necessary to decide which rule will be fired next so as to get a solution as efficiently as possible. To this end, the ROMES model proposes a control strategy with two processing phases:

- Filtering phase: For each type of chaining (forward and backward), a subset of candidate rules for firing is selected from all the rules in the knowledge base. Both subsets are stored in their respective conflict set.

- Conflict settlement phase: Using the specified selection criterion, a rule is selected from all the feasible rules and is then fired.

ROMES proposes another kind of control by means of metarules used to express knowledge on the rules themselves. For example, it may have rules that alter the priority of other rules. The class knowledgebase also includes other methods useful in system operation, like:

- Change the priority of a knowledge base rule;

- Update the conflict set;

- Locate a given knowledge base;

- Search for all the possible solutions for a given goal.

Figure 4.5 shows a diagram of general system behaviour, its structure and the interrelations between its parts. Each knowledge base, instance of the class knowledgebase, contains: a) a set of rules (R1, R2, ..., Rn) in which each rule, instance of the class rule, has knowledge on the variables it handles (the rule R1 handles the variables A, B, C in the Antecedent and D, E, F in the Consequent); b) the fact base, as a set of variables (A, B, C, D, ..., J), instances of the class datum or a derived class, that constitute an active part of both the antecedent and the consequent; c) the conflict set, composed of two lists of viable rules for firing one for forward chaining (Rf1, ..., Rfn) and another for backward chaining (Rb1, ..., Rbm); and 4) the inference engine, as a body containing the control and the priority rule (Rk) firing mechanism of the conflict set.

4.3.4   USER_INTERFACE Class

The objects in this class have the mission of interacting with the user both to ask for information and give explanations on the steps taken during the reasoning process. The model sets out two basic methods for this class:

- Analysis: This method is conceived to query the expert system, extracting concrete knowledge from the interface.

- Reasoning: It explains the reasoning of all of the rules fired after the last system query. This method should be inhibited when the system is first executed and will be activated after each query.

Both for value querying and system responses and information, the class user_interface will normally be implemented in a windows environment, providing for dialogue with the user.

4.4   ROMES MODEL APPLICATION

SEHO, an expert system for the homeopathic treatment of glaucoma [9, 1], developed at CETTICO (Centre of Technology Transfer in Knowledge Engineering) and transferred to the Spanish National Organisation for the Blind (ONCE) to assist therapists not specialised in homeopathic medicine, was chosen as an application to verify the adequacy and efficiency of the model.

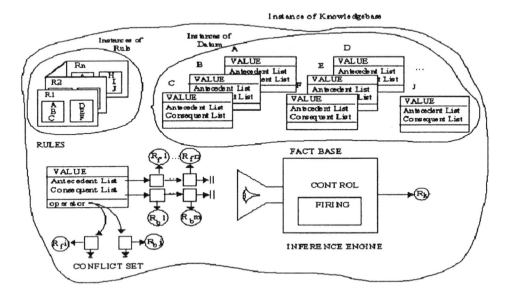

Figure 4.5: Overall System Diagram

The expert system architecture is supported by the GURU tool [15], which is a usual environment for the development of expert systems on PCs. GURU offers a wide range of information processing tools, such as: spreadsheet, word processor, graphics processor, report generator, communications processing and a natural language interface. Furthermore, it is compatible with SQL and supports forward, backward and mixed chaining, multivalue variables and fuzzy reasoning.

4.4.1 Description of SEHO

The expert system for homeopathic glaucoma treatment (SEHO) includes the expertise of a pluralist homeopathic doctor. This knowledge is divided into several knowledge bases modelled as rules which are applied to the symptomatology of a glaucoma sufferer on the basis of specific symptoms, category and field [9]. The specific symptoms are the symptoms suffered by the patient in the area affected by the disease. A distinction is made between major patient symptoms, which are acute symptoms or the symptoms considered most important by the doctor within the patient's symptomatology, and minor symptoms, which are less severe or considered to be of less relevance by the doctor. Atrophy of the optical nerve, retinal apoplexy, migraine, conjunctivitis, etc., are specific symptoms. The category refers to the worsening or improvement of the symptoms in given physical or atmospheric conditions (e.g., intensification of pain in the eyes when it is hot). The category is offset by the antagonistic category, the category opposed to the patient's (e.g., relief of eye pain when it is hot). The field refers to the patient's reactions to the disease and is characterised by typological data on the patient, his/her physical and mental health and his/her constitution (e.g. vomiting, vascular problems, ill humour, malnutrition, glandular problems, etc.). The pharmacopoeia used is composed of 18 homeopathic medicines, each of which covers an average of 12 symptoms per remedy. These medicines and the symptoms they cover were specified by the expert as the most suitable and most typical for treating each particular case of the disease. The final conclusion provided by the system is a choice of a series of medicines suited to the particular case of the patient and the dose at which these medicines should be administered, for how long and how many times a day. The system also provides the reasoning strategy followed during the inference process, explaining the reasons that led it to specify the medicine type and dilution to be administered in each case.

4.4.2 SERHO (Reusable expert system for homeopathic glaucoma treatment)

As the structure of ROMES is independent of the implementation language (e.g., C++, EIFFEL, SmallTalk, etc.), the generic classes (datum, knowledgebase, rule and user-interface) described in section 4.3 were designed in C++ so that the model could be applied to implement a particular expert system. Later, the SEHO expert system was redesigned according to this new OO approach to produce the expert system SERHO (the R of reusable has been incorporated as reusability is one of the major features of object-oriented components). For this purpose:

- The medicine class was designed. This class is a derivative of the class datum and includes data such as: name of the medicine, specific symptoms, categories and field characteristics it covers, appropriate dilution, etc. Thus each medicine constitutes an instance of this class.

- An instance of the class rule was created for each SEHO rule, assigning specific values to the name of the rule, priority, selection criteria, explanation, etc., that make up the rule structure. The fuzzy variables used in GURU that may have up to 256 values [13] have been substituted using generic ordered lists and sets.

- Seven knowledge bases derived from the class knowledgebase were instantiated with a similar structure to the one used in SEHO.

An ObjectWindows container class was used as the base class to implement the user interface, and the screens of questions requiring yes/no answers (62 on specific symptoms, 57 on category and 66 on field characteristics) in the SEHO system were substituted by 4 multiple choice windows with scroll bars (one for symptoms, one for category, one for field characteristics and another for important specific symptom selection). All the messages are displayed in a separate window with an option menu, managed by the application.

4.4.3 Comparative study of SEHO and SERHO

The human expert in homeopathy selected fifteen test cases, established as the system success criteria, along with another twenty frequent cases. These cases were used to validate the results of the system, and compare the SEHO and SERHO systems. Of the cases chosen, 10% were extreme cases generated artificially, 10% were ambiguous cases and the remaining were typical cases. The expert approved the system's procedure in all cases. Furthermore, fifteen typical cases were put to other experts in homeopathy, and they only disagreed on one ambiguous case, for which there were two equally acceptable forms of treatment and the choice of one or the other was a matter of preference. However, the system indicated the second possibility as an optional treatment. The results shown in Table 4.1 were obtained using a straightforward test case, several intermediate cases and the most unfavourable case, which entails considering all the specific symptoms, category and field characteristics as proper to the patient [12].

Table 4.1: SEHO and SERHO Execution Times

Case type ES	Straightforward	Intermediate	Unfavourable
SEHO	3 Minutes	8 Minutes	55 Minutes
SERHO	2 Seconds	50 Seconds	6 Minutes

The above results show that the ROMES model implemented in C++ has produced a much more efficient expert system than the one obtained using the GURU tool: it is actually 8.1 times faster in the most unfavourable case and 89 times faster in straightforward cases. There are three main explanations for this reduction in time:

- The use of an object-oriented model, which produces well-structured systems, thus cutting down the run time of the resulting code, apart from shortening system development time [7];

- Removal of the database accesses existing in SEHO;

- The use of a compiled language, like C++, for implementation instead of interpreters as in the case of GURU .

4.5   COMPARATIVE ANALYSIS BETWEEN ROMES AND OTHER EXPERT SYSTEM DEVELOPMENT TOOLS

Gaschnig [13] suggests that the following aspects be assessed to evaluate an expert system building tool:

- The quality of system queries and decisions;

- The adequacy of the reasoning techniques used;

- The man-machine interaction quality;

- System efficiency;

- Investment efficacy.

As these assessment criteria are very subjective and there are no specific evaluation metrics, Dreuth [10] introduces comparative criteria (knowledge representation formalisms, types of variables used, inheritance, type of inference, adaptation to external interfaces) that describe common capabilities and features of this kind of tool and others that define their efficiency. In this case, ROMES has been compared with the tools Crystal, Leonardo, Guru and ART-IM to obtain the results shown in Table 4.2, which reflect the power and efficiency of this expert system building tool.

4.6   CONCLUSIONS

When defining the different models for ES development, from the application domain to the implementation domain (conceptual model, formal model and implementation model), the transformation of the conceptual model into the formal model has always been a problem. Object-oriented techniques have emerged as a powerful lubricant to smooth this transformation, as the frontier between analysis and logical design disappears in OO. Alonso et al. [4] give a clear description of how these techniques can be used to derive the formal model from the conceptual model. With regard to the implementation model, tools like GURU, Crystal, ART-IM have typically been used to directly implement the ES without considering the design of this type of model. In this paper, we have defined a generic open model for ES implementation, called ROMES, which employs OO to structure and formalise the different architectural components of an ES. This model can be said to have the following strengths:

- It is a highly efficient system that produces expert systems with fast execution times;

- Taking a ROMES implementation in a programming language, expert system development time is substantially shorter than with other tools;

Table 4.2: Comparison of Different Tools

Characteristics	Crystal	Leonardo	Guru	ART-IM	ROMES
Knowledge Representation	Rules, Commands	Rules, Frames	Rules, Commands	Rules, Schemata	Rules, Frames
Variables	Strings, Numerals	Strings, Numerals, Lists	Strings, Integers, Numerals, Logic	Strings, Numerals, Sequences, Stream	Strings, Numerals, Lists, Integers, Logic, Sequences, Stream
Inheritance	NO	Multilevel	NO	Multilevel	Multilevel
Inference	Backward	Backward, Forward, Mixed	Backward, Forward, Mixed	Forward	Backward, Forward, Mixed
External Interfaces	Lotus 1-2-3, Symphony, dBase, ASCII	Lotus 1-2-3, dBase, Btrieve, DataEase	Lotus 1-2-3, Multiplan, dBase, SDF, Basic, ASCII	Generic Interface	Generic Interface
Relative Speed (*)	114.3	100	128.6	128.6	1214.3

- Being object oriented, its components can be reused (for example, instances of the same rule can be used for different knowledge bases) and it produces change-resistant systems;

- Object orientation makes the system easily extendible, allowing rapid and straightforward incorporation of new functionalities (like scripts, agendas, blackboards, etc.).

- As the user and inference interface modules are separate, the reasoning process can be adapted to any external interface;

- It is a robust system, easy to use and with a good basis for later growth.

4.7 REFERENCES

[1] F. Alonso Amo, A. Gómez Pérez, G. López Gómez and C. Montes. An Expert System For Homeopathic Glaucoma Treatment (SEHO), Expert Systems With Applications, vol. 8, no. 1, pp. 89–99, January-March, 1995.

[2] F. Alonso Amo, N. Juristo and J. Pazos. Trends in Life-Cycle Models for SE and KE: Proposal for a Spiral/Conical Life-Cycle Approach. International Journal of Software Engineering and Knowledge Engineering, vol. 5, no. 3, pp. 445–465, 1995.

[3] F. Alonso Amo, N. Juristo, J. L. Maté and J. Pazos. Software Engineering and Knowledge Engineering: Towards a Common Life Cycle. J. Systems Software, no. 33, pp. 65–79, 1996.

[4] F. Alonso Amo, J. L. Fuertes, L. Martínez and C. Montes. A Knowledge Engineering Software Development Methodology Applied to a Spiral/Conical Life Cycle. In Proceedings of the 9th International Conference on Software Engineering and Knowledge Engineering, pp. 30–38, Madrid, Spain, June 17-20, 1997.

[5] B. I. Blum. The Evaluation of SE. In Proceedings of the 1st International Conference on Information and Knowledge Management, Baltimore, MD, November 8-11, 1992.

[6] B. W. Boehm. A Spiral Model of Software Development and Enhancement. ACM Software Engineering Notes , vol. 11, no. 4, pp. 22–42, 1988.

[7] G. S. Booch. Object-Oriented Analysis and Design With Applications, Menlo Park, CA: Benjamin Cummings, 1991, chap. 7, pp. 267–287.

[8] J. W. Clancey. Knowledge-Based Tutoring: The Guidon, Cambridge, MA: MIT Press, 1987.

[9] R. Cristóbal and N. Ortiz. Sistema Experto Para El Tratamiento Homeopático Del Glaucoma, MSc Thesis, Facultad de Informática, Madrid, 1991.

[10] H. Dreuth and A. Moms. Prototyping Expert Solutions: An Evaluation of Crystal, Leonardo, GURU and ART-IM, Expert Systems, vol. 9, no. 1, pp. 35–55, February, 1992.

[11] C. Forgy. RETE: A Fast Algorithm for the Many Pattern/Many Object Match Problem, Artificial Intelligence, vol. 19, no. 1, pp. 17–38, September, 1982.

[12] M. M. García. CLASER: Conjunto De Librerías Abiertas Para El Desarrollo Y Consulta De Sistemas Expertos Reutilizable, Technical Report, Facultad de Informática, Madrid, 1993.

[13] J. Gaschnig et al. Evaluation Of Expert Systems: Issues And Case Studies, Reading, MA: Addison-Wesley, 1983.

[14] S. K. Padhy and S. N. Dwivedi. PCAAD - An Object-Oriented Expert System For Assembly Of Printed Circuit Boards, Expert Systems, vol. 9, no. 1, pp. 11–24, February, 1992.

[15] J. Shaw and A. Zeichick. Expert System Resource Guide, AI Expert, vol. 7, no. 12, pp. 42–49, December, 1992.

[16] E. H. Shortliffe. Computer-based medical consultation. MYCIN. New York: American Elsevier, 1976.

5

Re-engineering Requirements Specifications for Reuse: A Synthesis of 3 Years Industrial Experience

Wing Lam
Department of Computer Science, University of Hertfordshire
College Lane,
Hatfield,
Herts AL10 9AB,
UK
W.Lam@herts.ac.uk,
Phone: +44 (0)1707 284337, Fax: +44 (0)1707 284303

Abstract: This paper reflects on 3 years industrial experience of reuse. The specific focus of our work has been on reuse at the requirements level, and we outline some of the reasons why reuse at the requirements level is desirable. Our main contribution is a model of reuse (called R2) which highlights our observation that reusable requirements specifications tend to evolve through a process of re-engineering existing requirements specifications. Two case-studies are presented as evidence for the model's validity. We also present the results of a literature survey, and describe how our work differs in emphasis from related work.

5.1 MOTIVATION: TOWARDS REQUIREMENTS REUSE IN PRACTICE

Increasingly, many organisations are looking towards large-scale, systematic software reuse as a way of improving productivity, raising quality and reducing delivery time-scales [27, 20, 11]. Caper-Jones [12], in his book Patterns of software systems failure and success remarks "traditionally, full software re-usability programs have had the highest return on investment of any technology (about $ 30 returned for every $ 1 invested)". It is recognised that large-scale systematic reuse involves reuse at all levels of software engineering, from requirements through to code [31, 2]. However, industrial experiences of requirements reuse is an area that is underrepresented in the current literature. This paper synthesises the author's industrial experience of requirements reuse. This experience spans 3 years and 3 organisations operating in different domains (avionics, telecommunications and customer-services). The main contribution in this paper is a model of requirements reuse that places emphasis on the evolution of reusable requirements. This model is based on iterative re-engineering. Section 5.2 of this paper first presents the case for requirements reuse. Our model of requirements reuse, called R2, is introduced in Section 5.3. In Sections 5.4 and 5.5, we describe 2 industrial case-studies of requirements reuse which provide some validation for the R2 model. Section 5.6 discusses issues regarding the suitability, validation and generality of the R2 model. Section 5.7 gives a review of the current literature, and explains how the ideas in this paper differ from related work. Finally, Section 5.8 presents our conclusions.

5.2   THE CASE FOR REQUIREMENTS REUSE

Reuse will benefit some organisations more than others. A systematic reuse process is particularly desirable for organisations engaged in domain-specific or product-line software development [3], where a family of similar applications is developed and where the level of reuse is potentially very high. Macala et al. [21], for example, discuss the concept of a family of air vehicle training systems at Boeing, in which specific training aircraft are seen as part of the family. Specifically, the reuse of products and process at the requirements level can assist in the following ways:

- An existing requirements set can be used to rapidly develop a *new* requirements set for a similar system, thus reducing the time-to-specification.

- An existing requirements set can be used to aid completeness checking of a newly written requirements set for a similar system. For example, by triggering from the customer *forgotten*, assumed or unanticipated requirements.

- Requirements Engineering (RE) knowledge can be used to spotlight unrealistic or *troublesome* requirements based on the organisation's previous experience of similar systems.

- Requirements reuse facilitates reuse at later stages of development [32, 2]. For example, the work on domain-specific architectures [35, 36] focuses on the reuse of architectural designs that support established *reference* requirements in the domain.

- Cost and effort information recorded for a system with a given specification can be used to estimate cost and effort for a system with a similar specification; useful in a competitive bidding situation.

- RE, particularly in the early stages, involves the handling of uncertain and mutable problem models. Previously developed RE models can be used as tools for managing and reducing uncertainty and mutability.

In sum, it would seem that reuse at the RE level is desirable in most software organisations, but is particularly important to those that specialise in particular domains.

5.3   REFLECTING ON EXPERIENCE: THE R2 MODEL OF REUSE

The author has had three years industrially centred experience of reuse at the requirements level; some of this experience is documented in [14, 16]. In this paper, the author will propose (upon reflection) a model of reuse, called R2 (short for the 2 R's in *Re-engineering for Reuse*), and then explain how the model is supported and validated by his industrial experiences. The R2 model is depicted in Figure 5.1. It should be noted that a distinction is often made between reuse and re-engineering. Leach [19], for example, refers to re-engineering as "..an existing system is transformed to another system.." and reuse as "..artefact is used in more than one project or system". In our work, we still see re-engineering as a transformation process, but one that is an integral part of an evolutionary reuse process.

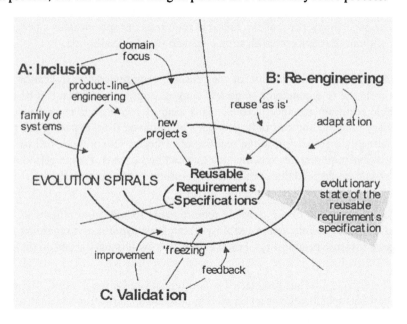

Figure 5.1: The R2 model of reuse

At the centre of the R2 model is the goal, a reusable requirements specification. One of our concerns is that there are few models of the reuse process that capture the *life-cycle* of reuse artefacts (a review of the current literature is given in Section 5.7). One of the central motivations behind the R2 model is the recognition that reusable requirements do not suddenly just *emerge*. In practice, what seems to happen is that reusable requirements evolve, improving with usage and feedback from project application. This is represented by the spiral nature of R2 and the notion that a reusable requirements specification has an *evolutionary state*. Each spiral is essentially a transition in the evolutionary state of the reusable requirements specification. Each transition consists of 3 basic phases:

Phase A, Inclusion: The treatment of a system as one where requirements reuse is both feasible and desirable. This might be determined in a number of different ways. Gomaa [10], for example, discusses the concept of a *family* of systems, where individual systems might be seen as belonging (or not belonging) to a particular family of systems. Lam [15] and Macala et al. [21] use the notion of *product-lines*, where similar systems are considered as part of the same product-line. Lam [14] also emphasises how systems that pertain to the same *domain* tend to have a high potential for reuse.

Phase B, Re-engineering: The re-engineering of an evolving reuse artefact, the reusable requirements specification, to produce a requirements specification for the current project/system. The nature of the re-engineering process is likely to change as the reuse artefact, the reusable requirements specification, becomes more mature. In the early stages of evolution, the reusable requirements specification is likely to be in a state that is difficult to reuse, where there is a high level of (time-consuming) adaptation. In the later stages of evolution, however, the re-engineering process becomes simpler, e.g. many parts of the reusable requirements specification can be reused *as-is* without adaptation or with simple instantiation/specialisation.

Phase C, Validation: The validation of the reusable requirements specification. Feedback from the re-engineering stage will suggest improvements that can be made to reusable requirements specification. This kind of feedback is central to the evolutionary process, and can only generally be obtained from exposing the reusable requirements specification to the realities of projects. Often, there will be parts of the reusable requirements specification that can be *frozen* (for some period of time), i.e. it has been decided that some state of re-usability has been reached.

The evolutionary state of the reusable requirements specification reflects its gradual maturity, in this case, its inherent re-usability (though we avoid issues regarding how we might judge or measure re-usability). For example, two evolutionary states might be:

Startup. The organisation has just started a requirements reuse programme. The reusable requirements specification is an actual requirements specification of an earlier system which is to be re-engineered for a new system. The reusable requirements specification is at a very early stage of evolution, and is not particularly easy to reuse, i.e. difficult and time-consuming to tailor for the new system.

Advanced. The reusable requirements specification has a high proportion (say >70%) of generic and reusable requirements. Many of the requirements can be reused *as-is*.

Note that, in practice, there is no endpoint for evolution; an organisation is likely to keep on evolving a reusable requirements specification as long as there is a desire to maintain reuse objectives. To provide some evidence of the soundness of the R2 model, we describe, in the following sections, 2 industrially (rather than academically)-centred case studies that provide some validation of the model.

5.4 MODEL ILLUSTRATION 1: THE AERO-ENGINE CONTROL SYSTEM STUDY

5.4.1 Phase A: Inclusion

The organisation specialises in avionics (aviation electronics) systems, the parent organisation being a major aircraft engine manufacturer. Modern passenger aircraft engines use a computer-based control system called a FADEC (Full Authority Digital Engine Controller). Though FADECs differ in their interface to airframe components, the software in FADECs tends to have similar control functionality. Aircraft engines are typically manufactured as part of an engine series, and significant savings can be accrued by having a FADEC software series where a high level of reuse is achieved across the series (Figure 5.2). Central to this reuse strategy is the notion of a generic piece of FADEC software (including requirements) that will evolve with an engine series; we refer to this as the reuse *chain*.

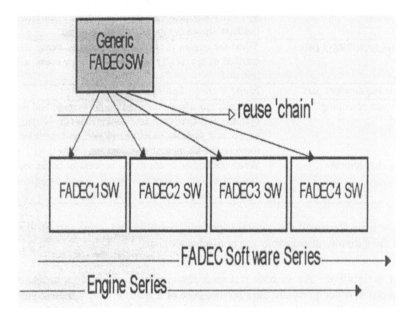

Figure 5.2: Reuse across a FADEC software series

5.4.2 Phase B: Re-engineering

A detailed description of our requirements specification re-engineering process can be found in [14, 16]. In this paper, we describe selected aspects of the re-engineering process.

Formulate generic requirements from concrete ones by reasoned abstraction. We identified equivalent or matching requirements in different requirements specifications for

FADEC software. As these requirements were in a concrete form, i.e. specific to a particular FADEC, it was necessary to abstract out the system-specific details to formulate generic requirements. Table 5.1 shows an example of this abstraction process.

Table 5.1: Use of abstraction to formulate a generic requirement

Element in Abstraction Process	Example
Concrete requirement from system A	When the engine is not in the process of being started, cranked or run, if the fuel switch is in the OFF position and the master crank switch is in the ON position, and the engine start switch is then turned to the ON position then a dry crank will be initiated.
Equivalent concrete requirement from system B	When the engine is not in the process of being started, cranked or run, if the fuel switch is in the OFF position and then the engine start switch is turned to the CRANK position, then a dry crank will be initiated.
Constant requirement part	When the engine is not in the process of being started, cranked or run, if (X) and then (Y), a dry crank will be initiated.
Variable requirement part	X and Y are cockpit-specific signals.
Abstraction reasoning	Cockpits are specific to a particular system, and not all systems will have the same cockpit layout. Hence, this aspect is a variable requirement part and must be factored out of the generic requirement.
generic requirement	When the engine is not in the process of being started, cranked or run, if (cockpit signal 1) and then (cockpit signal 2), a dry crank will be initiated.

Here, we have separated the constant (generic, reusable and core) part of the requirement from the variable (changeable and non-reusable) part.

Factor out variability.   As we have just seen, the variable parts in a requirement need to be factored out in order to isolate the reusable core of a requirement. Understanding what is variable in an application domain facilitates the re-engineering process. Discussion with domain experts allowed us to create factor-out lists, as shown in Table 5.2, which guided our abstraction and re-engineering efforts in general.

Identify the available choice sets.   By examining similar requirements across different requirements specifications, we found that some requirements had a defined range of options, which we chose to record as choice sets. For example, a FADEC system might have a requirement for *engine relight* which automatically energises the igniter when a flame-out occurs (such as in the event of severe water ingestion). Associated with this requirement is a number of choices:

- The igniters are energised for a minimum specified period of time.

- The igniters are energised for a maximum specified period of time.

Table 5.2: A factor-out list

Information to Factor-Out	Advice
Cockpit controls	Different aircraft will have a different cockpit layout. Instead, think in terms of a set of abstract signals such as engine start, engine stop, power on and power off which can be mapped onto a specific arrangement of cockpit controls.
Sensor-specifics	Different aircraft may use different sensors to achieve the same objective. For example, the sensors used for detecting that an aircraft is on the ground can vary from altimeter, weight on front wheels, weight on back wheels or any combination of sensors. Reference to specific sensors should therefore be replaced with what the sensor's objective is (such as to detect if the aircraft is on the ground).
EEC lanes	The EEC (Electronic Engine Controller at the heart of a FADEC) usually has a dual-lane architecture. However, hardware advancements or alternative designs may result in more sophisticated architectures being used. Therefore, the assumption that the EEC will always have a dual-lane architecture should not be made.
airframe-specifics	Airframes are rarely the same. Variance can occur in terms of power supply, aircraft electrics and hardware devices, just to mention a few. These specifics need to be generalised.
hard-coded values	Reference to specific values should be avoided. Instead use a *variable* instead, for example, 'Fuel_on_Speed', as opposed to a real number.

- The igniters are energised for a minimum and maximum specified period of time.

- The igniters are energised until manually switched off by the pilot.

In this case, the choice emerges from a balance of safety and maintenance issues (igniters have a limited life), but the key point here is that we have captured the typical forms in which the requirement is commonly used.

5.4.3 Phase C: Validation

Feedback. We validated our reusable requirements specification for FADEC software during reviews with domain experts. Using the reusable requirements specifications on a trial basis on individual FADEC projects helped us to:

- Identify the appropriate level of abstraction for our reusable requirements. Under-abstraction leads to requirements that are too specific to be reused as-is; over-abstraction leads to requirements that are too devoid of detail to be meaningful. Validation helps us move towards the right balance between over and under-abstraction.

- Gradually *weed out* variable and non-reusable details we had not accounted for in our factor-out lists.

- Recognise new options in choice sets.

- Gradually work towards a universal structure for the reusable requirements specification that would apply to all FADEC software systems.

5.5   MODEL ILLUSTRATION 2: THE BUSINESS PROCESS STUDY

5.5.1   Phase A: Inclusion

The organisation is a major telecommunications services supplier, supplying hundreds of different services (e.g. telephony, video-conferencing, Internet connection, LAN installation). Time-to-market and time-to-use is crucial in the telecommunications business, and the organisation needs to ensure that its services are available on the market to potential customers and ready to use before its competitors. The *provision* process describes the business requirements (which include system requirements) that cover all the procedures between the receipt of an order from a customer and the point at which a service is ready to use. To shorten provisioning times for a service, the organisation wished to standardise a generic provisioning process (GPP), for which provisioning processes for individual divisions and the individual services offered by each division can be rapidly created. This concept of process reuse can be depicted hierarchically (Figure 5.3).

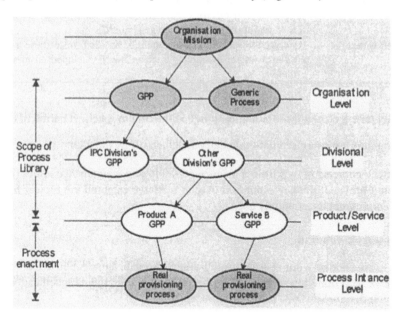

Figure 5.3: The process reuse hierarchy

5.5.2   Phase B: Re-engineering

A detailed description of our process re-engineering process can be found in [17]. Again, we describe only selected aspects of the re-engineering process.

The domain analysis process.   Prieto-Diaz [28] defines domain analysis as "a process by which information used in developing software systems is identified, captured, and organised with the purpose of making it reusable when creating new systems". Our overall domain analysis process involved the following steps:

1. Defining and refining a process domain.

2. Identifying the key *issues* in the process domain.

3. Selecting concrete instances of the process (in our case, provisioning processes for particular services).

4. Gathering the evidence for process instances (e.g. existing documentation, interview and observation studies) in order to model the process.

5. Identifying commonalities and variability between the process instances.

6. Deciding on appropriate and valid generalisations in the generic process (GPP).

7. Validation of generic processes through review and inspection.

8. Performing a variability analysis to anticipate future changes in process.

Steps 2-6 can be seen as the core re-engineering process in the R2 model.

Re-engineering allows the correction of defective processes.   It makes sense to re-use *good* processes, not *bad* (e.g. inefficient, slow) ones. As such, the development of a generic process may sensibly entail a degree of process re-engineering. We realised that our existing provision processes were not *perfect*. We identified certain improvements that could be made in a number of provision processes. Briefly, these included:

• Improving productivity on provisioning processes.

• Improving customer-perceived quality of the provisioning process.

• Identifying and removing redundant processing (e.g. keying in the same information).

• Identifying and introducing automated tasks (e.g. computer notification rather than relying on the human).

These improvements were incorporated into the GPP so that subsequent provisioning processes would *inherit* these improvements. However, some pitfalls were:

• Getting sidetracked by radical re-engineering rather than reuse ideas.

• Failing to simulate or *walk-through* newly re-engineered processes (e.g. in order to identify bottlenecks).

• Failing to get user acceptance for newly re-engineering processes.

5.5.3   Phase C: Validation

Review checkpoints.   We expected the GPP to undergo review, particularly at the following points in time:

- Casual validation of the GPP with staff and provisioning *experts*.

- Formal inspection and review meetings.

- Planned periodical organisational reviews of the GPP.

- Whenever a change in the organisation's provisioning policy occurs.

Maturity levels.   We defined a process reuse maturity model, based on the following levels (with brief entry criteria):

Recognition: Commonality in processes is recognised.

Conception: A generic version of the process exists.

Trial: The generic process has been tried out on a number of case studies.

Junior: The generic process has been successfully used for *real* in a variety of situations.

Senior: The generic process has undergone substantial reuse within the organisation and is considered the accepted way of doing something.

Refinement: The generic process is being continuously improved and optimised.

Unlike process maturity models such as the Capability-Maturity-Model, our process reuse maturity model applies to individual processes rather than at the level of the organisation as a whole (this is because different processes can be at different levels of maturity).

5.6   FURTHER ISSUES: SUITABILITY, VALIDATION AND GENERALITY

There are a number of other case studies that we could also have presented, though for brevity, we choose not to describe them here. Our main point is to highlight the iterative nature of the R2 model of reuse, which explicitly recognises the role of re-engineering in the evolution of reusable requirements specifications. We believe that this notion of evolution is an inescapable part of creating *good* reuse artefacts. In this section, we would like to consider further issues regarding suitability, validation and generality:

Suitability. The R2 model, as presented in this paper, represents a general paradigm of reuse, the re-engineering for reuse paradigm. We feel this is suitable for requirements, as requirements tend to be complex engineering artefacts (requirements specifications for complex systems can be hundreds of pages in length). For simpler artefacts, e.g. a code module, it may be that an experienced developer can immediately identify the necessary modifications to make a code module generic for a wide range of situations. We would contend, however, that for complex artefacts a more engaging re-engineering process is required.

Generality. On the surface, it would seem that the R2 model applies to all kinds of reuse
artefacts, not just reusable requirements. Our basis for this statement is that all reuse
artefacts tend to follow an evolutionary path, from a *concrete* form to a more abstract
form. A reusable design, for example, is one that is likely to have been used on many
occasions, undergoing improvements and refinements with each usage. We envisage
significant differences, however, in the treatment of the R2 model for different kinds
of reuse artefacts. For example, in Phase A: Inclusion, the domain for reuse requirements artefacts might be an *application* domain, e.g. telecommunication switching
systems. For an architectural design, the domain might span several application domains, e.g. the client-server architecture domain. Hence, concepts in the R2 model
needed to be redefined in the context of the reusable artefact.

Validation. As indicated earlier, the R2 model as presented in this paper is fairly general,
e.g. independent of organisation or application domain. We believe that most benefit
will accrue from our work from organisations taking the R2 model and specialising
it to their organisations and domains of interest. Therefore, as part of a broader
validation process, we need to investigate the *tailorability* of the R2 model. For
example, what kinds of guidance can be given to individuals wishing to tailor the R2
model? Also, one of the weaknesses of the R2 model is that there is little mention of
external factors that might influence the re-usability of a reuse artefact. For example,
a design aim might be incorporate flexibility for some new functionality anticipated
in the future. The R2 model needs to explicitly incorporate a much richer view of
re-usability.

5.7 LITERATURE REVIEW

In [18], we carry out a survey of existing requirements reuse approaches. We found that
there was a great deal of similarity between approaches. This, however, should not be too
surprising; after all, the common objective shared by all these approaches is to develop useful abstractions at the requirements level. Where we feel there are significant differences,
however, is in the emphasis (i.e. problem solving viewpoint) taken by different approaches,
which we summarise in Table 5.3.

Table 5.3: Review and comparison of related work on requirements reuse

Approach/ Emphasis	Sources	Description
Analogy	[7, 22, 24]	Borrowing from work in cognitive psychology [9], reuse re- volves around recognising the similarity between individual systems through the matching of a common abstract prob- lem model.
Case-based reasoning	[13]	In AI, automated case-based reasoners retrieve past cases from a case-base and adapt them in order to solve similar problems [33]. Such a framework can also be used to drive a reuse process where existing specifications (past cases) are modified to produce *new* specifications for similar systems.

Difference-based reasoning	[1, 25]	Overlapping with many of the concepts in case-based reasoning, difference-based reasoning considers the construction of new systems as *deltas* of existing systems.
Problem abstraction	[31, 30]	Problem abstraction attempts to capture essential elements of a particular type of problem, such as resource management systems. The problem abstraction can then be used to guide the acquisition of more specialised concepts for problem instances (for example, a library system can be considered an instance of a resource management problem). Reubenstein's [29] early work on the *Requirements Apprentice* system showed how problem abstraction could be used to semi-automate aspects of the reuse process.
Domain analysis	[28, 34]	Prieto-Diaz [28] defines domain analysis as "a process by which information used in developing software systems is identified, captured and organised with the purpose of making it reusable when creating new systems". In domain analysis, one is concerned with RE over a range of typical applications in a domain rather than on an individual system.
Goal-oriented domain modelling	[4]	This concentrates on identifying the *typical* goals in a domain, on the basis that individual systems in a particular domain are likely to share many of the same goals. Most library systems, for example, would wish to promote equal access to library stock even though the specifics of how this is achieved (maximum loan limit, no loaning of reference material etc.) may vary.
Parameterised requirements	[16]	While most approaches focus on developing generic artefacts, parameterisation addresses the question of how such generic artefacts can be tailored to individual systems. In the same way that code reuse is effected via parameterisation, the same principles are shown to be useful in the context of requirements.
Patterns	[6, 7, 8]	Code reuse has long been argued as one of the attractions of object-oriented software development. The notion of patterns attempts to leverage reuse at higher levels of abstraction. A pattern refers to a commonly re-occurring collection of related objects. Although patterns are seen primarily as a design artefact [8], Coad [5] discusses the use of analysis patterns at the requirements level.
Application families	[14, 16]	An extension of Parnas's [26] original idea of the *program family*. An application family approach encourages the study of commonalities between a set of applications, and the properties that distinguish on application from another. Importantly, systems are not viewed as isolated development projects, but as members of a family.

Domain-specific architectures	[35, 36, 10]	Strictly speaking, domain-specific architectures do not directly focus on reuse at the requirements level, but examine the relationship between requirements and generic software architecture. Specifically, the work of Tracz [35, 36] attempts to formalise domain-specific software architectures, and how they support the notion of *reference* requirements.
Re-engineering and evolution	This paper	The production of a reusable requirements specification as an evolutionary and iterative process that involves the re-engineering of existing requirements specifications.

Most of the approaches would appear to focus on the *product* of requirements reuse (e.g. models of reusable requirements), with little or no discussion of the process that is used to create the product. We would argue that the R2 model places much greater emphasis on the nature of the process used to create the *product*.

5.8 CONCLUSIONS

This paper has discussed reuse, focusing primarily on reuse at the requirements level. The specific contributions of this paper are:

- A 6-point case for requirements reuse which puts forward a qualitative argument.

- A new model of reuse, R2, which describes a re-engineering for reuse paradigm.

- The retrospective analysis of 2 industrially centred case studies of requirements reuse which validate concepts in the R2 model.

- A review of, and comparison with, existing approaches in the area of requirements reuse.

We do not claim that the R2 model is universally valid. Rather, we feel that what the R2 does best is to highlight the iterative and evolutionary nature associated with the maturity of complex reuse artefacts. It would be a useful exercise to track and log, in detail, the kinds of changes made to a complex reuse artefact. This might shed more light on the exact nature of the evolutionary process, as well as providing an opportunity to gather empirical data. It would also be worthwhile to identify the factors (technical and non-technical) which influence the evolutionary *pathway* of a reuse artefact. This may provide guidance on how we as software engineers can actively steer reuse artefacts to become highly reusable and high-value reuse artefacts.

5.9 REFERENCES

[1] S. Bailin. Difference-based engineering, In Proceedings of the 7th Annual Workshop on Software Reuse, St. Charles, Illinois, August 28-30, 1995.

[2] T. Biggerstaff and C. Ritcher. Reusability framework, assessment and directions, IEEE Software, 41(3), March, 1987.

[3] B. Boehm and W. Scherlis. Mega-programming, Proceedings of the STARS 92 Conference, December 1992.

[4] D. Bolton, S. Jones, D. Till, D. Furber, and S. Green. Using domain knowledge in requirements capture and formal specification construction. In Jirotka, M. and Goguen, J. (Eds.), Requirements Engineering: Social and Technical Issues, Academic Press, London, 1994.

[5] P. Coad. Object-Oriented Patterns, Communications of the ACM, 35(9):152-159, 1992.

[6] J.O. Coplien and D.C. Schmidt (Eds.). Pattern Languages of Program Design, Addison-Wesley, ISBN 0-201-6073-4, 1995.

[7] A. Finkelstein. Reuse of formatted requirements specifications, Software Engineering Journal, 3(5):186–197, 1988.

[8] E. Gamma, R. Helm, R. Johnson and J. Vlissides. Design Patterns: Elements of reusable object-oriented software, Reading MA, Addison-Wesley.

[9] D. Gentner. Structure mapping: a theoretical framework for analogy, Cognitive Science, 7:155–170.

[10] H. Gomaa. Reusable software requirements and architectures for families of systems, Journal of Systems and Software, 28:189–202, 1995.

[11] E. Horowitz and J.B. Munson. An Expansive View of reusable software, In T. Biggerstaff and A. Perlis, editors, Software Reusability: Concepts and Models, Volume 1, Chapter 2, pp. 19–41, ACM press/Addison-Wesley, New York, 1989.

[12] C. Jones. Patterns of Software Systems Failure and Success, International Thompson Computer Press, Boston USA.

[13] W. Lam. Reasoning about requirements from past cases, PhD thesis, Kings College, University of London, 1994.

[14] W. Lam. Achieving Requirements Reuse: a Domain-Specific Approach from Avionics, Journal of Systems and Software, 38(3): 197–209, 1997.

[15] W. Lam. A Case-study of Requirements Reuse through Product Families, Annals of Software Engineering (to appear).

[16] W. Lam, J.A. McDermid and A.J. Vickers. Ten Steps Towards Systematic Requirements Reuse, Journal of Requirements Engineering, 2:102–113, 1997.

[17] W. Lam, R. Davis, J. Hutton, R. Shortland and B. Whittle. Process reuse: 10 lessons for practitioners, IASTED International Conference on Software Engineering 98 (Submitted).

[18] W. Lam, S. Jones and C. Britton. Technology Transfer for Reuse: A Management Model and Process Improvement Framework, Third IEEE International Conference on Requirements Engineering, April 6-10, Colorado Springs, Colorado, USA, 1998.

[19] R. Leach. Software Reuse: Methods, Models and Costs, McGraw-Hill, New York, 1997.

[20] W.C. Lim. Effects of Reuse on Quality, Productivity, and Economics, IEEE Software, 11(5):23–30, 1994.

[21] R. Macala, L. Stuckey and D. Gross. Managing domain-specific, product-line development, IEEE Software, May 1996.

[22] N. Maiden and A. Sutcliffe. Exploiting reusable specification through analogy, Communications of the ACM, 35(4):55–64, 1993.

[23] N. Maiden. Acquiring Requirements: a domain-specific approach, In Proceedings of IFIP Working Groups 8.1/13.2 Conference, Domain Knowledge for Interactive System Design, (Eds. Sutcliffe, A.G., Benyon, D. and Assche, F.V.), Geneva, May 8-10, 1996.

[24] P. Massonet and A. Lamsweerde. Analogical reuse of requirements frameworks, In Proceedings of the 3rd IEEE International Conference on Requirements Engineering, 1997.

[25] K. Miriyala and T.H. Harandi. Automatic derivation of formal software specifications from informal descriptions, IEEE Transactions on Software Engineering, 17(10):1126–1142, 1991.

[26] D.L. Parnas. On the design and development of program families, IEEE Transactions on Software Engineering, Vol SE-2, March, 1976.

[27] J.S. Poulin, J.M. Caruso and D.R. Hancock. The Business Case for Software Reuse, IBM Systems Journal, 32(4):567–594, 1993.

[28] R. Prieto-Diaz. Domain analysis: an introduction, ACM SIGSOFT Software Engineering Notes, 15(2):47–54, 1990

[29] H.B. Reubenstein. Automated Acquisition of Evolving Informal Descriptions, Report No. AI-TR 1205, Artificial Intelligence Laboratory, Massachusetts Institute of Technology, 545 Technology Square, Cambridge, MA 02139, 1990.

[30] S. Robertson and K. Strunch. Reusing the products of analysis, Atlantic Systems Guild, 11 St. Mary's Terrace, London W2 1SU, UK.

[31] K. Ryan and B. Mathews. Matching conceptual graphs as an aid to requirements reuse, In Proceedings of the IEEE International Symposium on Requirements Engineering, ISBN 0-8186-3120-1, pp. 112-120, 1993.

[32] SPC. Software Productivity Consortium Reuse Adoption Guidebook, Version 01.00.03, SPC-92051-CMC, November, 1992.

[33] S. Slade. Case-based reasoning: a research paradigm, AI Magazine, 12(1):42–55, 1991.

[34] STARS. Organisation Domain Modeling Guidebook, STARS-VC-A023/011/00, March, 1995.

[35] W. Tracz. DSSA (Domain-Specific Software Architecture) pedagogical example, ACM SIGSOFT Software Engineering Notes, 20(3):49–62, 1995.

[36] W. Tracz, T. Angeline, S. Shafer and L. Coglianese. Experience Using an Avionics Domain-Specific Software Architecture, In the proceedings of NAECON'95, May 22-27, Dayton, Ohio, pp. 646–653, February 1995.

6

Object-Oriented Development Of X-Ray Spectrometer Software

Tuomas Ihme

VTT Electronics
P.O.Box 1100, FIN-90571
Oulu,
Finland
Tuomas.Ihme@vtt.fi
telephone +358-8-551 2111
telefax +358-8-551 2320

Abstract: Embedded computer systems, incorporated in various types of products and systems, are common in a wide range of everyday commodities as well as industrial and scientific equipment. In connection with the increasing use of object-oriented methodologies in the development of real-time computer systems, better means are provided for reusable embedded software architectures and components, as well. Yet, there is still no large-scale application and routine utilisation of commercial object-oriented technology in the development of hard real-time embedded software.

Commercial object-oriented technology usually has to be tailored to the specific characteristics and needs of individual embedded computer system domains. This paper is concerned with the object-oriented development process of scientific on-board X-ray spectrometer control software. It discusses the experiences gained through the utilisation of object-oriented real-time methods and tools based on OMT (Object Modelling Technique), MSC (Message Sequence Charts) and formal SDL (Specification and Description Language) notations.

6.1   INTRODUCTION

Although there are several commercial general-purpose object-oriented methods and tools available, these seem inadequate to manage the complexity of embedded software. Although there are some commercial object-oriented methods for real-time systems available, these have only been used to a limited extent for real-time embedded software, because of the following reasons, for example:

- The tool support for the method is unreliable due to a small number of users, e.g. the Hood method [8],

- No commercial tool support is available, e.g. the Octopus [1], Gomaa's [5], and Ellison's [4] methods,

- Some methods are very new, e.g. Real-Time UML [3],

- The target code produced on the basis of design models occupies too much memory (the ROOM method [9] supported by the ObjecTime tool), and

- CASE tools are often very expensive

Industry is presently showing great interest in formal and standard behavioural description techniques such as SDL, to be used for consistency checking, validating specifications and designs and for automatic generation of code from design models. Object-oriented techniques and notations such as OMT (Object Modelling Technique) and MSC (Message Sequence Charts) provide means for reusable embedded software. Many object-oriented features are already incorporated in the new SDL standards. Some commercial methodologies, such as ObjectGEODE by Verilog SA and SDT by Telelogic AB, integrate OMT, MSC and SDL techniques. The ObjectGEODE methodology consists of the OORT method [7] and the ObjectGEODE tool. The SDT methodology consists of the SOMT method [10] and the SDT tool.

This document is concerned with the experiences gained in the evaluation of the support for object orientation in the ObjectGEODE and SDT methodologies. The development and documentation needs of the existing SIXA on-board software [11] are used as the basic evaluation criterion of the methods. The SIXA instrument is a multielement X-ray photon counting spectrometer.

This paper will also focus on the applicability, and tailoring needs, of the Object-GEODE and SDT methodologies to object-oriented modelling of the SIXA on-board software. An outline of a set of object-oriented software development activities for X-ray spectrometers will be given. Examples of the use of architectural patterns [2, 3] will be shown.

The presented examples are derived from the documentation of SIXA on-board software. In the construction of the example models some of the operations of SIXA were simplified in order to reduce the size of the model. The most important simplification is that the examples depict measurement functions of the SIXA instrument only, thus excluding housekeeping functions, for example. The system is called SIXA Measurement Controller hereafter.

6.2 SYSTEM REQUIREMENTS SPECIFICATION

The product requirements specification of embedded systems often ignores software. Software development is only one of the subprojects of the master project. The system requirements specification recaptures the relevant product requirements for the software in a way that supports software development. The following models may be needed for the system requirements specification document of the SIXA Measurement Controller software:

- Textual Requirements,
- Hardware Architecture,
- Concept Dictionary,
- Requirements Use Case Model and
- System Context Diagram

The textual requirements are necessary, but they are not adequately supported by the ObjectGEODE and SDT tools. There are also shortcomings in the integration of textual descriptions and graphical models with the specification document of system requirements. As the tools have no free drawing support, a separate drawing tool has to be used for capturing the hardware architecture of the SIXA Measurement Controller. Hardware architecture views show the hardware components and interfaces with which the software relates. The SOMT method provides a good example of the concept dictionary (data dictionary). The requirements use case model may include a list of actors and use cases and a number of MSCs [10]. Use cases are first recorded using natural text structured into a number of text fields. MSC scenarios are then created from these textual use cases. Two MSC scenarios for the SIXA Measurement Controller are shown in Figures 6.1 and 6.2, depicting typical observation sequences of the controller:

- Receive measurement parameters
- Repeat for each target:
    - Switch on analog electronics
    - Receive target coordinates
    - Start the observation time
    - Finish the observation time
- Begin the ground contact
- Transmit the science data

The operating modes of the controller are Standby, Measurement, Data Retention and Dumping.

The interaction relationships between the SIXA Measurement Controller and external actors from the point of view of the software to be developed are shown in Figure 6.3. The SIXA Measurement Controller is installed in a satellite and controlled by a ground station via the satellite. The controller is responsible for three energy-spectrum observing modes and three single event characterisation observing modes. An array detector is used for detecting X-ray photons.

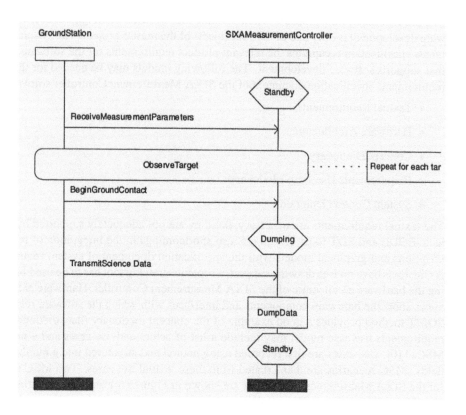

Figure 6.1: The Observation scenario for the SIXA Measurement Controller

6.3   SYSTEM ARCHITECTURE DEFINITION

The Broker architectural pattern [2, 3] is applied to the architectural design of the SIXA measurement system as shown in Figure 6.4. The Broker pattern is used to structure a complex system as a set of decoupled interoperating components. This results in better flexibility, maintainability, changeability and reusability. The Broker pattern includes another pattern that is called the Proxy pattern. The role of a proxy is to decouple clients from their servers. The ground station plays the role of a client in the Broker pattern as shown in Figure 6.4. It sends ground commands to the space craft service system that has the role of the broker in the pattern. Each ground command is given a time stamp, which specifies when it is to be sent to the SIXA Measurement Controller. When the time is reached to execute a command, the service system will give the command to the Satellite Computer BIUS, which plays the role of Server Proxy in the pattern. The SIXA Measurement Controller software is decomposed into two independent and almost identical subsystems, called Energy Measurement Controller and SEC Measurement Controller. These play the

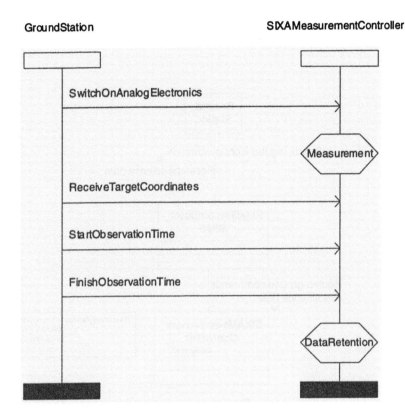

Figure 6.2: The Observe Target scenario.

role of servers in the Broker pattern. The ground station addresses ground commands to
the SIXA Measurement Controller, not to the separated subsystems. The Energy and SEC
Measurement Controller subsystems are allocated to independent processors. The role of
the Energy Measurement Controller is to control three observing modes: Energy-Spectrum
Mode (ESM), Window-Counting Mode (WCM) and Time-Interval Mode (TIM). The role
of the SEC Measurement Controller is to control three single event characterisation observing modes.

6.4 SUBSYSTEM ANALYSIS

The Energy and SEC Measurement Controller subsystems are very similar. The results of
a partial analysis of the Energy Measurement subsystem are represented by the following
models:

- External Event List,

- Analysis Use Case Models, an MSC scenario is shown in Figure 6.5, and

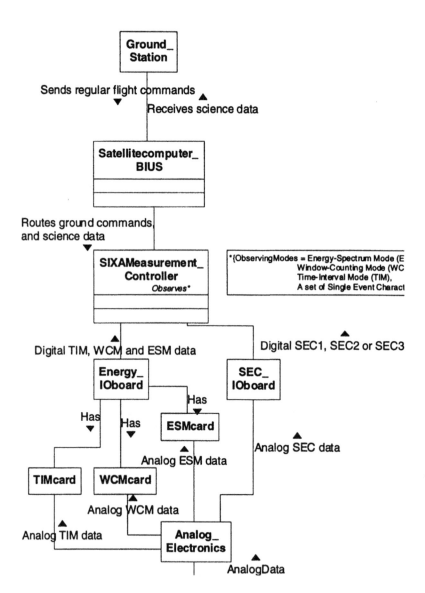

Figure 6.3: The system context diagram of the SIXA Measurement Controller.

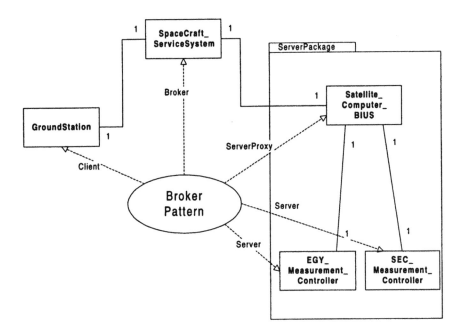

Figure 6.4: The architecture model of the SIXA Measurement system.

- Analysis Object Models.

The external event list defines the external events and their parameters, the sources and arrival patterns of the events, and the expected system response. The Analysis Object Model of the Energy Measurement subsystem is shown in Figure 6.6. The model comprises the main concepts of the subsystem, the most important properties of the concepts and the relationships between the concepts. Centralised control architecture is very common in the embedded control software of various products, as well as in industrial equipment and scientific instruments. The architecture is also known as master-slave architecture. The complexity of control is centralised on the master. This makes it easy to modify and maintain the software, provided that the system does not get too complex when the distributed control architecture becomes simpler. The master-slave architecture is well suited to hard-real-time systems requiring complete timing predictability. The centralised control architecture is adjusted to the Energy Measurement subsystem, see Figure 6.6. The Measurement Control class is responsible for controlling and timing the main functions of the subsystem. It provides methods to control the electronics and instances of rather passive Energy Data Acquisition and Energy File Management classes. The Energy Data Acquisition class is responsible for the acquisition of energy data chunks. It provides interfaces for controlling the science data acquisition and includes as well as hides data acquisition details. The Energy File Management class is responsible for the storing of energy data chunks. It provides interfaces for storing data chunks and controlling the transmission of the stored data to the ground station, as well as hiding data storing details.

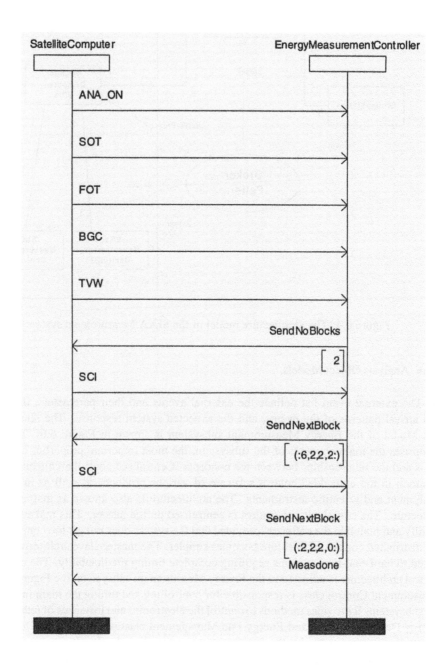

Figure 6.5: An MSC scenario of the Energy Measurement subsystem.

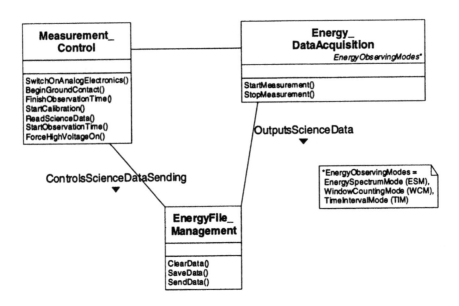

Figure 6.6: The analysis object model of the Energy Measurement subsystem.

6.5 SUBSYSTEM DESIGN

In the following paragraphs the suitability of the SDL language and ObjectGEODE and SDT tools for the modelling of the Energy Measurement subsystem is treated from different points of view.

6.5.1 Architectural and behavioural design

The mapping of concepts from the analysis object model of the Energy Measurement subsystem into SDL models is very straightforward in this case. The documentation structure of the Energy Measurement subsystem design models is shown in Figure 6.7. The Energy Measurement subsystem is mapped into the EGY Measurement block, the Measurement Control class into the MeasControl process, the Energy Data Acquisition class into the Data Acquisition process and the Energy File Management class into the File Management process. It is also easy to refine the analysis MSC of the Energy Measurement subsystem into a design MSC.

The block and processes can be identified also in the existing SIXA software, which consists of a few parallel state machines communicating with each other using asynchronous messages. The state machines were modelled using Statecharts [6] or RT-SA and the connections between the state machines were modelled with RT-SA data flow diagrams. The final code was either hand-written or generated automatically from RT-SA diagrams. The block diagrams and processes of SDL are semantically quite close to RT-SA semantics used in SIXA modelling. The reverse engineering of SIXA state diagrams and data flow diagrams into corresponding SDL diagrams is quite straightforward. It is not that signif-

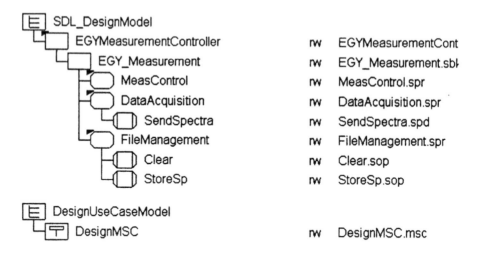

Figure 6.7: The structure of the subsystem design models of the Energy Measurement subsystem.

icant, if the SDL or RT-SA notation is used. SDL is well suited for the architectural and behavioural modelling of the Energy Measurement subsystem. As a language, SDL is not offering anything remarkably new. However, the tools supporting SDL (especially simulators and validators) are much more advanced than those of the CASE tool - code generator pair used in the SIXA development. The availability of such a tool would certainly have increased productivity and quality in the design, implementation and testing of SIXA.

6.5.2   Data and algorithm modelling

The features of basic SDL for modelling data and corresponding algorithms are rather poor. As the science data structures and algorithms of SIXA are somewhat complex, it would have been really difficult to carry out the modelling with SDL. Furthermore, the data structures of SIXA used in external communications (protocol frame structures) are defined at bit level and also the expressing of data format issues is not within the scope of SDL. Therefore, SDL is not suitable for modelling the data and algorithms of the SIXA software. A weak support for data descriptions may cause problems in the automatic system validation process. The data structures and algorithms may be defined outside SDL with the C language, for example. However, if these C functions are called from within the SDL model the validator tool will have no control over the activities and data structures implemented in C code. Due to this parts of the system state space will be hidden from the validator, and thus the automatic validation process will not work properly.

6.5.3   Concurrency of processes

The science data collection of SIXA is based on polling the hardware/software interface. The detector electronics insert science data into the hardware FIFO queues, while the software reads data from the FIFOs to data memory. The reading of FIFOs is extremely time-critical. Due to this, the FIFO polling loop is written in assembly and highly speed-optimised by hand. During observation SIXA stays several hours in the polling loop. Therefore the polling loop must be somehow interruptible, so as to allow the other subsystems to operate during data acquisition. In SIXA a pre-emptive operating system was used and the polling loop was assigned to task with relatively low priority, thus allowing interruptions by other tasks. The SDL language itself does not contain any task definition properties like, e.g., the Ada language. The assignment of SDL processes and blocks to tasks must be performed outside the scope of SDL language. The SDT tool supports this, but the support was not studied during this experimentation. The need of a pre-emptive operating system is an indication of a broader modelling restriction: SDL is not well-suited for the modelling of continuous processing. With the aid of a pre-emptive scheduler and task concept the "continuous" processing of a process will be easier to model and implement. In the SDL model of the Energy Measurement subsystem the continuos polling loop was simulated with a timer-triggered transition i.e. the continuous polling was replaced with periodic polling. Although this works well in the simulation phase, in practice the polling will have to be continuous in order to meet the requirements set on the data collection speed of SIXA.

6.5.4   Hardware interface

SDL has no means of expressing features required in hardware interfaces (such as interrupts, specific I/O address space instructions, and the like). These features have to be coded outside the SDL system and then exported to SDL, or else the hardware interface has to be completely hidden from the SDL system, e.g. by separating the hardware-dependent code into hand-written tasks and modules.

6.5.5   Code generation

In addition to the simulation and validation support, the possibility to generate the final application code from the SDL model is a very tempting feature. Many difficulties were encountered during the experimentation with the code generators of the ObjectGEODE and SDT tools. The quality of the generated code ranges from good to useless. The most important features of the generated code are code size, execution speed and the ease of interfacing to other parts of the system. Typically the size of the generated code is always larger than achieved with hand-coding. The speed of the generated code can easily be as high as in hand-coding, provided that appropriate coding rules are used. The interfacing to other parts of the system (e.g. operating system timer and message passing primitives) is typically not uncomplicated.

6.5.6 Testing

The classic way of unit testing is to draw up a test driver sending input to module, calling module and checking the generated output and internal state of the module after the call. During the testing, the internal activities of the module will not be visible to the test driver; this is called "black box" testing. The use of the test driver enables easy repetition of the tests, since the test cases and expected results are coded into the test driver. The use of MSCs as test drivers is a very promising idea. MSCs can be used to generate black box test cases, if only the signals between the system under test and environment are charted. The use of MSCs also enables white box and grey box testing, since all or some of the internal events can be included in the test MSC. In the SDT environment, the use of the Coverage Viewer tool will further enhance the testing phase. After all the test MSCs have been executed, the Coverage Viewer can be used to check the completeness of the test session.

6.6 DISCUSSION

Domain models and descriptions are used to collect and organise domain knowledge in such a way that will enable faster and more effective product development, configuration and production of systems. However, domain models and descriptions are not easy to develop and maintain. The OORT and SOMT methods do not include the domain analysis phase, which was not addressed in this paper either. The system requirements specification recaptures the relevant product requirements for the software in a way that supports software development. This viewpoint is addressed for example by the Octopus and Ellison's methods but not by the OORT and SOMT methods. The OORT and SOMT methods provide basic guidelines for specifying use cases and scenarios. More sophisticated guidelines are provided by the Real-Time UML method, for example. The system context diagram and the external event list are necessary for the SIXA Measurement Controller, but they are not supported by the OORT method. The external event list is not supported by the SOMT method. The ObjectGEODE and SDT methodologies support OMT for object-oriented analysis, i.e. for understanding the problem domain and analysing it using classes and objects. The methodologies support only those features of OMT that can easily be mapped into SDL designs. This will probably constrain the UML [12] support of the methodologies in the future. UML is the next version of the OMT notation. Object-oriented analysis models are useful but they cannot be regarded as the best foundation for the object-oriented design structure. They do not directly convey the benefits of the technology of object-oriented design. Good object-oriented design should be based upon the decoupling facilities of polymorphism and encapsulation. This allows object-oriented software to be more flexible, maintainable and reusable. It is difficult to apply object-oriented design patterns in SDL design using object-oriented extensions in SDL. The OORT and SOMT methods do not provide any guidelines for that. The ObjectGEODE and SDT tools do not support the description of design patterns and the use of object-oriented languages in the implementation of SDL models. The ObjectGEODE and SDT methodologies emphasise the use of the SDL language and pay less attention to specific design problems of real-time embedded systems, such as timing constraints and performance analysis.

6.7 CONCLUSIONS

The ObjectGEODE and SDT methodologies fail to support all the required viewpoints of the system requirements specification, system architecture definition and subsystem analysis of the SIXA Measurement Controller. The methodologies support only those features of object-oriented analysis that can easily be mapped into SDL designs. However, most of the essential specification and analysis models could be modelled with these methodologies. The SDL language is well suited for the behaviour modelling of the SIXA Measurement Controller. The modelling of state behaviour with SDL state machines and the communication between state machines with block diagrams is natural. The disadvantages of SDL include poor efficiency of the generated code and inadequate support for complex data type, algorithm, concurrency and hardware interface descriptions. These shortcomings restrict the use of SDL for system designing and implementation. Some parts of the system will have to be implemented by other means than SDL. It is difficult to apply good object-oriented design principles in SDL design. The benefits of the technology of object-oriented design can be only partially achieved. The experiments with the ObjectGEODE and SDT tools showed these tools to be very useful in system modelling, simulation and testing. The benefits of the simulation and validation capacities are so convincing that the use of these tools will be worth considering, even if the final coding had to be done manually due to the poor quality of the code generated with these tools. The ObjectGEODE and SDT methodologies as well as other object-oriented methods and tools for real-time embedded software are changing all the time and it is very difficult to know which method and tool to choose. Most object-oriented life cycle approaches support developing independent application systems. They generally consider the possibility of model reuse between systems very little. However, if several related control systems are to be developed, it often makes sense to create and acquire a set of reusable components, design patterns and frameworks. Thus, there is a case for developing a systematic approach for reuse-driven embedded software.

6.8 ACKNOWLEDGEMENTS

The work reported in this paper was funded by the Technology Development Centre of Finland (TEKES), Finnish industry and VTT Electronics.

6.9 REFERENCES

[1] M. Awad, J. Kuusela and J. Ziegler. Object-Oriented Technology for Real-Time Systems: A Practical Approach Using OMT and FUSION. New Jersey: Prentice-Hall Inc., 276 p., 1996.

[2] F. Buschman, R. Meunier, H. Rohnert, P. Sommerlad and M. Stal. Pattern-Oriented Software Architecture, a System of Patterns. Chichester, England: John Wiley & Sons., 457 p., 1996.

[3] B. Douglass. Real-Time UML, Developing Efficient Objects for Embedded Systems. Reading, Massachusetts: Addison-Wesley., 365 p., 1998.

[4] K. Ellison. Developing Real-Time Embedded Software in a Market-Driven Company. New York: John Wiley & Sons., 351 p., ISBN 0-471-59459-8, 1994.

[5] H. Gomaa. Software Design Methods for Concurrent and Real-Time Systems. Reading, Massachusetts: Addison-Wesley., 447 p., 1993.

[6] D. Harel and S. Rolph. Modelling and Analysing Complex Reactive Systems. In Proc. AIAA Computers in Aerospace VII Conf., Monterey, CA, 1989.

[7] OORT. ObjectGEODE Method Guidelines, Version 1.0. Toulouse, France: Verilog SA. 146 p., 1996.

[8] P. Robinson. HOOD: Hierarchical Object-Oriented Design. Hemel Hempstead: Prentice-Hall Inc., 238 p., 1992.

[9] B. Selic, G. Gullekson and P. Ward. Real-Time Object-Oriented Modeling. New York: John Wiley & Sons., 525 p., 1994.

[10] SOMT. SDT 3.1 Methodology Guidelines Part1: The SOMT Method. Malmö, Sweden: Telelogic AB., 196 p., 1996.

[11] J. Toivanen. SIXA On Board Software Requirements Document, Version 3.0. Oulu: VTT Electronics., 75 p., (SIXA-FM-05), 1995.

[12] UML. UML Summary, Version 1.1. Santa Clara, California: Rational Software Corporation., 19 p., 1997.

7

Pre-processing COBOL Programs for Reverse Engineering in A Software Maintenance Tool

Jan Kwiatkowski and Ireneusz Puchalski

Computer Science Department
Wroclaw University of Technology
50-370 Wroclaw,
ul. Wybrzeże Wyspiańskiego 27
Poland
tel. (+48)(+71) 320 36 02
E-mail: kwiatkowski@ci-1.ci.pwr.wroc.pl

Hongji Yang

Department of Computer Science
De Montfort University
Leicester
The Gateway Leicester LE1 9BH
England
tel. +44 (0) 116 255 1561 Ext. 8474
E-mail: hjy@dmu.ac.uk

Abstract: The Maintainer's Assistant is an interactive software maintenance tool which helps the user to extract a specification from an existing source code program. It is based on a program transformation system, in which a program is converted to a semantically equivalent form using proven transformations selected from a catalogue. This paper describes an environmental support tool, the COBOL pre-processor, for the Maintainer's Assistant. The requirements of the tool are stated and the technical methods used in the tool are summarised. The current implementation is then described and results achieved discussed. Finally, both the research into the tool and the experience obtained via implementing the tool are summarised.

7.1   INTRODUCTION AND BACKGROUND

It is a well-established view that in order to achieve major productivity gains, software maintenance must be performed at a higher abstraction level than the code level i.e. at the design level or specification level. Advantages of maintaining at high level are more compact representation and hence less to understand and the way in which algorithms are expressed is more closely linked to the application domain. In other words, whether it is corrective, perfective, adaptive, or preventive maintenance, the key to effective maintenance is program comprehension [2, 5]. Maintainers need to understand what the code does and what it is supposed to do before implementing a change. High level abstractions provide an easy way to gain such understanding. This important step in the software maintenance process of acquiring high level abstract views from existing code is called Reverse Engineering [6]. Reverse engineering involves the identification or "recovery" of the program requirements and/or design specifications that can aid in understanding and modifying the program. They are then used to discover the underlying features of a software system including the requirements, specification, design and implementation. The purposes of reverse engineering can be separated into the quality issues (e.g. to simplify complex software, to improve the quality of software which contains errors, to remove side effects from software, etc.), management issues (e.g. to enforce a programming standard, to enable better software maintenance management techniques, etc.) and technical issues (e.g. to allow major changes in a software to be implemented, to discover and record the design of the system, and to discover and represent the underlying business model implicit in the software, etc.). One example of reverse engineering is to extract the specification from the program source code. This is necessary, firstly because the documentation and relevant reference materials are not complete, and the personnel who may have relevant knowledge have already forgotten about it or left the company. Secondly, although there might be some documents available, the software may not be implemented consistently with the documents. Thirdly, the original documents and reference materials were not written in a modern specification language and they cannot be used in a modern software maintenance environment. This means that the extraction of the specification of old program code is a vital step especially when the program code is the only available documentation or is the only source to rely on.

7.1.1   The maintainer's assistant (MA)

The Maintainer's Assistant is the name given to a tool whose main objective is to develop a formal specification from old code [3]. It will also reduce the costs of maintenance by the application of new technology and increase quality, so producing improved customer satisfaction. The source code can be a program written in any language such as COBOL. The ultimate specification will be written in a specification language such as Z [19]. To move from the low-level source code to the high-level specification, different levels of abstraction have to be presented. To express the broad range of the stages (all forms of code) in the maintenance of a program, a Wide Spectrum Language (WSL) is used in the Maintainer's Assistant. This incorporates a variety of constructs, from low-level machine-oriented constructs up to high-level specification ones. It is natural for specification constructs to be mixed freely with programming constructs in the intermediate steps of transformation, by using the wide spectrum language, so that programs are gradually abstracted to high-level specification. The formal definition of WSL can be seen in [23] and examples of WSL programs will be given in later sections of this paper. The external format of a WSL program looks like a commonly-used programming language such as PASCAL. Furthermore, the system is able to cope with program source code written in any programming language, as long as a pre-processor is built to translate that language into WSL. The Maintainer's Assistant is based on a formal system developed by Ward [22, 23] in which it is possible to prove that two versions of a program are equivalent. The formal system is independent of any particular programming language and allows the inclusion of arbitrary specifications as statements in a program. Hence it can be used to prove that a program is equivalent to a given specification. Programs are defined to be equivalent if they have the same denotational semantics. Hence equivalent programs are identical in terms of their input-output behaviour, although they may have different running times and use different internal data structures. A refinement of a program, or specification, is another program which will terminate on each initial state for which the first program terminates, and will terminate in one of the possible final states for the first program. In other words a refinement of a specification is an acceptable implementation of the specification and a refinement of a program is an acceptable substitute for the program.

7.1.2 Reverse engineering using program transformation

Program transformation is the process of formally changing a program to a different program with the same semantics as the original program. Much work has been focused on the program transformation as one kind of programming paradigm in which the development from specification to implementation is a formal, mechanically supported process. The long range objective of this approach is dramatically to improve the construction, reliability, maintenance, and extensibility of software. There have been several transformational system implemented based on this idea [1, 8, 9]. Generally speaking, these systems have the following features:

- The main goal is to experiment with the mechanically assisted development of a broad range of programs. This includes: general support for program modification, e.g. optimisation of control structures, efficient implementation of data structures, and the adaptation of data structures and given programs to particular styles of programming; program synthesis, e.g. the generation of a program from a formal description of the problem; program adaptation to particular environments and verification of the correctness of programs.

- Their functions are to provide a transformation data base for keeping the information collected by the user; user guidance for offering the user advise on the choice of transformations; history recording for documenting the development process; assessment of programs for measuring the effect of transformations.

- Their working modes are mainly semi-automatic, working both autonomously and manually, e.g., the CIP (Computer-Aided, Intuition-Guided Programming) System [1]; while a manual system or a fully automatic system may have certain disadvantages, e.g., the user being responsible for every single transformation step in a manual system, or the system not having enough built-in heuristics in a fully automatic system.

- Basic types of transformation are the catalogue approach and the generative set approach. A catalogue of rules is a linearly or hierarchically structured collection of transformation rules relevant for a particular aspect of the development process. A generative set means a small set of powerful elementary transformations to be used as a basis for constructing new rules.

The transformation system used in reverse engineering should support the particular demands of the maintenance programmer, i.e. helping the maintainer to understand the program transformed. There are a number of benefits to using formal transformations:

- Increased reliability: errors and inconsistencies are easier to spot at high level of abstraction.

- Formal links between the specification and code can be maintained.

- Maintenance can be carried out at the specification level.

- Large restructuring changes can be made to the program with the confidence that the program's functionality is unchanged.

- Programs can be incrementally improved instead of being incrementally degraded.

- Data structures and the implementations of abstract data types can be changed easily.

Distinguishing features of the program transformer of the Maintainer's Assistant include:

- A wide spectrum language is used. The wide spectrum language is an intermediate language, which means that program transformations as well as the tool itself only needs to be built once and programs in any programming language can be dealt with by the tool.

- The applicability of a transformation is tested before it is applied.

- A history/future database is built-in to allow back-tracking and "forward-tracking".

- The system is interactive and incorporates a browser which provides a graphical mouse-driven front end and pretty-printer.

7.1.3   Requirements of the supporting environment for MA

The success of building systems is dependent both on the application of the method and on the method itself. A method typically consists of a sequence of steps combining management procedures, technical methods, and automated support to produce systems [24]. When a good technical method is found and a good management procedure is adopted, the automated support or environment becomes a very crucial part of producing systems. The software maintenance environment provides a framework for describing the way that software maintainers make use of a software maintenance methodology. In deciding what are needed in the MA, the following points must be addressed:

1. *Reverse Engineering* — An important requirement of reverse engineering is to understand software that is probably without any available specification, documentation, or, indeed, any helpful information.

2. *Program Transformation* — The key elements of the environment of the Maintainer's Assistant are those which support program transformations.

3. *Rapid Prototyping* — There are several advantages of rapid prototyping which can be taken to develop the Maintainer's Assistant itself. For instance, the system can be developed much faster by rapid prototyping, so that it can speed up the implementation. The user is involved in the process, so that he or she (mainly the builder in our system) can determine if the development is moving in the right direction. Rapid prototyping produces a model of the final system, so that the user, as well as builder, can see the final system in the early development stage.

From the above, the environment of the Maintainer's Assistant should support the following characteristics:

1. It should support the maintenance of large, to very large, software.

2. It should support software independently of its source programming language so that specifications and programs can both be included in the environment in the form of the Wide Spectrum Language.

3. It should provide a set of tools covering all the activities required by, and provided by the current technical methods and make provision for other possible tools in the future.

It should provide a set of tools covering all the activities required by, and provided by the current technical methods and make provision for other possible tools in the future.

7.1.4   Architecture of MA

MA supports the transformation of an existing source code to a specification in three phases (Figure 7.1). In phase 1, a "Source-to-WSL" translator will take source code in COBOL or other language and translate it into its equivalent WSL form. The maintainer does all his operation through the Browser. Then the Browser checks the program and uses the Program Slicer to chop the program into manageable sized lumps. The maintainer may conduct the process more than once until he realises that he has split the code in such a way that it is ready for transformation. Eventually, this code is saved to the Repository, together with other information, such as the relations among these code modules, in order to assemble specifications of those code modules. In the second phase, the maintainer will take one piece of code out from the Repository to work with. The Browser allows the maintainer to look at and alter the code under strict conditions and the maintainer can also select transformations to apply to the code. The program transformer works in an interactive mode. It presents WSL on screen in Human Computer Interface (HCI) format and searches a catalogue of proven transformations to find applicable transformations for any selected piece of code. These are displayed in the user interface's window system.

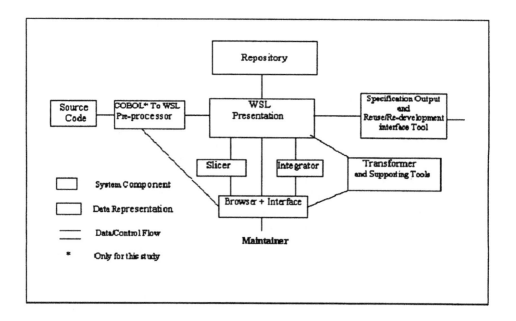

Figure 7.1: Components of MA

When the Program Transformer is working, it also depends on the supporting tools such as General Simplifier, the Program Structure Database and the Knowledge Base System by sending them requests. The maintainer can apply these transformations or get help from the Knowledge Base as to which transformation are applicable. Once a transformation is selected it is automatically applied. These transformations can be used to simplify code and expose errors. Finally, the code is transformed to a certain high level of abstraction and the code is saved back to the Repository.

The third phase comes when all the source code in the Repository has been transformed. The Program Integrator is called to assemble the code into a single program in high-level WSL. A WSL to Z translator will translate this highly abstracted specification in WSL into specification in Z.

7.1.5   Components of MA

From the outset of the project, attention has been paid to the particular aspects of the environment for supporting the program transformation of reverse engineering. The Maintainer's Assistant system has been implemented on a SUN workstation system and the Program Transformer itself is written in Common LISP. Other tools are discussed below.

- *COBOL-to-WSL Pre-processor* — In this study, the COBOL Pre-processor is addressed. Pre-processors for other languages such as an IBM-Assembler to WSL Pre-processor have been implemented.

- *Program Slicer* — With the maintainer's assistance, the Program Slicer pre-process the program code split before saving the code in the Repository. Its main function is to help in naming program modules to be transformed.

- *Program Integrator* — Using the information stored in the Repository when the program was split, the Program Integrator will reassemble those pieces of WSL code after transformation.

- *Specification Output and Reuse/Redevelopment Interface Tool* — This mainly consists of two parts (1) WSL to Z Translator, dealing with both the symbolic translation and the output in Z notation to both the screen and the printer; and (2) Reuse/Redevelopment Interface, dealing with output obtained high-level WSL programs for the purposes of reuse and redevelopment.

- *Transformer Supporting tools* — These include: (1) A History/Future Database, which allows the maintainer to go back to an older version of the program he has transformed. It is usual for the maintainer to move forwards and backwards several times through a sequence of transformations in order to reach an optimal version of the program. Two commands "Undo" and "Redo" are provided. (2) A Program Structure Database, which is a dynamic database mainly serving the Program Transformer. The Program Transformer accesses the Database via the Database Manager. When the Program Transformer is transforming a section of program code, queries about the program are sent to the Database Manager. When a query is made for the first time, the Database Manager will go through the program structure and calculate the answer to that query. The result will both be sent to the Program Transformer and saved in the database. When the question is asked again, the database manager will check the database and simply return the result. (3) A General Simplifier, which carries out symbolic calculations in mathematics and logic for helps the Program Transformer. Mathematical and logical operations defined in the system are: +, -, *, /, **, Min, Max, Div, Mod, =, >, <, <>, Not, And, Or, etc.

- *Browser and Interface* — The Browser and Interface is implemented together as a graphical user interface to the other subsystems of the Maintainer's Assistant using the X-Windows System. It provides all the commands necessary to use other Maintainer's Assistant programs via buttons and pop-up menus and uses several windows to display the output from the system and to receive text input from the user. In particular it provides a browser to display the program being transformed by the Transformer, and this has facilities not provided by the transformer such as pretty printing the program and a mechanism to fold or unfold sections of code. It runs displaying a frame made up of three windows. The first window is a box containing several buttons and labels. By clicking these buttons the user can invoke various commands, change options, and pop-up other windows. The second window (the application window) is an interface to the transformer command driven user interface and the third window (the display window) is used to display the program being transformed by the user. A manual page for the front end is available for the novice user.

In the remaining of the paper, Section 7.2 presents an overview and the design of the COBOL Pre-processor for MA; Section 7.3 explains how to implement the COBOL Pre-processor and Section 7.4 concludes our study.

7.2   OVERVIEW AND DESIGN OF COBOL PRE-PROCESSOR

7.2.1   COBOL pre-processor

It is believed that there are 800 billion lines of COBOL programs existing in the world [14] today and they are a big portion of legacy systems still used in industry. Therefore building a COBOL Pre-processor for MA is an inevitable task.

The COBOL language was first developed in 1959. The CODASYL committee (Conference on Data Systems Languages) produced the initial specification of COBOL in 1960, and a revised version appeared in 1961. The first ANSI (American National Standard Institute) specification of the COBOL language was published in 1968. Later standards were the ANSI 1974 and the ANSI 1985 Standard. COBOL offers the following advantages within the standard language [12], which are related to the research:

- Uniform treatment of all data as records.

- Extensive capabilities for defining and handling files.

- Incorporation of many functions which in other contexts would be regarded as the province of system utilities.

- The ability to construct large programs from independently compiled modules which communicate with each other by passing parameters or by using common files.

The COBOL language used in this research not only is unrestricted to any dialect of COBOL but also covers features written in ANSI COBOL Standard 1985. More importantly, this research will be not only of benefit to COBOL programs but also to other data intensive programs written in other languages.

7.2.2   Compiler writing techniques and available tools (flex and bison)

After studying different techniques of implementing a pre-processor of this kind, we have chosen a technique that, in our opinion, is the easiest in respect of available tools. The BISON and FLEX are today belonging to the most popular tools, and the technique based on using them is simple and clear. Briefly, it is working like this: firstly descriptions of the syntax and semantics of COBOL are written; then FLEX and BISON will convert the descriptions into a code of the scanner and the parser respectively written in C language; finally that a code generator is needed to develop data structures and a set of procedures for creating WSL code.

Flex, Fast Lexical Analyser generator, is a tool for generating scanner which recognise lexical patterns in text. Flex reads the given input files, or its standard input if no file names are given, for a description of a scanner to generate. The description is in the form of pairs of regular expressions and C code, called rules. Flex generates as output a C language source file, which is a scanner. The Flex is the newest version of Lex, a Unix's systems tool.

Bison is a parser generator in the style of YACC. It should be upwardly compatible with input files designed for YACC. Bison converts a grammar description for an LALR(1) context-free grammar into s C program to parse that grammar. The most common formal systems for presenting such rules for humans to read is Backus-Naur-Form (BNF), which was developed in order to specify the language Algol 60. Any grammar expressed in BNF is a context-free grammar. The input to Bison is essentially machine-readable BNF.

7.2.3   COBOL program structure

A COBOL program consists of four parts (divisions):

1. *Identification division* — An identification of the program. This division identifies both the source program and the resultant output listing. In addition, the user may include the date when program was written, the date of the source program compilation and some other information as desired under the paragraphs in this section [15].

2. *Environment division* — A description of the equipment to be used to compile and run program. This division specifies standard method of expressing those aspects of a data processing problem that are dependent upon the physical characteristics of a specific computer. The Environment Division allows specification of the configuration of the source computer and the object computer. In addition, information relating to input-output control, special hardware characteristics and control techniques can be given.

3. *Data division* — A description of the data to be processed. This division describes the data that the object program is to accept as input, to manipulate, to create, or to produce as output.

4. *Procedure division* — A set of procedures to specify the operations to be performed on the data. This Division may contain declarative and non-declarative procedures [15].

Each division is divided into sections which are further divided into paragraphs, which in turn are made up of sentences.

7.2.4   Rules of pre-processing COBOL into WSL

The key problem of pre-processing a COBOL program into a WSL programs for MA is to retain the semantics of the original COBOL program. This has been consistently considered throughout the design of the COBOL Pre-processor.

The COBOL specification is composed of four divisions and therefore all rules of COBOL into WSL conversion will be divided using these divisions.

Identification division — All the information from this division will be converted into a standard comment statement in WSL, e.g.:

COBOL

PROGRAM-ID.*program-name.*   **comment:**"program-id:*program-name,*
AUTHOR.*comment-entry.*   author:*comment-entry.*";

Environment division — Almost all constructions of this division will be converted into comment statements (e.g. description of source and object computers) with the exception of SPECIAL-NAMES in CONFIGURATION SECTION and FILE CONTROL in INPUT-OUTPUT SECTION, which are used to describe data in COBOL language. These two statements will not be converted into comment statement but names of these statements will be put on the table of names with the following prefixes:

- **spe**, i.e. special name,

- **sfc**, i.e. sequential files,

- **rfc**, i.e. relative files,

- **ifc**, i.e. indexed files,

- **srt**, i.e. sorted files.

Both in the Environment division and Data division there are sections not included in the standards of COBOL. For such sections a syntax element called "unknown section" has been created. All "unknown sections" will be dealt with as follows:

1. <Name of section> will be converted into comment state with warning:
    comment: "WARNING !!! Unknown section: name."
2. <Body of section> will be ignored.

Data division — Data division is made up of elements which describes the structure of data in COBOL programs. It is similar to var statement in Pascal. This division is composed of six sections:

- FILE SECTION which will be converted into **file** - the new extension of WSL,

- WORKING-STORAGE SECTION which will be converted into **record**,

- LINKAGE SECTION which will be converted into **record**,

- COMMUNICATION SECTION which will be converted into **record**,

- REPORT SECTION which will be ignored,

- SCREEN SECTION which will be converted into **record**.

These sections are based on the statement called record description entry. Record description entry is a basic statement record of WSL - a standard type WSL describing data structure - with the following extensions, which identifies structural data:

- keyword **asc-key** - used before the field name in the record statement for marking fields which are an ascending key,

- keyword **dsc-key** - used before the field name in the record statement for marking fields which are an descending key,

- keyword **index** - used before the field name in the record statement for marking fields which are index,

- keyword **redefine** - used after the name of the record for redefining one record into another.

	COBOL		WSL
01	test	**record**	test **with**
	02 field-three		**index** filed-one;
	02 field-four REDEFINES field-three		**asc-key** field-two;
	02 field-five		**record** field-three;
01	test INDEXED BY field-one		**record** field-four;
01	test ASCENDING KEY IS field-two		**redefine** field-three **with** field-four;
			record field-five;
			end;

Special numbers in COBOL record description entry will be converted into "normal" names (variable) with prefixes:

- COBOL level 77 will be converted into a name with the prefix **nsb** (non subdivided name),

- COBOL level 78 will be converted into a name with the prefix **cnt** (constant name),

- COBOL level 88 will be converted into a name with the prefix **cnd** (conditional name).

Procedure division — Rules for this division are as follows:

- Main program procedure is:

- name of program == body of program.

- All sections from *Procedure division* are converted into separate procedures. The names of these procedures are named by names with the prefix: **section**.

- All paragraphs from *Procedure division* are converted into separate procedures. The names of these procedures are named by names with the prefix: **paragraph**.

- COBOL statement: *Declaratives* are ignored.

- Functions present in *Procedure division* are converted into their counterparts in WSL.

7.2.5 Structure of the pre-processor

The Pre-processor consist of three modules: a parser, a scanner and a code generator. Figure 7.2 presents the way in which it has been created.

On the basis of the description of the COBOL grammar the BISON creates the parser's source code in C language (y.tab.c). The parser's task is to analyse the semantics of the COBOL grammar. The analyser divides the COBOL program into syntax elements and checks whether or not it can apply to them the rules described in the analyser. If the

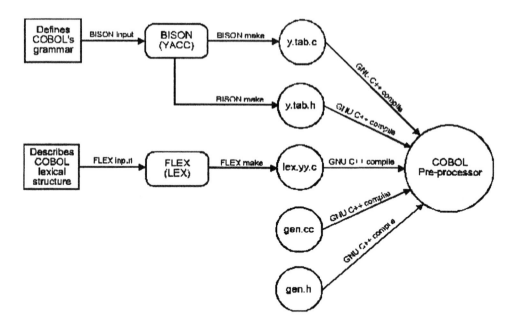

Figure 7.2: Generation of COBOL Pre-processor

application of a rule is possible, a suitable procedure of the code generator is called. If not, an error is indicated. While generating the parser, the BISON creates an additional file (y.tab.h) containing a declaration of all the tokens required by the parser. The second module of the Pre-processor is the scanner, which is generated by the FLEX (the generated file: yy.lex.c). The scanner is created on the basis of the lexical description of COBOL, i.e. the description of the COBOL syntax. The task performed by the scanner is the division of the input file of the COBOL program into a set of tokens which will then be put into the parser's input. The set of the tokens required by the parser is declared in the file (y.tab.h). The tokens of the input file are identified according to their type and allocated in the names table of the code generator. They will be used in the procedures of the generator called by the parser. The last module of the Pre-processor is the code generator (gen.cc, gen.h) controlled by the parser and provided with data by the scanner, it generates the WSL code. It consists of the set of procedures called by the parser, the names table, and the object data structure that organizes information from the scanner.

7.2.6   Description of code generator structure using object oriented methodology

The internal structure of the code generator consists of two parts. One part is the set of the procedures called by the parser, the other part is the data structure that organises information from the scanner. The structure has been implemented by means of object oriented methodology (Coad-Yourdon) and presented in Fig. 7.3

The classes of the structure perform the following functions:

• *Streamble* - this class contains the methods of operating the input/output streams and

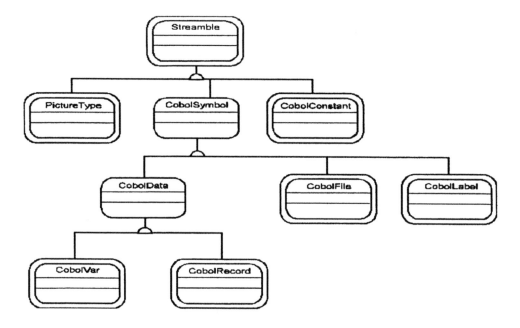

Figure 7.3: Object Oriented Data Structure of Code Generator.

the file streams,

- *CobolSymbol* - this class is an abstract class describing the COBOL data; the table of name is made up of the elements of CobolSymbol,

- *CobolConstant* - this class describes the constants of COBOL; the table of names does not contain this class,

- *PictureType* - this class contains all the functions operating the types of the COBOL data,

- *CobolData* - this class in an abstract class defining the basic type of the COBOL data,

- *CobolFile* - this class defines the COBOL file descriptor,

- *CobolLabels* - this class defines the COBOL labels and is used for making the control flow in the WSL program,

- *CobolRecord* - this class defines the COBOL record,

- *CobolVar* - this class defines the COBOL variable.

7.3 IMPLEMENTATION

7.3.1 Ambiguity problem of COBOL language specification

The main problem of COBOL's specification is its ambiguity. The ambiguity results from the fact that almost all of the specification of COBOL consists of optional parts. Additionally, a state called: unknown section has been included, because the "real" COBOL code often contains sections which are not described by international standards. The ambiguity has been increased by the parser's capacity to understand COBOL code compatible with the following standards:

- ANSI'74 X2.23-1974,

- ANSI'85 X3.23-1985,

- IBM VS COBOL II,

- MICRO FOCUS VS COBOL.

All of the grounds cause the final specification of COBOL grammar to be a COBOL "X" specification. The COBOL "X" grammar is compatible with the above mentioned standards, and it is more extensive. This means, that it accepts syntactic constructions which are not standard. The reasons for such a solution to the problem are as follows:

- COBOL grammar is not LALR(1) and this solution makes the COBOL grammar suitable for the BISON, i.e., a tool working with grammars LALR(1),

- the parser built on the basis of this grammar will be used by the COBOL Pre-processor,

- this parser will be used by the Maintainer's Assistant, and will be working with a semantically correct code of COBOL.

7.3.2 Implementation of scanner

Part of the context problems of the COBOL grammar is solved by a proper construction of scanner. Special features of FLEX: "Start Conditions" have been used in it. Start conditions are useful when certain constructions have to be analysed differently, depending on a left context, and when multiple lexical analysers have to work simultaneously. In this case a scanner is divided into four individual parts:

- *declaration scanner*, which analyses declaration sections of COBOL, like: Environment Division and Data Division,

- *picture scanner*, which analyses the correctness of the Picture state of COBOL,

- *comment scanner*, which analyses the Comment state of COBOL,

- *unknown section scanner*, which analyses the extension of the specification of the COBOL language.

This mechanism guarantees an efficient control of a left context of the COBOL grammar, provided that start and end point of the scanners has been precisely determined. To illustrate the uses of "Start Conditions", here is a part of scanner which provides the comment scanner:

```
% s COMMENT_STATE
%%
^[0-9]{6}[\t]*"*"|
^[\t]*"*"{BEGIN COMMENT_STATE;
  /* startpoint of the comment scanner -it starts from asterix */ }
<COMMENT_STATE>[something]{
  /* the body of the comment scanner */ }
<COMMENT_STATE>.*\n {BEGIN INITIAL;
  /* end point of the comment scanner -it finishes on the end
     of the line */}
```

7.3.3 Implementation of parser

BISON has been used to analyse the semantics of COBOL. The BISON's limitations require introducing further changes to the specification of the COBOL's semantics. The alterations, however, have been restricted in order to preserve the meaning of the semantics. LALR(1) parsers are restricted to one-symbol look ahead on which they have to base their parsing decision. If a grammar is ambiguous (like COBOL's grammar), or cannot be parsed unambiguously using one-symbol look ahead, BISON will generate parsing conflicts when constructing the parse table. There are two types of such conflicts:

- shift/reduce (also called for enhanced understanding: read/reduce [11]) - when both a shift (read) and reduce action take place for a given input symbol in a given state,

- reduce/reduce - if there is more than one reduce action for a given input symbol in a given state.

The first conflict occurs in most constructions, in which optional key-words are present. The BISON could reduce such a key-word immediately, or carry on the analysis of the input stream. Luckily, the parser has been designed in such a way that it analyses the longest input stream. Thus a built-in rule of COBOL will always be applied, i.e. the choice of action shift (read). Conflicts of the kind are not dangerous for the COBOL grammar, however they must be clearly described. The second conflict is a much serious one. Although some built-in rules of the parser's construction exist also in this case, they are not reliable. The clearest example of this conflict and a solution to it can be the construction of a "unknown section". An example including reduce/reduce conflicts:

```
description_part:    unknown_section_op
                     environment_division_op
                     unknown_section_op
                     configuration_section_op
                     unknown_section_op
                     input_output_section_op
                     unknown_section_op
                     data_division_op
                     unknown_section_op
                     file_section_op
                     unknown_section_op
                     working_storage_op
                     unknown_section_op
                     linkage_section_op
                     unknown_section_op
                     communication_section_op
                     unknown_section_op
                     report_section_op
                     unknown_section_op
                     screen_section_op
                     ;
unknown_section_op: identifier TOK_SECTION
                     ;
environment_division_op: environment_division
                     |
                     ;
```

An example of a correct solution of the problem:

```
description_part:    unknown_section_op
                     environment_division_op
                     configuration_section_op
                     input_output_section_op
                     data_division_op
                     file_section_op
                     working_storage_op
                     linkage_section_op
                     communication_section_op
                     report_section_op
                     screen_section_op
                     ;
unknown_section_op: identifier TOK_SECTION
                     |
                     ;
environment_division_op: environment_division
                     unknown_section_op
                     ;
```

The problem can be solved by prescribing the unknown section to other individual sections (as explained above). In other parts of the COBOL grammar an analogous mechanism has been applied.

7.3.4   Experiments

The Pre-processor has been strictly tested according to the COBOL standard and definitions WSL. So far no errors have been discovered. Although it may not be entirely free of flaws (Murphy's Laws), we are convinced that the Pre-processor can be a very useful tool for the Maintainer's Assistant. We will carry on close observation into the COBOL Pre-processor, continuing to seek new scope for enhancement. Here an illustration is given on a self-contained full COBOL program being pre-processed into a WSL program:

COBOL:

```
IDENTIFICATION DIVISION.
  PROGRAM-ID. TEST-PROGRAM.
ENVIRONMENT DIVISION.
DATA DIVISION.
WORKING-STORAGE SECTION.
01  VARX.
   05  VARY PICTURE IS 9999 VALUE IS ZEROES.
   05  VARZ PICTURE IS 9(5) VALUE IS ZEROS.
   05  VARF PICTURE IS 9(5) VALUE IS ZERO.
   05  FILLER PICTURE IS X VALUE IS "".
   05  NAME PICTURE IS X(18) VALUE IS SPACES.
   05  FILLER PICTURE IS X VALUE IS "".
   05  NAMES PICTURE IS X(18) VALUE IS SPACES.
   05  FILLER PICTURE IS X VALUE IS "".
   05  CITY PICTURE IS X(15) VALUE IS SPACES.


PROCEDURE DIVISION
  DISPLAY "THIS IS A COBOL PROGRAM".
  DISPLAY VARX.
  MOVE 5 TO VARY,VARZ.
  MOVE "JOHN" TO NAME,NAMES.
  DISPLAY VARX.
```

   WSL:

```
comment: "test.wsl
         Generated by Cobol-to-WSL Pre-processor from test.cob.";
comment: "program-id: test-program.";
record varx with
   record vary;
   record varz;
   record varf;
   record filler000;
   record name;
   record filler001;
   record names;
   record filler002;
   record city;
end;
paragraph-set-var-values ==
    space-var := '';
   varx.vary := 0;
   varx.varz := 0;
   varx.varf := 0;
   varx.filler000 := " ";
   varx.name, := ' ';
   varx.filler001 := " ";
   varx.names := ' ';
   varx.filler002 := " ";
   varx.city :=   ' ';
   paragraph-first.
```

```
paragraph-first ==
    write(stdout, "This is a cobol program");
    write(stdout, varx);
    varx.varz := 5;
    varx.vary := 5;
    varx.names := "John";
    varx.name := "John";
    write(stdout, varx);
    test-program.
test-program ==
    paragraph-set-var-values;
    cpi := 0;
    while cpi <= 0 do
      if cpi = 0 then cpi := cpi + 1;
                      paragraph-first;
        else write(stderr, "Broken paragraph chain!");
             cpi := 1;
    od;
    exit.
```

7.4   CONCLUSIONS AND FUTURE WORK

The current prototype of the COBOL Pre-processor consists of

- a scanner of COBOL lexical,

- a parser of COBOL grammar, and

- a generator of WSL code.

With the support provided by the COBOL Pre-processor, a user can easily translate a COBOL program into WSL and then operate MA to reverse engineer the original program. Results on a number of programs of up to 500 lines show that:

- COBOL programs have been pre-processed into WSL programs and the resulting programs have been inspected to be semantically correct.

- The experimented include real programs, not just on artificial examples.

- Performance of the COBOL Pre-processor is satisfactory.

It is not hard to conclude this study by saying that MA is much more powerful and practical after being equipped with a COBOL Pre-processor, in particular when dealing with a large COBOL program. Enhancing the implementation of the COBOL Pre-processor represents the next major thrust of the next stage of the project.

7.5   REFERENCES

[1] F. L. Bauer, B. Moller, H. Partach and P. Pepper. Formal Program Construction by Transformation — Computer-Aided, Intuition-Guided Programming, IEEE Transactions on Software Engineering, Vol. 15, No. 2, Feb. 1989.

[2] K. H. Bennett, J. Denier and J. Estublier. Environments for Software Maintenance, Technical report, Centre for Software Maintenance, 1989.

[3] K. H. Bennett, T. Bull and H. Yang. A Transformation System for Maintenance - Turning Theory into Practice, IEEE Conference on Software Maintenance-92, Orlando, Florida, Nov., 1992.

[4] T. Bull. An Introduction to the WSL Program Transformer, IEEE Conference on Software Maintenance-1990, San Diego, California, 1990.

[5] N. Chapin. Software Maintenance Life Cycle, IEEE Conference on Software Maintenance-1988, Phoenix, Arizona, 1988.

[6] E.J. Chikofsky and J.H. Cross. Reverse Engineering and Design Recovery: A Taxonomy, IEEE Software, Vol. 7, No. 1, 1990.

[7] C. Donnelly and R. Stallman. BISON v.1.2 - The YACC-compatible Parser Generator, Free Software Foundation, Cambridge USA, December 1992.

[8] M.S. Feather. A Survey and Classification of Some Program Transformation Techniques, Program Specification and Transformation, 1987.

[9] S.F. Fickas. Automating the Transformational Development of Software, IEEE Transactions on Software Engineering, Vol. SE-11, No. 11, November 1985.

[10] M. Gawrys. UNIX - Narzedzia programistyczne - YACC & LEX, Wydawnictwo PLJ, Warszawa, November 1993.

[11] J. Grosch and H. Emmelmann. A Tool Box for Compiler Construction, Compiler Generation Report No. 20, GMD Forschungsstelle and der Universität Karlsruhe, January 1990.

[12] J. Inglis. COBOL 85 Programming, John Wiley and Sons, Inc., Chichester, 1989.

[13] E. Kurzydem, A. Macielinski, U. Szmidt and E. Wiecek. COBOL - Jezyk Programowania, Panstwowe Wydawnictwo Ekonomiczne, Warszawa, July, 1978.

[14] P. Layzell. The Identification and Management of Latent Software Assets, International Journal of Information Management, Vol. 14, No. 6, pp. 427-442, 1994.

[15] Micro Focus. COBOL/2 Language Reference, Micro Focus Ltd. Palo Alto USA, Issue 7, September 1988.

[16] P. Oman. Maintenance Tools, IEEE Software, May 1990.

[17] H. Partsch and R. Steinbruggen. Program Transformation Systems, Computing Surveys, Vol. 15, No. 3, September 1983.

[18] H.M. Sneed and G. Jandrasics. Inverse Transformation of Software from Code to Specification, IEEE Conference on Software Maintenance-1988, Phoenix, Arizona, 1988.

[19] J.M. Spivey. Understanding Z, Cambridge University Press, 1988.

[20] M. Szaniawska. Programowanie Komputerów - COBOL, Panstwowe Wydawnictwo Ekonomiczne, Warszawa, September, 1979.

[21] P. Vern. FLEX v. 2.3 - Fast lexical Analyser Generator, Free Software Foundation, Cambridge USA, May 1990.

[22] M. Ward. Proving Program Refinements and Transformations, PhD thesis, Oxford Univ., 1988.

[23] M. Ward, M. Munro and F.W. Calliss. The Maintainer's Assistant, IEEE Conference on Software Maintenance-1989, Miami, Florida, 1989.

[24] A.T. Wasserman. Software Engineering Environments, Advances In Computers, Vol. 22, 1983.

8

Agent Oriented Programming Language *LASS*

Mihal Badjonski, Mirjana Ivanović, Zoran Budimac

University of Novi Sad, Faculty of Science, Institute of Mathematics
Trg D. Obradovića 4
21000 Novi Sad,
Yugoslavia
e-mail: {mihal,mira,zjb}@unsim.ns.ac.yu

Abstract: This paper presents a new agent-oriented programming language named *LASS*. *LASS* is aimed for agent-oriented programming in multi-agent systems. It enables programming using new, agent-oriented concepts. Agents programmed with *LASS* can have deliberative properties (plans, intentions) as well as the reactive ones (behaviors). Agent can execute its plans and/or behaviors simultaneously. It can communicate with other agents. *LASS* has been used for specifying a personal digital assistant.

8.1 INTRODUCTION

Multi-agent systems (MASs) ([5, 6, 19]) are a new and promising area in the field of distributed artificial intelligence (DAI), as well as in the mainstream computer science. These systems are compound of relatively autonomous and intelligent parts, called agents. Even if we restrict ourselves to computer science, a word 'agent' has many meanings. In [19] agent is defined as: "... a hardware or (more usually) software based computer system that enjoys the following properties:

- autonomy: agents operate without the direct intervention of humans or others, and have some kind of control over their actions and internal state;

- social ability: agents interact with other agents (and possibly humans) via some kind of agent-communication language;

- reactivity: agents perceive their environment (which may be the physical world, a user via a graphical user interface, a collection of other agents, the Internet, or perhaps all of these combined), and respond in a timely fashion to changes that occur in it;

- pro-activeness: agents do not simply act in response to their environment, they are able to exhibit goal-directed behavior by taking the initiative."

This definition does not specify the size of agents. They can be as big as expert system and as small as the part of an application interface. Agent can be static (permanently located in some computer) or mobile (moving across the computer network, such as Internet). The amount of agent intelligence is also not specified. A collection of agent definitions is given in [10].

Agent-oriented programming languages are programming languages developed for programming of agents. Agent-oriented programming (AOP) can also be seen as a post-object-oriented paradigm.

An advantage of the usage of agents in software development instead of objects stems from the primitives used for programming. AOP introduces new concepts such as mental categories, reactivity, pro-activeness, concurrent execution inside and between agents, communication, meta-level reasoning, etc.

This paper presents an AOP language named *LASS*. Agent programmed with *LASS* possesses intentions, beliefs, and plans for its public and internal services. Besides deliberative properties, agent specified with *LASS* can behave reactively as well. *LASS* introduces the usage of behaviors - programming primitives enabling agent to react immediately when it is necessary [2]. *LASS* enables powerful communication between agents which is based on agent public services. Services are used similarly like remote procedure calls.

Most of the concepts in *LASS* are already seen in other programming languages. However, the usage of all of them in one computer language is unique [1]. Once the software system is identified as a MAS, *LASS* can be used for its implementation. Trivial software systems may be also programmed with *LASS*, using only one agent. However, the benefits that *LASS* provides are more evident when it is used for the programming of more complex systems.

This paper is organized as follows. The programming language *LASS* is presented in the Section 8.2. In the Section 8.3 an example of *LASS* in action is given. Section 8.4 compares *LASS* with other AOP languages. A conclusion is given in Section 8.5.

8.2 *LASS*

Every program written in *LASS* is intended for the specification of exactly one agent. If there are *n* agents in MAS, *n* programs in *LASS* will be written.

The main part of the *LASS* syntax and the description of the syntax categories are as follows.

```
program =
        'AGENT' agent_name ';'
        [known_agents_decl ';']
```

```
[fact_types_def ';']
[facts_decl ';']
[public_services_decl ';']
[private_services_decl ';']
[behaviors_decl ';']
[init_beliefs ';']
[init_intentions ';']
'END' agent_name
```

Other agents that will communicate with the agent are specified in the first part. The agent can ask services from each of these agents and it can be asked for service by each one of them. If the agent will not communicate, program will not contain this part.

The facts important to agent have to be declared. Before that, their types have to be defined in the second part of the program.

Besides public services, agent can perform its own, private services as well.

Agent can possess behaviors. They monitor the agent's beliefs and use them to activate or deactivate themselves.

At the beginning of its existence, agent can have initial beliefs about the facts in its environment. If agent does not have belief about some fact, it believes that fact has unknown value. It can also have initial intentions.

In the following subsections, parts of a *LASS* program will be further explained.

8.2.1 Other agents

```
known_agents_decl =
            'KNOWN' 'AGENT' agent_decl {';' agent_decl}
agent_decl = agent_name ':' (internet_adr | 'LOCAL')
```

There are two types of agents from the viewpoint of an agent: the agents located in the same machine where the agent is located and the agents located in remote machines.

8.2.2 Facts

```
fact_types_def = 'FACT' 'TYPE' ftype_def {';' ftype_def}
ftype_def = ftype_name '=' ftype
ftype = prim_type | record_type | array_type
```

Fact can be of a primitive type, a record, or an array.

```
facts_decl = 'FACTS' fdecl {';' fdecl}
fdecl = fact_names ':' ftype_name
fact_names = fname {',' fname}
```

Facts are used as variables in traditional languages. Besides user-defined facts, meta-level facts CURRINT and CURRBEH are also available. They contain information about current intentions and active behaviors.

8.2.3 Services

```
public_services_decl =
        'PUBLIC' 'SERVICES' serv_decl {';' serv_decl}
serv_decl =
        serv_name '(' [ par_decl {';' par_decl} ] ')' ';'
        ('ALWAYS' | 'WHEN' bool_expr ';')
        'PLAN' body
        'END' serv_name
```

Service can contain parameters, that can be INPUT or INPUT-OUTPUT. par_decl represents the declaration of parameter(s). It consists of parameter names optionally preceded with the word VAR and followed by the type of parameter(s). Service will not be performed if bool_exp in WHEN condition is not satisfied. Every service has its plan for an execution.

```
bool_expr =
    'TRUE' |
    'FALSE' |
    'KNOWN' '(' fname ')' |
    '(' bool_expr ')' |
    test_service |
    term relation term |
    'NOT' bool_expr |
    bool_expr ('AND' | 'OR') bool_expr
```

test_service is a special type of private service that returns logical value TRUE or FALSE after its execution.

```
body = action {';' action}
action =
        communicative_action |
        service_action |
        loop_action |
        cond_action |
        modify_fact_action |
        input_output_action
```

LASS supports standard constructs from procedural programming languages such as loop_action, cond_action, modify_fact_action and input_output_action. In addition, *LASS* possesses special communicative primitives characteristic for agent-oriented languages.

```
communicative_action =   ask_service_wait | ask_service
ask_service_wait =
        'SENDWAIT' serv_name '(' [params] ')'
        'TO' agent_name
        'REPORT' 'IN' rep_fact_name
```

```
ask_service =
        'SEND' serv_name '(' [params] ')'
        'TO' agent_name
        'STATUS' 'IN' stat_fact_name
```

Communication is used when some service is asked from a local or remote agent. Agent that asks other agent service may stop the execution of the action sequence while remote service is being performed or it may continue to perform its actions. Agent can have several intentions and/or behaviors active simultaneously. If it uses remote service with wait, only one plan/behavior will be paused, while other will continue to execute. Report can have one of the following values: 'DONE' or 'DENIED'. Status of the service can be either: 'DENIED', 'EXECUTING', or 'DONE'.

```
service_action = service_wait | service
```

Agent may execute its own service in two ways. The plan or behavior that invoked the service may continue to execute simultaneously with the new service or it may wait until the new service finish its execution. Like with remote services, service is accompanied with report (service_wait) or status information (service).

Private services are similar to public services, but they can be called only by the agent itself.

```
private_services_decl =
        'PRIVATE' 'SERVICES' pri_serv_decl {';' pri_serv_decl}
pri_serv_decl = test_serv_decl | serv_decl
behaviors_decl = 'BEHAVIORS' beh_decl {';' beh_decl}
beh_decl =
        beh_name ';'
        [ 'PRIORITY' integer ';' ]
        'ACTIVE' 'WHILE' bool_expr
        'BEGIN' body 'END' beh_name
```

Behavior activation depends on the truth value of bool_expr defined in 'ACTIVE WHILE' part of the declaration. When bool_expr is true, the behavior will be active. There can be several behaviors active at the same time. However, only the active behaviors with the highest priority (lowest integer number) are executed, while other active behaviors are paused. By default, behavior has highest level priority.

8.2.4 Beliefs and intentions

```
init_beliefs = 'BELIEFS' 'INITIALIZATION' body
```

body should be used for the assignment of values to various facts. Facts that are not initialized have the special value: UNKNOWN.

```
init_intentions =
        'INITIAL' 'INTENTIONS' intention {';' intention}
intention = serv_name '(' [params] ')'
params = par {',' par}
```

Intentions are the list of services that are being performed.

8.2.5   A special service `system`

All actions specific to all particular problem domains cannot be covered with any AOP language.

So, in order to use *LASS* in every particular MAS domain, domain specific services should be grouped in the special agent named SYSTEM. SYSTEM should be able to provide its services to every local *LASS* agent. From the viewpoint of any *LASS* agent, it would act like another *LASS* agent. However, it would not be programmed in *LASS*. It would provide domain specific actions represented as *LASS* services. It would serve as an effector common to all local agents.

To every hardware component in MAS, exactly one SYSTEM agent is attached.

8.3   *LASS* SPECIFICATION OF A PERSONAL DIGITAL ASSISTANT

Personal digital assistants (PDAs) are special types of computer programs. They have properties that categorize them as software agents. Personal digital assistant performs some activity that is usually performed by human assistant or secretary. As suggested in [11] and [12], PDA can handle the owner's e-mail, it may monitor or find interesting newsgroups or web sites on the Internet, filter 'interesting' information, maintain the owner's appointment schedule and solely make or cancel appointments. PDA may communicate with others PDAs and perform many tasks which would otherwise have to be performed by owner.

PDA is an agent. Its purpose is to perform some tasks that are usually performed by human personal assistant (secretary) or to act as an intelligent interface to some application. If PDA cooperates with other PDAs, they form a MAS. However, PDA can be isolated as well.

In this paper, a MAS compound of many PDAs is proposed. Agents (PDAs) in the MAS communicate using each other's public services. These agents are actually *LASS* programs. Every PDA in the system is built in the same manner, using the same *LASS* program.

LASS proved as a suitable language for a PDA creation. The PDA program contains all main *LASS* constructs: beliefs about facts, three public services, several private services and one behavior. The PDA has its initial beliefs and one initial intention that never stops - getting new data from its owner.

8.3.1   Beliefs

There are three main facts that constitute the PDA's beliefs:

- `time_intervals_with_availability_levels` - this is an array of records. It stores the owner's time intervals that can be with various level of availability for appointment making.

- `people_and_importance` - this is also an array of records. Every person that may ask appointment has its degree of importance for the PDA's owner.

- importance - the priority of appointment, the priority of the person, and the availability levels of the owner's time intervals are used for the determination of the owner's time intervals that can be used for the appointment. Determined intervals are matched with the time intervals proposed by another PDA that asks appointment.

- appointment_schedule - this fact is used for storing of already made appointments.

- people_and_agents - information about known people and theirs agents.

8.3.2 Public services

There are three public services available to others PDAs.

```
make_appointment(name : name_type;
                 available : ARRAY OF time_type;
                 priority : INTEGER;
                 VAR when : time_type;
                 VAR done : BOOLEAN);
```

The service has three input and two output parameters. Remote PDA that uses this service has to specify the name of its owner (person that wants an appointment), available time intervals proposed by its owner and the priority of an appointment. As the result of the service execution, parameters when and done get theirs values. If done is TRUE, then the appointment is made and when contains the time when it will take a place. Otherwise, the appropriate time for appointment was not found.

```
get_time_intervals( name : name_type;
                    VAR times : ARRAY OF time_type;
```

This service is used by remote PDA when its owner wants to know appropriate times for an appointment with the owner of the PDA

```
cancel_appointment(name : name_type;
                   when : time_type)
```

When some person wants to cancel an appointment with the PDA's owner, that person's PDA will use this public service.

8.3.3 Private services

```
calculate_availability_level( importance,
                              priority : INTEGER;
                              VAR level : INTEGER);
```

It uses the importance of the person and the priority of the appointment and determines the lowest level of availability of time interval that can be used for the appointment.

```
input_output()
```

This service is executed all the time. It is used for information exchange between PDA and its owner. The service constantly displays the menu of available commands and handles the owner's requests. This service invokes executions of services enlisted below.

```
request_appointment(with : name_type;
                    priority : INTEGER;
                    VAR when : time_type;
                    VAR done : BOOLEAN)
```

The service is used when the PDA's owner wants to make an appointment with somebody.

```
get_request_from_owner(VAR name : name_type;
                       VAR priority : INTEGER;
                       VAR available : ARRAY OF time_type)
get_data_from_owner()
display_schedule()
```

The three last services are used for the communication with the PDA's owner.

8.3.4   Behavior

PDA possesses one simple behavior. It becomes active whenever some change occurs in the appointment schedule without the knowledge of the PDA's owner. Such situations happen when another PDA successfully makes or cancels appointment. In both cases the behavior writes an appropriate message on the status line of an agent window.

8.4   RELATED WORK

The first AOP language that uses mental categories is AGENT0 [14]. Agents programmed in AGENT0 have their initial beliefs and capabilities to perform private and communicative actions. The main part of AGENT0 program are the commitment rules. Each commitment rule determines the new commitments and other mental changes that will occur if particular message is received. Types of messages are chosen from the speech acts theory ('inform', 'request', and 'unrequest'). Agents programmed with AGENT0 are synchronized with a common clock. The language is loosely coupled with modal temporal logic. This logic is used for the specification of the language.

Unlike AGENT0, *LASS* is intended for practical usage. The purpose of AGENT0 was to introduce new concepts in an elegant manner. *LASS* is not bound to any logic. It uses some procedural constructs and its expressive power is greater than it is in AGENT0. Agents programmed in *LASS* do not use clocks and references to time points to synchronize their actions. ask_service_wait can be used for synchronization. While AGENT0 possesses some elements of logic programming, *LASS* is more oriented to procedural constructs.

PLACA ([15, 16]) is the descendant of AGENT0. PLACA introduces planning capabilities of agents. Agent in PLACA uses plans to achieve the desired state of the world.

Agents in *LASS* also use plans, but plans cannot be generated at run-time as they can be in PLACA.

In Concurrent MetateM ([8, 9, 18]) MAS is specified with the logic. The logic is modal and linear temporal. Specification of MAS is directly executed. Concurrent MetateM is only in experimental stage and so far it has no common features with *LASS*.

A different approach to MAS programming is proposed in [13]. In HOMAGE, the language for agent specification has two levels. The lower level uses objects of Java, Common Lisp and C++ instead of menta categories. Higher level contains constructs for organization of objects from the lower level into agent's program. Agents in HOMAGE communicate and received messages are handled with rules similar to those in AGENT0 and PLACA.

LASS does not allow the use of other languages. However, two types of primitives in *LASS* can be identified. Primitives that are specific for AOP languages (communicative actions, services, plans, intentions, behaviors, etc.) correspond to higher level in HOMAGE. Primitives inherited from procedural languages (loop_action, cond_action, modify_fact_action, input_output_action, ...) correspond to lower level in HOMAGE.

The AOP language with the greatest influence on our research is AgentSpeak ([17]). Creators of AgentSpeak aimed to join object oriented programming and MAS concepts such as: mental categories, reactive and proactive properties, distribution over wide area network, real-time response, communication with speech acts, concurrent execution of plans in and between agents and meta-level reasoning. The main difference between *LASS* and AgentSpeak is in communication. We believe that *LASS* introduces more powerful communicative primitives than those existing in languages enlisted above. Speech acts can be easily implemented in *LASS* using services. Sending of a speech act performative then corresponds to a request for a service execution.

None of the above languages possesses such a powerful construct for agent reactivity such as behaviors. Behavioral approach to artificial intelligence is developed at MIT. Its creator, R. Brooks ([5, 6, 7]), has developed many simple robots that are able to perform complex tasks. Broks proposes Subsumption Architecture for the organization of behaviors. Behaviors in *LASS* are organized in the similar manner, but with a big difference – Brooks' behaviours are triggered by robot sensors, while *LASS* behaviours are bound to agent beliefs. .

Most of the concepts used in *LASS* are already seen in other programming languages. The significance of *LASS* is in the inclusion of all these concepts into one programming language.

8.5 CONCLUSION

This paper presents a new programming language called *LASS*. *LASS* enables programming using agent-oriented concepts.

Besides other concepts, *LASS* provide the usage of behaviors. Behaviors can be used for programming of reactive agent features. *LASS* and/or ideas on which *LASS* is based were conceptually applied in [3, 4].

In the paper, as a simple example of using *LASS*, PDA for appointment schedule, has been presented. The main contribution of this paper is twofold. It suggests an usable application that exploits concepts proposed by multi-agent system theory. Secondly, it confirms the expectations about the usefulness of *LASS* in the development of multi-agent systems. This application serves as a test example for exploration of *LASS* capabilities.

The proposed PDA has two main advantages over PDAs proposed in [11] and [12]. It is simpler and more reliable. It will never make an undesired appointment. The future work on proposed PDA may include expanding the PDA with new services. Services may be added that provide various information about the PDA's owner. When and where will the owner be, on which telephone numbers will he/she be available, what are his/her current activities, etc. Other new services may be used for the realization of messaging system similar to e-mail.

LASS is not yet available for practical use, but authors are working on its implementation. *LASS* is being implemented in Java. *LASS* is suitable for agent-oriented software engineering. This approach to software engineering has several advantages. It facilitates the usage of divide-and-conquer strategy. It also enables the exploitation of parallelism. Software system can be easily deployed on the wide area network and executed on several machines simultaneously. Whereas agents are encapsulated entities, the system behaves robustly when the addition of new agents or the modification or removal of existing ones occurs.

8.6   REFERENCES

[1] M. Badjonski and M. Ivanović. *LASS* - A Language for Agent-Oriented Software Specification. In Proc. of VIII Int. Conf. on Logic and Computer Science (Novi Sad, Yugoslavia), eds. Tošić, R. and Budimac, Z., pp. 9–18, 1997.

[2] M. Badjonski and M. Ivanović and Z. Budimac. Software Specification Using *LASS*. In Proc. of ASIAN '97 (Kathmandu, Nepal), Lecture Notes in Computer Science Series vol. 1345, Springer Verlag , (Eds. Shyamasundar, R. K. and Ueda, K.), pp. 375–376. 1997.

[3] M. Badjonski and M. Ivanović. Multi-agent System for Determination of Optimal Hybrid for Seeding. In Proc. of EFITA '97 (Copenhagen, Denmark), pp. 401–404, 1997.

[4] M. Badjonski, M. Ivanović and Z. Budimac. Possibility of using Multi-Agent System in Education. In Proc. of IEEE International SMC '97 Conference (Orlando, Florida, USA), pp. 588–593, 1997.

[5] R. A. Brooks. Intelligence without Reason. In Proc. of the Twelfth International Joint Conference on Artificial Intelligence (IJCAI-91), Sydney, Australia, pp 569–595, 1991.

[6] R. A. Brooks. Intelligence without Representation. Artificial Intelligence 47, pp. 139–159, 1991.

[7] R. A. Brooks. A robust layered control system for a mobile robot. IEEE Journal of Robotics and Automation, 2(1), pp. 14–23, 1986.

[8] M. Fisher. Representing and Executing Agent-Based Systems. Intelligent Agents, Lecture Notes in Artificial Intelligence Vol 890, Springer-Verlag, pp. 307–323, 1994.

[9] M. Fisher. A Survey of Concurrent MetateM - the Language and its Applications. Temporal Logic - Proc. of the 1. Int. Conference, Lecture Notes in Artificial Intelligence Vol 827), Springer Verlag pp. 480–505, 1994.

[10] S. Franklin and A. Graesser. Is it and Agent, or just a Program?: A Taxonomy for Autonomous Agents. Working Notes of the 3. Int. Workshop on Agent Theories, Architectures and Languages, ECAI '96, Budapest, Hungary, pp. 193–206, 1996.

[11] P. Maes. Agent that Reduce Work and Information Overload. Comm. ACM, 37(7), pp. 31–40, 1995.

[12] T. M. Michell, R. Caruana, D. Freitag, J. McDermott and D. Zabowski. Experience with a Learning Personal Assistant. Comm. ACM, 37(7), pp. 80–91, 1994.

[13] A. Poggi and G. Adorni. A Multi Language Environment to Develop Multi Agent Applications. Working Notes of the 3. Int. Workshop on Agent Theories, Architectures and Languages ECAI '96, Budapest, Hungary, pp. 249–261, 1996.

[14] Y. Shoham. Agent-Oriented Programming. Artificial Intelligence, 60(1), pp. 51–92, 1993.

[15] S. R. Thomas. The PLACA Agent Programming Language. Intelligent Agents, Lecture Notes in Artificial Intelligence Vol 890, Springer-Verlag, pp. 356–370, 1994.

[16] R. S. Thomas. PLACA, an Agent Oriented Programming Language. Ph.D. thesis, Computer Science Department, Stanford University, Stanford, CA, 1993, (available as technical report STAN-CS-93-1487).

[17] D. Weerasooriga, A. Rao and K. Ramamohanarao. Design of a Concurrent Agent-Oriented Language. Intelligent Agents, Lecture Notes in Artificial Intelligence Vol. 890, Springer-Verlag, pp. 386–401, 1994.

[18] M. Wooldridge. A Knowledge-Theoretic Semantics for Concurrent MetateM. Working Notes of the 3. Int. Workshop on Agent Theories, Architectures and Languages ECAI '96, Budapest, Hungary, pp. 279–293, 1996.

[19] M. Wooldridge and N. R. Jennings. Agent Theories, Architectures, and Languages: A Survey. Intelligent Agents, Lecture Notes in Artificial Intelligence Vol 890, Springer-Verlag, pp. 1–39, 1994.

9

Fair Objects

Paul Gibson and Dominique Méry

Université Henri Poincaré (Nancy I)
UMR 7503 LORIA, Campus Scientifique,
BP 239, 54506 VANDOEUVRE-LES-NANCY, FRANCE.
Email: {gibson,mery}@loria.fr), WWW: http://www.loria.fr/~mery.

Abstract: The temporal logic of actions (TLA) provides operators to express liveness requirements in an abstract specification model. TLA does not, however, provide high level composition mechanisms which are essential for synthesising and analysing complex behaviour. Contrastingly, the object oriented paradigm has proven itself in the development of structured specifications. However, most, if not all, of the object oriented formalisms are based on the specification of safety properties and, as such, they do not provide an adequate means of expressing liveness conditions. This paper examines how we combine temporal semantics and object oriented concepts in a complementary fashion. High level re-usable concepts are formalised as different kinds of *fair objects*. The object oriented semantics aid validation and customer communication, whilst the TLA semantics provide a means of formally verifying liveness requirements. The fairness concepts are founded on the notion of objects as servers which may have multiple (concurrent) clients. Some simple telephone feature specifications illustrate the practical application of our *fair object* semantics.

9.1 INTRODUCTION

We believe a complementary integration of object oriented concepts and TLA[19] within one formal framework is an aid to requirements modelling. Our main goal is to draw together the object oriented, concurrency and fairness concepts into one formalism. Combining the different semantic frameworks is not an easy task. We are currently following two different approaches which, we hope, will meet in the middle. Firstly, we are examining the means by which we can imporve Lamport's proposals for structural mechanisms in TLA[21], which will reflect the object oriented semantics of classification, composition, subclassing and polymorphism. Secondly, we are extending the object oriented semantics to include the notion of different forms of *fair objects*. This paper reports on this second line of work. Namely, we report on the different forms of *fair object* which act as high level reusable components during requirements modelling. Throughout this paper we do not report on the formal integration of our two different semantic models. Rather, specifications are given pairwise and the intuitive relationship between each model in a pair is informally, yet rigorously, explained.

9.1.1 Objects

Object oriented methods encompass a set of techniques which have been, and will continue to be, applied in the successful production of complex software systems. The methods are based on the simple mathematical models of abstraction and classification. We adopt a simple object-labelled state transition system semantics (O-LSTS) which regards an object as a state transition machine [14]. The true advantage of the O-LSTS approach is in the initial requirements modelling phase of development. It improves the communication with the customer and aids in synthesis, analysis and validation. However, we have found the inability to express liveness requirements a main weakness when applying the O-LSTS approach. Without liveness we can specify only what cannot happen (i.e. saftey properties) rather than what must happen. Furthermore, without temporal semantics based on liveness, the nondeterminism in a system can be specified only at one level of abstraction: namely that of an internal choice of events. This can lead, as we shall later see, to many problems in development.

9.1.2 Temporal logic and liveness

Consider the specification of a shared database. This database must handle multiple, parallel requests from clients. The order in which these requests are processed is required to be nondeterministic. This is easily specified without liveness. However, if the requirements are now refined to state that every request must be eventually served (this is a fairness requirement which we cannot express in a safety-only semantic framework). Our only choice is to *over-specify* the requirement by defining how this fairness is to be achieved (for example, by explicitly queueing the requests). This is bad because we are enforcing implementation decisions at the requirements level.

TLA [19] provides a simple and effective means of expressing fairness properties. The semantics incorporate the notions of *always* (represented by the $\Box$ operator) and *eventually* (represented by the $\Diamond$ operator). Using these, we can specify different categories of fairness within the object oriented framework. The ability to model nondeterminism at different levels of abstraction is the key to TLA's utility in requirements modelling. Unfortunately, TLA does not provide the means for easily constructing and validating initial customer requirements. By combining TLA and object oriented semantics we can alleviate these problems.

9.1.3   Telephone feature specification

Features are observable behaviour and are therefore a requirements specification problem
[23]. We concentrate on the domain of telephone features [4, 5]. The feature interaction
problem is stated simply, and informally, as follows: A *feature interaction* is a situation
in which system behaviour (specified as some set of features) does not as a whole satisfy
each of its component features individually. Most feature interaction problems can be (and
should be) resolved at the requirements capture stage of development[15]. The telephone
feature examples in section 9.4 are taken from a large list of specifications which we have
developed using our *fair object* concepts. Telephone feature specification is well suited to
our semantic approach because it requires a high degree of structuring to cope with the
highly compositional and incremental nature of such systems; and there is a clear need for
fairness requirements [16].

9.2   SEMANTIC FRAMEWORK

9.2.1   Objects as state machines: Different views

Labelled state transition systems are often used to provide executable models during analysis, design and implementation stages of software development [7, 9, 10]. In particular,
such models are found in the classic analysis and design methods of [3, 6, 8]. However,
a major problem with state models is that it can be difficult to provide a good system
(de)composition when the underlying state and state transitions are not easily conceptu-
alised. The object oriented paradigm provides a natural solution to this problem. By equat-
ing the notion of class with the state transition system model and allowing the state of
one class to be defined as a composition of states of other classes, the O-LSTS approach
provides a means of specifying such models in a constructive fashion.

The O-LSTS semantics also permit us to view objects at different levels of abstraction.
Firstly, using an abstract data type (ADT) we can specify the functionality of an object at a
level of abstraction suitable for requirements capture[22]. Secondly, we can transform our
ADT requirements into a parameterised process algebra (LOTOS[2, 11]) specification for
the design stage. Finally, as we approach an implementation environment, we can view the
objects in our designs as clients and servers in a distributed, concurrent network. At each
of these levels of abstraction we provide a means of incorporating fairness requirements.

ADT view

The simplest way to introduce the ADT view is through a *standard* example: A Queue
of Integers is specified using the OO ACT ONE specification language from [13]. An
equivalent graphical representation of the state transition system is also given.

The Queue uses a predefined class Integer (which itself uses Bool) The literal and
structure members define all the possible (states of the) objects in the class. There is one
non-structured literal value empty. All other elements are structured from two components,
namely a Queue and an Integer, using the AQueue operator.

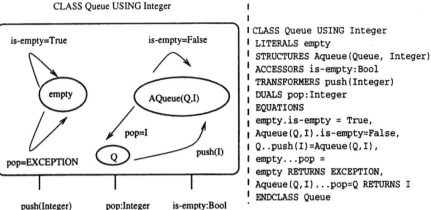

CLASS Queue USING Integer

```
CLASS Queue USING Integer
LITERALS empty
STRUCTURES Aqueue(Queue, Integer)
ACCESSORS is-empty:Bool
TRANSFORMERS push(Integer)
DUALS pop:Integer
EQUATIONS
empty.is-empty = True,
Aqueue(Q,I).is-empty=False,
Q..push(I)=Aqueue(Q,I),
empty...pop =
empty RETURNS EXCEPTION,
Aqueue(Q,I)...pop=Q RETURNS I
ENDCLASS Queue
```

push(Integer)   pop:Integer   is-empty:Bool

The class interface is defined by the three different sets of services offered: a transformer changes the internal state of an object, an accessor returns some value without changing internal state, a dual returns a value and may also change the internal state. The services may be parametrised (e.g. push) to represent the input data passed to the server object when a service is requested. The equations are used to define a semantics for the interface services. The syntax (including the *dot notation*) should be easy to follow: *one dot* defines the value returned when a service is completed, *two dots* defines the new state of an object after a service is fulfilled, and *three dots* defines both these values. It should be noted that every class has, by default, an implicit EXCEPTION value which can be used in cases like the popping of an element from an empty queue. Furthermore, variables which are not typed explicitly may have their types inferred where there is no ambiguity. We also have tools for verifying the completeness and consistency of such specifications.

Process algebra view

Consider a system made up of two Queues, as specified above, whose behaviour is illustrated by the O-LSTS diagram for class TwoQs. (The corresponding OO ACT ONE code can be easily deduced from the diagram: the only new construct is the *dotted* move transition which represents an internal, nondeterministic state trabsformer.) A corresponding full LOTOS design[1] is found to the right of the diagram. The ADT part of the LOTOS specification, not shown, is generated automatically from the OO ACT ONE specification, and is used to parameterise the process definition for the corresponding behaviour. In this case, type TwoQs parameterises the behaviour of process TwoQs.

The TwoQs provides two services: push (which pushes elements onto the first queue component) and pop (which pops elements from the second queue component); and the internal state transition move transfers elements from the first queue onto the second queue. The full LOTOS design moves us a step closer to an implementation because our specification is now modelled as a process with which we can communicate. This particular LOTOS design, chosen for its simplicity, specifies that a *remote procedure call* protocol[2] is used for communication with the TwoQs process.

---

[1]For simplicity, we use a shorthand '[...]' to represent a gate list which is the same as that found in the process definition header.

[2]Other types of protocol can also be generated automatically.

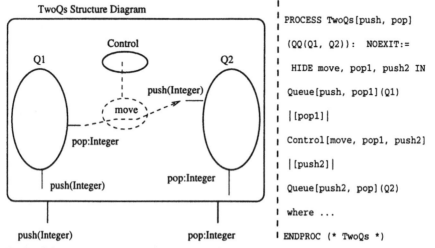

CLASS TwoQS Using Queue

```
PROCESS TwoQs[push, pop](QQ:TwoQs):

NOEXIT:=

HIDE move IN

( push?  Integer1:Integer;

TwoQs[...](push(QQ,Integer1))

)[]

( pop; pop! popRESULT(QQ);

TwoQs[...](pop(QQ))

)[]

( move; TwoQs[...](move(QQ)) )

ENDPROC (* TwoQs *)
```

The push operation is carried out synchronously between the object and its environment. The pop operator requires some result to be returned and we model the communication of the result as an event different from the service request. The move operation is hidden from the environment of the TwoQs process: as such, the movement of elements between the two queues cannot be determined by the TwoQs client(s).

It is now possible, using a pre-defined correctness preserving transformation, to reuse the compositional structure found in the OO ACT ONE specification in a structurally equivalent compositional LOTOS specification. This results in an equivalent specification with two Queue processes synchronising on an internal move event. We illustrate this below, in a partial specification together with an equivalent O-LSTS structure diagram:

TwoQs Structure Diagram

```
PROCESS TwoQs[push, pop]

(QQ(Q1, Q2)):  NOEXIT:=

HIDE move, popl, push2 IN

Queue[push, popl](Q1)

|[popl]|

Control[move, popl, push2]

|[push2]|

Queue[push2, pop](Q2)

where ...

ENDPROC (* TwoQs *)
```

Each of the component Queue processes is generated directly from the ADT specification. The names of the external services of these components are indiced to avoid name clashes, and all synchronisation between the two components is controlled by a `Control` process. This `Control` is generated through analysis of the equations defined in the `TwoQs` ADT. There will (nearly) always be a need for such a control process: we consider it as a refinement of the actions which are shared between the component parts. In this example, we note that push and pop do not require co-operation between the two components and so these can be routed directly to the internal components.

Client-Server view

The type of LOTOS design seen above is quite close to the type of *client-server* model that is found in many reference models for software development, see [17, 18], for example. We can say that the environment of a `TwoQs` process is its client. Now let us consider a *liveness* property which we would reasonably require such a system to fulfil. The nondeterministic move operation cannot be guaranteed to be carried out when we specify only *safety* properties. We may require that if an element is pushed onto the first queue, then it will eventually be moved to the second queue. We do not wish to specify how this happens, only that it does. This is the essence of abstraction with regards to the nondeterminism in our system: we need to be able to specify *fairness* at the 'class level of abstraction'.

Furthermore, we need to consider what happens when a server has multiple (concurrent) clients. If an object in the server's environment requests a push how can we be sure that it will be carried out even though, in this case, it is always enabled? The problem is as follows: if the server is shared between other clients then how do we guarantee that one client's requests will eventually be carried out? Certainly, we could specify some sort of queueing protocol, for example. However, again we believe that at this stage of design we do not want to impose such implementation decisions. A *fair object* should guarantee, wherever possible, the eventuality of meeting clients' requests in a concurrent environment. Using TLA, we shall show how different types of *fair objects* can be used to fulfil such eventuality requirements.

9.2.2 Temporal logic

Introducing TLA

TLA is a linear temporal logic introduced by Lamport [19] and based on the action-as-relation principle. A system is considered as a set of actions, namely a logical disjunction of predicates relating values of variables before the activation of an action and values of variables after the activation of an action; a system is modeled as a set of traces over a set of states. The specifier may decide to ignore traces that do not satisfy a scheduling policy, such as strong or weak fairness; and temporal operators such as $\Box$ (Always) or $\Diamond$ (Eventually) are combined to express these assumptions over the set of traces.

The meaning $[\![\Pi]\!]$ of a linear temporal-logic formula Π is a Boolean-valued function on behaviors. We say that the behavior σ satisfies Π iff $[\![\Pi]\!](\sigma)$ equals TRUE. Formula Π is valid, written $\models \Pi$, iff every behavior satisfies Π. To use temporal logic to specify (a mathematical model of) a system, we consider states to represent possible system states and events to represent possible system actions, so a behavior represents a conceivable execution of a system. A system is specified by a formula Π that is satisfied by precisely those behaviors that represent a legal system execution.

The power of TLA with respect to verification is its simplicity. One model is verified against another simply by logical implication. The means of verification are built into the language semantics.

Liveness and safety

A safety property expresses that something bad will never happen. More precisely, a safety property is a formula on traces that is satisfied by an infinite behavior σ if, and only if, it is satisfied by every prefix of σ. It is finitely refutable. Alpern and Schneider have shown that a safety property is a closed set in an adequate topology[1]. Intuitively, a safety property Π constrains only the finite behavior of a system—any behavior that fails to satisfy Π fails at some specific instant.

A liveness property states that something good will eventually happen. The two most commonly seen liveness properties, within the TLA framework, are weak fairness and strong fairness. We examine these below, where we incorporate them into our *fair object* framework.

Weak fairness

Consider the simple O-LSTS for System1. (We represent only internal actions and abstract away from the state values that play no role in deciding which internal actions are enabled. In this way the example is trivial, but it does illustrate the need for fairness.) The system permits traces a;a;a;... and b;b;b;.... In other words, we cannot guarantee that either a or b will ever be performed. The corresponding temporal logic specification (based on TLA syntax) is also given.

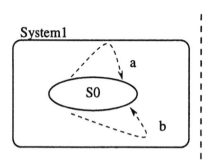

————module *System1*————

extends DATA
x,s : VARIABLE
definitions
STATES $\triangleq$ { s0 }
Initial_System1 $\triangleq$
$(s = s0) \wedge (x \in DATA)$
$\mathcal{A} \triangleq R_a(x,x') \wedge$ UNCHANGED s
$\mathcal{B} \triangleq R_b(x,x') \wedge$ UNCHANGED s
Nofairness_System1 $\triangleq$
$\wedge$ *Initial_System1*
$\wedge \Box[\mathcal{A} \vee \mathcal{B}]_x$

The specification of *Nofairness_System1* guarantees, through the always operator $\Box$, the eventuality of some action being carried out. It does not guarantee either of the actions individually: for that we need the notion of *weak fairness*. Weak fairness states that if an action is continually enabled then it will be eventually carried out. This is defined below, together with other useful concepts:

Fundamental TLA concepts

p in the next state: $p' \triangleq p(\forall v : v'/v)$

Eventually p in a linear temporal model: $\Diamond F \triangleq \neg \Box \neg F$

Either action $\mathcal{A}$ or a stuttering step: $[\mathcal{A}]_f \triangleq \mathcal{A} \vee (f' = f)$

F Leads to G: $F \rightsquigarrow G \triangleq \Box (F \Rightarrow \Diamond G)$

An $\mathcal{A}$ step without stuttering: $< \mathcal{A} >_f \triangleq \mathcal{A} \wedge (f' \neq f)$

Unchanged: UNCHANGED $f \triangleq f' = f$

Definition **Weak fairness:**

$$\mathrm{WF}_f \mathcal{A} \triangleq \Box \Diamond < \mathcal{A} >_f \vee \Box \Diamond \neg \text{ ENABLED } < \mathcal{A} >_f$$

We define weak fairness on an object (system), written *WF(system)* to be the system together with weak fairness requirements on all the internal events in its alphabet. Using the TLA theorem prover TLP [12], we can now prove that neither a nor b actions in *WF(System1)* will be continually refused in order to carried out the other (see *Property1* in the specification).

─────────**module** *WF_System1*─────────

> **extends** System1
> **definitions**
> $WF\_System1 \triangleq \wedge Initial\_System1$
> $\qquad\qquad\qquad \wedge \Box[\mathcal{A} \vee \mathcal{B}]_x$
> $\qquad\qquad\qquad \wedge \mathrm{WF}_{<x,s>} \mathcal{A}$
> $\qquad\qquad\qquad \wedge \mathrm{WF}_{<x,s>} \mathcal{B}$
> **theorems**
> $Property1 \triangleq WF\_System1 \Rightarrow \Box \Diamond < \mathcal{A} >_{<x,s>} \wedge \Box \Diamond < \mathcal{B} >_{<x,s>}$
> **assumptions**
> $Assumption\_\mathcal{A} \triangleq \forall x \in DATA, \exists x' \in DATA : R_a(x,x')$
> $Assumption\_\mathcal{B} \triangleq \forall x \in DATA, \exists x' \in DATA : R_b(x,x')$

├──────────────────────────────────┤

Now, in the specification of the TwoQs system we can use weak fairness to guarantee that the move operation cannot be continually ignored. Thus, specifying WF(TwoQs) guarantees that we shall always eventually be able to pop off an element (from the second queue component) provided we have already pushed an element (onto the first queue component). Using TLP, we can now prove that WF(TwoQs) => Queue, i.e. the system of two queues is an implementation of a simple queue.

Strong fairness

Weak fairness guarantees the eventual execution of an action when that action is continually enabled. If the action is not continually enabled, but is enabled an infinite number of times, then weak fairness does not guarantee its execution. This is the role of strong fairness. Consider the simple O-LSTS for System2. The system permits the trace a;b;a;b;a;b;.... We may require that event e always eventually happens. However, stating weak fairness on System2 (i.e. weak fairness on all its actions) does not guarantee the execution of any e events. For this we require strong fairness. By stating strong fairness, as defined below, on action $\mathcal{E}$ in System2, we can prove its eventual execution:

Definition **Strong fairness**

$$\text{SF}_f \mathcal{A} \triangleq \Box\Diamond < \mathcal{A} >_f \lor \Diamond\Box\neg \text{ENABLED} < A >_f$$

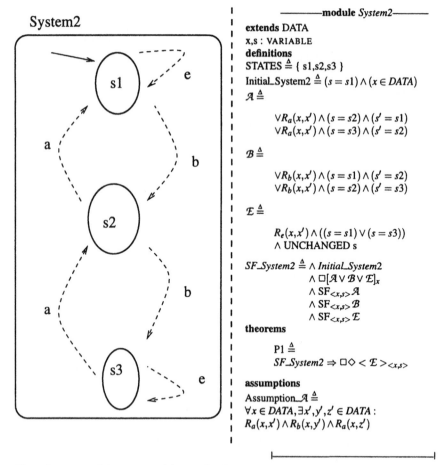

```
                                               ———————module System2———————
     System2                                   extends DATA
                                               x,s : VARIABLE
                                               definitions
                                               STATES ≜ { s1,s2,s3 }
                                               Initial_System2 ≜ (s = s1) ∧ (x ∈ DATA)
                                               𝒜 ≜

                                                       ∨ R_a(x,x′) ∧ (s = s2) ∧ (s′ = s1)
                                                       ∨ R_a(x,x′) ∧ (s = s3) ∧ (s′ = s2)

                                               ℬ ≜

                                                       ∨ R_b(x,x′) ∧ (s = s1) ∧ (s′ = s2)
                                                       ∨ R_b(x,x′) ∧ (s = s2) ∧ (s′ = s3)

                                               𝓔 ≜

                                                       R_e(x,x′) ∧ ((s = s1) ∨ (s = s3))
                                                       ∧ UNCHANGED s

                                               SF_System2 ≜ ∧ Initial_System2
                                                              ∧ □[𝒜 ∨ ℬ ∨ 𝓔]_x
                                                              ∧ SF_<x,s> 𝒜
                                                              ∧ SF_<x,s> ℬ
                                                              ∧ SF_<x,s> 𝓔
                                               theorems

                                                   P1 ≜
                                                   SF_System2 ⇒ □◇ < 𝓔 >_<x,s>

                                               assumptions
                                               Assumption_𝒜 ≜
                                               ∀x ∈ DATA, ∃x′,y′,z′ ∈ DATA :
                                               R_a(x,x′) ∧ R_b(x,y′) ∧ R_a(x,z′)
```

There is no need for strong fairness in the TwoQs system to guarantee the movement of elements. However, imagine a similar system where a move is enabled only directly after a push event. In this instance, we would need to define strong fairness on this system to guarantee the movement of elements between the two queues. We define SF(system) as the system in which all its internal actions have the strong fairness requirement. We note that SF is more commonly found than WF: it is not often that internal actions are continually enabled since in most specifications there are intermediate states, like s2 in System2, where a required action is not enabled but is sure to be enabled in the next state.

9.3 FAIR OBJECTS

The goal of our research is to identify high-level fairness concepts within our object oriented framework. The O-LSTS specifications can then be extended to include fairness requirements, which are to be reasoned about using TLA. *Weakly fair objects* and *strongly fair objects* provide us with two such concepts; five additional high-level concepts are described below. Each of these has played an important role in the development of telephone feature specifications.

9.3.1 Progression

The notion of progression arises from the way in which concurrent processes are modelled through an interleaving of events. We can "view" such interleaving as though there is a scheduler which randomly chooses which process to be executed at any particular time. In such systems we wish to specify that each of the component processes is *fairly scheduled*. Consider the simple example in the diagram below, where we consider concurrent TwoQs component objects which do not need to communicate within the system in which they are found:

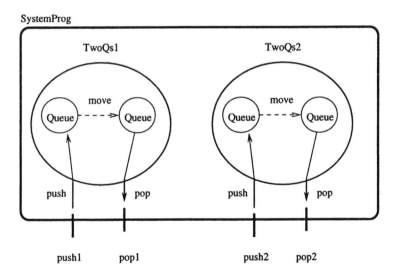

In SystemProg we cannot guarantee the internal movement of elements in either of the two components, even if we specify the component objects to be fair (strong or weak). The reasoning is simple: the interleaving semantics, of the process algebra, would allow either one of the two processes never to be scheduled and thus the internal moves may never be enabled. Thus, we require some means of saying that the scheduling in SystemProg is *fair*. Furthermore, we want to be able to do this without having to change the specifications of the two components. *Progression* corresponds to this notion. In this simple example, we can see that Prog(SystemProg) could be defined as strong fairness on the action ($move_{TwoQs1}$ ∨ $move_{TwoQs2}$). This can be easily formalised, and generated automatically, in TLA.

A more complex situation occurs if there is synchronisation between two, or more, components of a system. In such a case, we require strong fairness on the synchronising action(s) and progression in the individual components:

Definition **Progression**

A process P is said to (strongly) progress, written $Prog(P)$, when:

- If P has no component processes then we require $SF(\bigvee_{i \in I} i)$, where I is the internal action set of P.

- If P has components $C1$ and $C2$ then each of these components progress and $SF(\bigvee_{i \in J} i)$, where J is the set of internal actions on which $C1$ and $C2$ synchronise.

This definition is easily generalised to processes with more than two components.

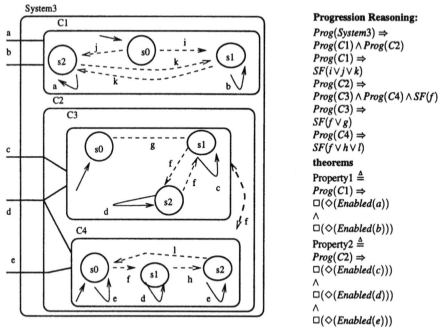

Progression Reasoning:

$Prog(System3) \Rightarrow$
$Prog(C1) \wedge Prog(C2)$
$Prog(C1) \Rightarrow$
$SF(i \vee j \vee k)$
$Prog(C2) \Rightarrow$
$Prog(C3) \wedge Prog(C4) \wedge SF(f)$
$Prog(C3) \Rightarrow$
$SF(f \vee g)$
$Prog(C4) \Rightarrow$
$SF(f \vee h \vee l)$

theorems

Property1 $\triangleq$
$Prog(C1) \Rightarrow$
$\square(\lozenge(Enabled(a))$
$\wedge$
$\square(\lozenge(Enabled(b)))$

Property2 $\triangleq$
$Prog(C2) \Rightarrow$
$\square(\lozenge(Enabled(c)))$
$\wedge$
$\square(\lozenge(Enabled(d)))$
$\wedge$
$\square(\lozenge(Enabled(e)))$

A weaker form of progression can be defined by placing only WF constraints on the internal action sets. By default, when talking about progression, we mean strong progression. The utility of progression is illustrated by System3, where we see that progression is needed to guarantee the *eventuality obligations* (see 9.3.5): $\forall x \in \{a, b, c, d, e\}$:

$\Box\Diamond Enabled(x)$. Thus, using progression, we can prove that the environment of System3 will never have to wait indefinitely for a requested service to be enabled.

9.3.2 Possible fairness

Nondeterminism often gives rise to systems in which it is always possible for an action to be enabled (by following a certain sequence of interal actions) yet the action cannot be guaranteed to be executed through the use of strong fairness or progression (see system4, below). In such cases, we require the notion of *possible fairness*. (Lamport has also considered the notion of possibility[20] but our approach, we believe, is much simpler with respect to the development of *fair objects*.)

We construct our definition of possible fairness from the notion of a system which may give rise to a certain property. The properties of interest, with respect to *fair objects*, is the eventual enabling of their external events.

May — *System Π may lead to P*
$$[\![\mathbf{May}_\Pi(P)]\!](\sigma) \triangleq [\![\Pi]\!](\sigma) => \exists\rho \sqsubset \sigma : \exists\tau : [\![\Pi]\!](\rho\cdot\tau) \wedge [\![\Diamond P]\!](\tau)$$

Always possible — *P is always possible in Π*
$$\mathbf{P}_\Pi(P) \triangleq [\![\Pi]\!](\sigma) => \forall\rho \sqsubset \sigma : \exists\tau : [\![\Pi]\!](\rho\cdot\tau) \wedge [\![\Diamond P]\!](\tau)$$

Possible fairness —
An action $\mathcal{A}$ is possible-fair, written $PF(\mathcal{A})$, if it is guaranteed to be enabled when it is always possible. $PF_\Pi(\mathcal{A}) \triangleq \mathbf{P}_\Pi(P) \Rightarrow \Diamond Enabled\mathcal{A}$

A system is said to be possible-fair if all its internal actions are possible-fair, written PF(system). Consider the O-LSTS for System4. We see that event c is always possible, i.e. no matter what state we are in we can always find a sequence of actions which will lead to c being enabled. In such a situation we may wish to specify $\Box\Diamond C$. Specifying strong fairness does not, however, disallow the trace b;a;d;b;a;d;.... To disallow this behaviour we require a possible fairness on event c.

We note that strong fairness on event a implies $\Box((\Diamond c) \vee (\Diamond d))$. An a event must always eventually be taken (due to the strong fairness condition) and so this a event enables either event c or event d. System4 is thus modelling a deferred nondeterministic choice between actions c and d. It is possible to model the same behaviour by renaming all the a events, and specifying strong fairness on each of them. This approach would give rise to many complications if the a events corresponded to synchronisations between different component objects. Possible fairness lets us reason about such complex cases in a very simple manner.

System4

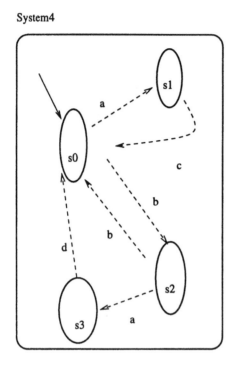

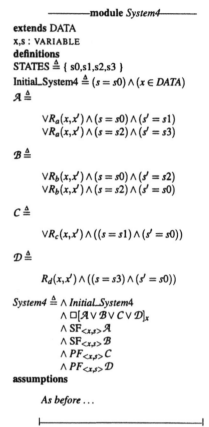

module *System4*

extends DATA

X,S : VARIABLE

definitions

STATES $\triangleq$ { s0,s1,s2,s3 }

Initial_System4 $\triangleq (s = s0) \wedge (x \in DATA)$

$\mathcal{A} \triangleq$

$\quad \vee R_a(x,x') \wedge (s = s0) \wedge (s' = s1)$
$\quad \vee R_a(x,x') \wedge (s = s2) \wedge (s' = s3)$

$\mathcal{B} \triangleq$

$\quad \vee R_b(x,x') \wedge (s = s0) \wedge (s' = s2)$
$\quad \vee R_b(x,x') \wedge (s = s2) \wedge (s' = s0)$

$C \triangleq$

$\quad \vee R_c(x,x') \wedge ((s = s1) \wedge (s' = s0))$

$\mathcal{D} \triangleq$

$\quad R_d(x,x') \wedge ((s = s3) \wedge (s' = s0))$

$System4 \triangleq \wedge Initial\_System4$
$\qquad\qquad \wedge \Box[\mathcal{A} \vee \mathcal{B} \vee C \vee \mathcal{D}]_x$
$\qquad\qquad \wedge SF_{<x,s>} \mathcal{A}$
$\qquad\qquad \wedge SF_{<x,s>} \mathcal{B}$
$\qquad\qquad \wedge PF_{<x,s>} C$
$\qquad\qquad \wedge PF_{<x,s>} \mathcal{D}$

assumptions

As before ...

9.3.3 Compositional fairness

There are many different ways in which we may wish to define new *fair objects* in terms of
already specified *fair objects*. One such composition mechanism is illustrated by System5,
where we require the following behaviour with respect to fairness:

> Event c should act like a fairness switch (which is *on* in state s0 and *off* in state
> s1). When *on*, events a and b should be weakly fair. When *off*, there should
> be no fairness on these events.

Thus, we allow the traces a;c;b;b;b; ... and a;b;b;c;a;a;a; ..., but disallow an
infinite sequence of a's or b's when there has been an even number of c events. We cannot
specify this behaviour in a satisfactory way by using the global fairness operators. (We can
specify the behaviour in a contrived fashion by relabelling events and hiding the specification behind an interface which decodes the relabelling.) Rather, we require a means of
specifying System5 as a composition of two different types (with respect to the fairness)
of System1. In this way we localise the fairness to system components rather than forcing
fairness upon the whole system. This simplifies the proving of theorems using TLA and
aids implementation.

System5   System5 (compositional style)

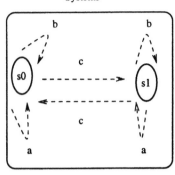
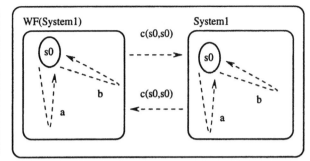

9.3.4   Politeness and eventuality

We now examine the composition of *fair objects* in such a way that nondeterminism must
be resolved by co-operation. First, we need some new definitions:

Eventuality

Action a is said to be *eventual* in Process P, written $ev_a(P)$, iff

$P \Rightarrow \Box \Diamond Enabled(a)$

Eventuality set

The *eventuality set* of Process P, written $Ev(P)$, is defined to be: $\{x : ev_a(P)\}$

   We say that one system is *polite* to another, with respect to some construction operator,
if the *eventuality* properties of the events in the first system are maintained in the composed
system. This is illustrated by the TCS example, below.

TCS

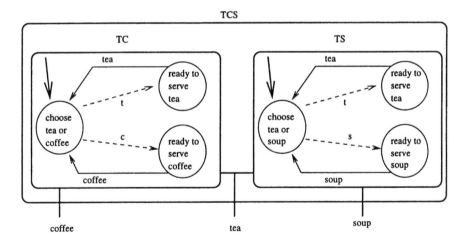

   TC is a nondeterministic tea-coffee machine. TS is a nondeterministic tea-soup machine. The machine TCS is a composition of the two which requires synchronisation on the
external tea action. The example is trivial but it does illustrate the *politness* concept.

   In system TCS we say that the components are *impolite* because either one can cause

deadlock in the other. Consider a client of TCS who requires tea, and is willing to wait
(a finite period of time) while others are served coffee or soup. Now, if either machine
reaches the ready to serve tea state then that component cannot serve another drink
until the other is also ready to serve tea. Thus, the client may never get their tea
request served. However, if we specify SF(TC) then the tea-coffee machine cannot forever
choose to serve coffee and so cannot deadlock the tea-soup machine. In other words SF(TC)
is polite to TS when they synchronise on tea. Similarly, SF(TS) ensures that the tea-soup
machine cannot cause deadlock in the tea-coffee machine.

To formalise this notion, we say that synchronised machines are polite (in a certain
composition) if the eventuality sets of each machine is a subset of the eventuality set of the
complete system in which they are composed.

9.3.5   Eventuality protocols

Consider a queue object which allows the pushing and popping of *elements*; there is one
particular exception case which we must consider: what happens when the queue is empty
and a pop is requested. Is it the responsibility of the server or the client to cope with such
an instance?

In the first instance we consider *client responsibility*. Here, the server queue cannot
enable the pop request and thus refuses to participate in it. The client must then either wait
until some other client pushes an element onto the queue or decide to do something else (or
both). However, the client is unable to distinguish between a queue that is empty and not
serving the request, and a queue that is taking its time to service the request. This approach
is fundamentally flawed.

In the second instance, we consider *server responsibility*. Here, the notion of politeness
is fundamental. If the queue server can always guarantee the enabledness of the pop action
(even when the queue is empty) then the client has no additional worries. Within our fair
objects framework we have a wide range of means of achieving responsible servers.

Client eventuality requirements

We have identified five different types of *client eventuality requirements* which could provide high level reusable concepts. A client may require that a service request be serviced
immediately. A client may require that a service is carried out **eventually**. A client may
wish a service to be performed **immediately on condition** that if it cannot be done without
delay then it will be informed. A client may wish a service to be performed **eventually on
condition** that if it cannot be guaranteed to be done in a finite period of time then it will
be informed. The client wants the service but places **no eventuality** requirements on when
the service must be performed (if ever).

Server eventuality properties

Each service that a server offers can be classified dynamically, during execution. An **immediate** service is now enabled. An **eventual** service is guaranteed to be enabled in a finite
period of time. An **possible** service may be enabled but it depends on the environment
of the server in forcing certain state transitions; no internal action can make the service

impossible to fulfil eventually. A **probable** service can possibly be enabled but it depends on some internal nondeterminism; no external service request can make it impossible to service the request (eventually). An **impossible** service will never be enabled.

Client-Server eventuality protocols

Within a fair object system, the *server* properties can, we hope, be made to match the *client* requirements. This is the job of an *interface protocol* which seperates clients from servers. In a formal model of requirements we should be able to prove that eventuality needs are fulfilled by servers. For now, we concentrate on how such needs can be specified and how eventuality properties can be guaranteed. The *fairness* classifications which we identified earlier in this paper may be used to provide server guarantees to clients.

9.4   TELEPHONE FEATURE EXAMPLES

In each of the following examples, we specify the behaviour requirements from the telephone user's point of view. All network operations are modelled as internal nondeterministic operations.

9.4.1   The phone

The O-LSTS specification of a telephone is given below.

State invariant properties define restrictions on the possible sets of component values, using the □ operator of TLA. For example, as is shown in the figure below, we may require that when onhook the Phone *must* be ringing or silent. These properties are verified, for more complex cases, by proving that all transitions are closed with respect to the invariant, and the invariant is true for initial state(s). Note that the state invariants specified in this way are explicit requirements of the client that must be respected by the model. A specification where the invariants are not true is said to be *inconsistent*.

Liveness conditions can be specified on the nondeterministic events in the model, using the ◇ operator of TLA. For example, we require that when off and connecting the user does not wait forever for a state transition if they refuse to drop the phone. This must be specified in a separate TLA (temporal) clause. We specify *weak fairness* on the noconnection action. Note that we cannot specify the Phone to be a weakly fair object since we cannot expect someone to phone us (even if we would like them to).

9.4.2   An answering machine

Without giving the actual specification, it is clear that an answering machine requires fairness semantics. The standard functionality is for the phone to ring for a finite period of time and then a message to be taken.

An *eventuality* requirement is that when I ring someone with an answering machine I will eventually talk with them or get to leave a message. This requirement can be proven with TLP, using a fair object model of the answering machine. However, as we shall see below, when combined with other features, such an eventuality requirement can be lost (and we have an interaction).

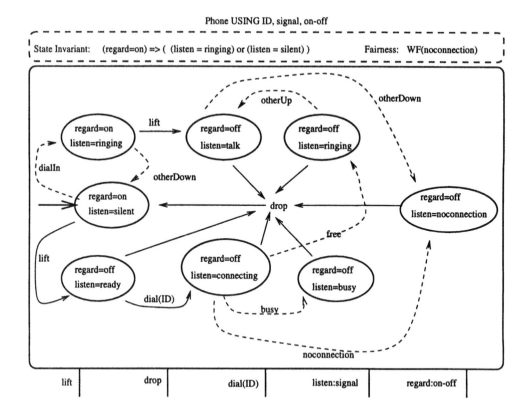

9.4.3 Call forwarding

Informally, call forwarding can be used to transfer an incoming call to another line. Thus, if I am not at home I can, for example, forward my calls to my portable phone. Here the transfer is an internal action and it must be completed in a finite period of time, and so we once again we have an eventuality requirement. In the specification, we make the requirement conditional on the forwarding number being connectable.

9.4.4 Answering machine with call forwarding

Combining these two features illustrates the difference between a fair object model and a standard object model. Without fairness, when I telephone someone with an answering machine who has forwarded their call to another number then, if there is no answering machine at the second phone, I cannot leave a message if they do not reply. With the fair object requirements model, I must be able to leave a message if the person doesn't reply (independent of whether the call is forwarded or not). Thus, if the telephone at the forwarded address does not have an answering machine my specification requires that the call control is returned to the original phone so that a message can be left there.

9.5   CONCLUSION

We have shown how the integration of object oriented semantics and temporal logic is appealing. Different types of *fair object* have been introduced and the means of re-using these high-level concepts has been shown. The formalisation of a specification language based on *fair object* concepts is incomplete and we have been forced to specify our problems using the two different semantics. Such a dual-model approach has proven itself in the domain of telecom feature development. We believe that our research could also be useful in any problem domain where clients and servers act in a distributed framework. Certainly, our work is not yet complete, but we are already finding our *fair objects* to be useful conceptualisations during different stages of formal development.

9.6   REFERENCES

[1] B. Alpern and F. B. Schneider. Defining liveness. Information Processing Letters 21(4), 1985, pp. 180–185.

[2] T. Bolognesi and E. Brinksma. Introduction to the ISO specification language LOTOS. Computer Networks and ISDN Systems 14, 1987, pp. 25–59.

[3] G. Booch. Object oriented design with applications. Benjamin Cummings, 1991.

[4] L.G. Bouma and H. Velthuijsen. Feature Interactions In Telecommunications. IOS Press, 1994.

[5] K.E. Cheng and T. Ohta. Feature Interactions In Telecommunications III. IOS Press, 1995.

[6] P. Coad and E. Yourdon. Object oriented design. Prentice-Hall, 1990.

[7] L. Constantine. Beyond the madness of methods: System structure methods and converging design. Software Development. Miller-Freeman, 1989.

[8] B. Cox. Object oriented programming: an evolutionary approach. Addison-Wesley, 1986.

[9] G. Cutts. Structured system analysis and design method. Blackwell Scientific Publishers, 1991.

[10] T. DeMarco. Structured analysis and system specification. Prentice-Hall, 1979.

[11] van Eijk, Vissers and Diaz. The Formal Description Technique LOTOS. North-Holland, 1989.

[12] U. Engberg. TLP Manual- (release 2. 5a)- preliminary. Department of Computer Science, Aarhus University, 1994.

[13] J.P. Gibson. Formal Object Oriented Development of Software Systems Using LOTOS. PhD Thesis CSM-114, Stirling University, 1993.

[14] J.P. Gibson. Formal Object based Design in LOTOS. Stirling University Computing Science TR-113, 1994.

[15] J.P. Gibson. Feature Requirements Models: Understanding Interactions. Feature Interactions In Telecommunications IV, pp. 46–60, IOS Press, 1997.

[16] J.P. Gibson, B. Mermet and D. Méry. Feature Interactions: A Mixed Semantic Model Approach. Irish Workshop on Formal Methods, Dublin, 1997.

[17] ISO/IEC. Working Document on Topic 6.2 - Formalisms and Specifications. Information Retrieval, Transfer and Management for OSI ISO/IEC-JTC1/SC21/WG7, 1989.

[18] ISO/IEC. Specification Styles for Structuring of OSI Formal Descriptions ISO/IEC JTC1/SC21/N669, 1989.

[19] L. Lamport. The Temporal Logic of Actions. ACM transactions on programming languages and systems 16, May 1994, pp. 872–923.

[20] L. Lamport. Proving Possibility Properties. DEC technical report, 1995.

[21] L. Lamport. The Syntax and Semantics of TLA+ Part 1: Definitions and Modules. Technical Report (Web Pages), 1996.

[22] B. Liskov. and S. Zilles. Programming with Abstract Data Types. ACM SIGPLAN Notices 9(4), 1974, pp. 50–59.

[23] P. Zave. Feature Interactions and Formal Specifications in Telecommunications. IEEE Computer Magazine, Aug 1993, pp. 18–23

10

Systems of Systems as Communicating Structures

Vadim Kotov
Hewlett-Packard Laboratories
1501 Page Mill Road
Palo Alto, CA 94303
fax: (415) 857 5548, email: kotov•hpl.hp.com

Abstract: By **Systems of Systems (SoS)** we mean large-scale distributed systems the components of which are complex systems themselves (e.g. enterprise intranets). **Communicating Structures** are represent SoS in a uniform, systematic way as composition of a small number of basic system objects and notions.

Communicating Structures are focused on SoS the performance of which largely depends on **data traffic** and **data placement**. The subsystems and components are represented as **nodes** with **memory** that stores **items**. **Nets** are sets of **links** that connect the nodes. The items move from node to node along links. All these objects may have hierarchical structure.

CSL is an object-oriented core environment for the modeling and analysis of SoS in the framework of Communicating Structures. It includes both simulation and analytical options as well as GUI and visualization tools for analysis of the modeling results. A case study in which CSL was used to analyze a global enterprise distributed computing environment is presented.

10.1 INTRODUCTION

Hardware, software, network, and application systems are merging into *integrated information systems*. As a result, the variety of feasible system architectures and their complexity is rapidly increasing. Such systems become very large and very complex systems which are, in fact, *Systems of Systems* as their components are themselves complex systems.

Some examples of today's Systems of Systems (SoS) are:

- multiprocessor servers and clusters;

- enterprise intranets supporting common business processes;

- distributed global mission-critical applications;

- distributed control systems;

- distributed design/manufacturing systems;

- World-Wide Web;

- their combinations.

Typical SoS have to satisfy many strict requirements, among which are: cost effectiveness (SoS are often unique and very expensive); responsiveness; throughput; scalability and flexibility; availability; maintainability; reliability, fault tolerance, and recoverability; data and application integrity; security.

Many of these requirements are conflicting. Only modeling can help to find the best compromise solution. The competitive market does not give much time for experimenting with prototypes. There is a clear need for design methods, techniques, and tools that allow designers to construct and analyze quickly and reliably various architectural hypothesis and evaluate them against a wide spectrum of desired system properties.

However, SoS represent a challenge for the modeling and analysis as their solution space is huge and complex. Modeling methods and tools typically used in object-oriented analysis and design (for example, UML [1], statecharts [2]) are biased to the specification aspects as their main goal is to support the rigorous and efficient design and development process. For SoS, the main problem is to identify the satisfactory solutions among a sea of solutions.

SoS are also too complex and diverse to fit into formal semantics Procrustean framework.

To meet this challenge, SoS models should be as simple as possible, without, of course, losing those features that are important for system validation. The best way to simplify the models is to identify:

- modeling objectives and those global system features that are relevant to those objectives;

- a small number of concepts that are common to most of the SoS and in which terms the modeling objectives can be adequately specified;

- convenient modeling data handlers, statistics and analysis libraries, as well as visualization-animation tools.

10.2   COMMUNICATING STRUCTURES

Here we propose to view large information systems in a uniform and systematic way as *Communicating Structures* in which the main activities are related to the coordination of *data traffic* and *data placement*. The modeling objectives are:

- evaluation of system performance in terms of average latencies, throughput, utilization, sensitivity to variation in the system and workload parameters;

- identification of congestions, bottlenecks, non-fairness, and unpremeditated behavior.

Such a view emphasizes those system features and components that generate and manage the data traffic.

This paper presents the *Communicating Structures Library (CSL)*, an implementation of the Communicating Structures as a core environment for the modeling and synthesis of SoS. In its most general form, a Communicating Structure is a *hierarchical* and *concurrent* structure that represents the SoS components and communication between them. The system components are represented simply as *nodes*. Each node has *memory* that may contain *items*. *Nets* are sets of *links* that connect the nodes. The items are generated in some nodes and move from node to node along links with some delay. Items may be modified by nodes. The item traffic models the data traffic in the system, which is represented as a Communicating Structure.

Items, nodes, memories, and nets may be elementary or may have some structure. For example, an item may represent simple data such as frame, packet, as well as complex messages and large chunks of data. The nodes may represent relatively small units such as processors, memories, I/O and storage units, or systems such as multiprocessors, computer clusters, servers, networks, etc. Nets may represent simple point-to-point links as well as busses, crossbars, interconnects, cascaded switches, communication lines and networks, and other data transfer facilities.

Thus, the items, nodes, memories, and nets are Communicating Structures *objects* that are either simple or hierarchical. The objects may be assigned different attributes (numbers, variables, functions, and processes) that:

- define quantitative parameters such as the number of subobjects in an object; the memory capacity, delays, the current number of items in a memory, time constraints, etc.;

- locate an object in the model hierarchy such as the object's name and its relative address in the hierarchy tree;

- generate and control the item traffic;

- change the behavior of objects;

- provide input data for objects and register their behavior and for output and further analysis;

- provide data and functions for analytical modeling.

SoS are too complex and divers to fit into a unique formal semantics Procrustean frame-work. Instead, Communicating Structures provide default semantics for basic objects, functions and processes which may be changed by a user. This means that Communi-cating Structures provide a common base for future more specific and, if required, more rigorous "dialects" adjusted for particular tasks and level of detail of the SoS analysis and construction.

In general, any information that is relevant to a specific study of a modeled system may be easily added to a Communicating Structure describing the system. Communicating Structures allow easy abstraction/refinement modifications in order to be used at different levels of the specification and modeling detail.

CSL is accumulating generic or parameterized CSL objects, functions, and processes that may be quickly assembled into a particular model and tuned for a specific case study using input parameters.

10.3   C++/CSIM CONSTRUCTS

The CSL hierarchy is based on C++ classes, and CSL concurrency uses the main structures of C++/CSIM, a process-oriented discrete-event simulation package [3].

A set of modified CSIM structures is introduced to generate and coordinate concurrent processes (see Figure 10.1). A *process* is a C++ procedure that executes a *create* state-ment. This statement invokes a new thread that proceeds concurrently with the process that invoked it.

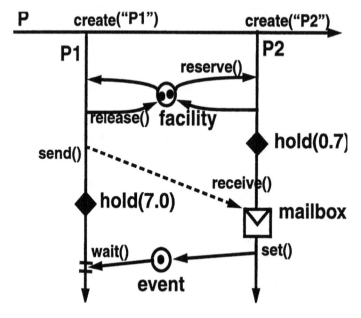

Figure 10.1: CSIM concurrency constructs

There can be several simultaneously active instances of the same process each of which has its own runtime environment. A process can be in one of four stages: *passive* (and ready to start), *active*, *holding* (allowing a modeling time to pass), and *waiting* (for permission to continue after it has been interrupted).

The mechanisms to organize the interactions between the processes are *mailboxes, facilities*, and *events*.

The CSL class *Mailbox* is used for interprocess communication. A process can *send* a message to a mailbox and *receive* a message from a mailbox. When a process does a receive operation on an empty mailbox, it automatically waits until a message is sent to this mailbox. The CSL Mailbox is augmented by an additional operation em send_with_delay that makes it possible to send a message to a mailbox with some time delay.

The class *Facility* models a resource. It contains a single queue and several servers. Only one process at a time can hold a server after executing the *reserve* statement. If there is no available server, the process waits in the queue until one of the servers is *released* and there is no process waiting in the facility queue ahead of this process.

Events are used to synchronize processes. An event is a state variable with two states, *occurred* and *not occurred*, and two queues for waiting processes. One of these queues is for processes that have executed the *wait* statement (and are in a waiting state) and another is for processes that have executed the *queue* statement (and are also in the waiting stage). When the event occurs, by executing the *set* statement, all waiting processes and only one of the queued processes are allowed to proceed.

10.4 THE COMMUNICATING STRUCTURE OBJECTS

The basic elements of Communicating Structures are *items*, *memory*, *nets* and *nodes*.

Nodes typically generate, receive, store, forward, and, perhaps, modify data abstractly presented as items. They store and retrieve items in the node's memory. Items are "dynamic" objects which are born, travel and perish. Nets connect the nodes into a Communicating Structure in which the items travel from source nodes to destination nodes.

All these elements are derived from the common CSL class *Object*. As all CSL objects may have a hierarchical structure, the class Object represents tree-like hierarchies with the class members and functions, which help handle the hierarchy, for example, select subtrees and sets of subtrees, checking some properties of trees, to applying functions to objects-subtrees, etc.

The class Object is derived also from the class Facility. This makes the object to be a resource for a competition among concurrent processes. The number of servers in the object is set during the object construction.

A CSL *Memory* is an object to store items. In the general case, the Memory is a hierarchy of (sub)memories with the ability to store items at different levels of the hierarchy. The top memory of the hierarchy is contained in a node. At the bottom of this hierarchy are *Locations*, "simple" memories which are arrays consisting of *locations* that hold pointers to stored items. One location is capable of storing exactly one item.

In the general case, the net inherits a multilevel hierarchy from the class Object. So, a net may consist of subnets. A "top" net enters into a "docking" node for which it defines communication links among the node's subnodes. So, the constructor of the net contains a docking node as a potential argument.

At the bottom of this hierarchy are *Links*, "elementary" nets each of which connects just a pair of nodes. Each link delivers items from a *from-node* to a *to-node* with *link delay* which is either a constant or a function of some of that item's attributes. The from- and to-nodes are identified by their pointers. Being derived from the class Object, the link is a resource with some number of servers which define the maximal number of transfers that may occur along the link simultaneously.

The main building block of Communicating Structures and CSL models is the node. It contains a memory and, possibly, subnodes as well as an internal net with its links connecting subnodes. The whole model itself is a top level CSL node. The nodes are assigned different functions and processes which originate and control the items movement in the Communicating Structures simulation runs. Most of the basic node member functions and processes are virtual and may be customized by user for specific purposes. The default definitions of these functions provide some "generic" item traffic that is generated in some subset of nodes and destined for some subset of nodes with shortest path routing on the way.

To apply the queuing analysis, the CSL nodes is supplied by classes that implement queue models such as *M/M/m* or *G/G/m*. The analytical model of a communicating structure is built using a network of queue models, this network being derived from the topology of the structure.

10.5   THE COMMUNICATING PROCESSES

With each node, a *main process* and a *generation process* are associated.

When the generation process generates an item, the item is stored in the node's memory, and a message is sent to the node's mailbox in order to activate the node's main process. This message contains a pointer to the address of a location in which the item has been stored.

The *main_process* (see Figure 10.2) prescribes the node functionality and behavior. (A rectangle represents a function (procedure), a rounded rectangle represents a CSIM process, a rhombus is a condition, and a circle is a loop condition.) The process is awakened by a message to the node mailbox and starts with finding a location in the memory to work on. It may be either the location indicated in the message or any other location prescribed by the memory access function.

Then the main process analyzes the destination path of the item stored in this location. If the destination path is empty, the process completes its work without actually doing anything. Otherwise, the head of the path is extracted. If it is a pointer to this node and it is the only element of the path, the *transformation* procedure is initiated. This function may make some changes to the item. In particular, the function may change the item's destination, or make clones of this item for subsequent spawning into the communicating structure. The transformation function will almost always be customized, as it actually defines the node's functionality. The default version of transformation is an "empty action".

After the transformation, the main process either terminates or the *transfer* procedure is initiated. The decision to terminate or to transfer is made at the end of the transformation and is signaled in some way, for example, by using the memory pointer in the the default version of the main process.

The transfer function organizes the transfer of the item or the item's copies to other

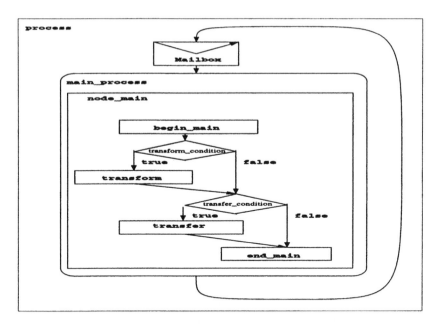

Figure 10.2: Main node process

nodes. In the default definition, it analyzes the item's destination path and selects one of the possible transfer modes: monotransfer or multicast; synchronous or asynchronous transfer.

10.6 CSL PARTS KIT

The parts kit contains sublibraries that accumulate those system structures, functions, and processes that are frequently used. Some of these parts are generic, that is, they are used quite often but are not basic CSL objects or functions. Others may be specialized and often used in domain-specific models.

For example, specific types of memories which are derived from the class *Memory* are introduced in the KIT.

The class *Buffer* contains a number of locations that are addressed by an integer index. One can put an item into a location only if the location is empty, that is, it does not contain any item. One can get an item from a location only if the location is not empty, that is, it contains an item. In a similar way, the classes *FIFO*, *Stack* and *PriorityQueue* are introduced. These memories often serve as "control memories" that help to implicitly control the traffic in Communicating Structures.

In many cases it is convenient to have a node memory with two submemories each of which hosts a portion of the traffic going through the node. For example, one submemory may take care of the ingoing traffic and another, the outgoing traffic. (In this way one can avoid deadlock situations.) To support such types of memory, the classes *DoubleBuffer*, *DoubleFIFO*, and *DoublePriorityQueue* are provided.

Often used topologies are accumulated in the "Nets" part of the CSL PARTS KIT.

Let us consider two sets of nodes that we will refer to as *input* nodes A and *output* nodes B. The input nodes represent the from-nodes for net links and the output nodes represent the to-nodes for net links. These sets may intersect or even be identical. In the last case, one set A will represent both sides of the transferring activities. Let N be the number of input nodes and M be the number of output nodes.

It is convenient to define the topology of the connections defined by a simple net using auxiliary *connectivity functions*. The connectivity functions are predicates that are valid for some subsets of integer pairs. The first element of each pair is in the range $[0, N]$; the second element is in the range $[0, M]$. There is a link between the i-th and j-th nodes in a connection defined by some connectivity function if and only if the value the function is **true** for the pair (i,j).

For example, the function *alwaysconnected* is the predicate that is **true** for any pair of integers in the range. The function *parallelconnected* is the predicate that is **true** only for pairs of the type (i,i).

Suppose we want to connect the node sets A and B by links that lead from every node of A to every node of B. This type of connection is represented by the *OneWayMultiBus* simple net. It is formed using a set of links that connect each input node with each output node (a bipartite graph constructed with the help of the connectivity function *alwaysconnected*). All links have the same basic delay. If the the node sets A and B coincide, the net *MultiBus* is derived.

The number of servers supplied to the nets *OneWayMultiBus* or *MultiBus* defines how many items are transferred concurrently between these nodes. If the number of servers is equal to the number of links (this is the default number of servers), there is no restriction on parallel traffic among the nodes. If, however, we supply the net with only one server, only one item can be transferred at a time.

The latter case is represented by the simple net *Bus* which is derived from the net *MultiBus* simply by setting the number of servers equal to one. Thus, the *Bus* net is a Communicating Structures abstraction of real bus-type nets. This abstraction captures the two basic properties of simple busses: (1) any input point is connected to any output point, and (2) only one item at a time may be transmitted.

The simple net *RightLoop* connects nodes in a loop by unidirectional links in such a way that the i-th node is connected to the $((i - 1) \bmod N)$-th node, where N is the total number of nodes. This type of connection is built with the help of the connectivity function *rightcyclicshift*.

The number of servers in the net defines the number of transfers that may occur simultaneously in the *RightLoop*. In a similar way, the simple net *LeftLoop* is constructed.

Restricting the number of servers to one, transforms the loop nets into ring nets in which only one transfer at a time may occur.

The combination of the *RightLoop* and *LeftLoop* makes a *Loop* that connects a node with both its left and right neighbors.

Quite complicated restrictions imposed on the item traffic in systems can be expressed through hierarchy of nets and the default scheme of reserving subnets and links.

10.6.1 A SoS case study

A project of a world-wide distributed system that represents a decentralized computing environment for a global transportation company has been analyzed using the Communicating Structures methodology and CSL.

The system does

- packages tracing and monitoring (hundreds of millions of transactions per day);

- statistics, billing data processing, and decision support ;

- customer services (including WWW) ;

- common enterprise business applications.

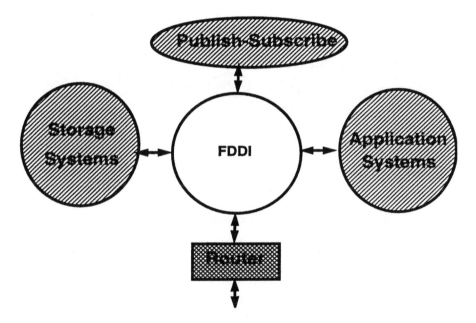

Figure 10.3: Three-Tiered computing Center

Three-level hierarchical network of three-tiered computing centers (see Figure 10.3):

- global Data Centers (DC), several of them;

- regional Processing Centers (PC), tens of them;

- local Operations Centers (OC), tens of thousands of them;

- mission critical, "almost real-time" computing environment;

- cost effectiveness is the dominant requirement;

- a client/server computing model;

- a publish/subscribe data distribution model.

So, this is a typical SoS and it is specified in the Communicating Structures terms in a natural way (see Figure 10.4). The computing centers are CSL nodes of different levels of hierarchy, the communication lines are links, the functionality of computing centers is modeled by the functionality of CSL nodes.

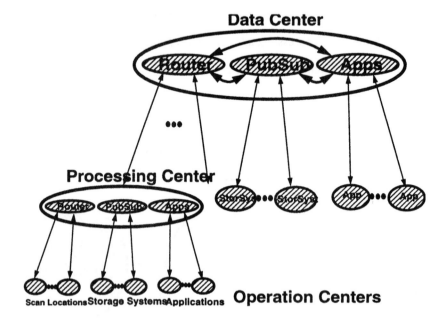

Figure 10.4: Three Level Network of Processing Center

Information is distributed and exchanged among centers according to the *Publish-Subscribe* paradigm: applications publish data for potential use by other applications and are subscribers for data published by others.

Point-to-Point dispatch and *data brokerage* are two alternative models for the implementation of the Publish-Subscribe methodology (see Figure 10.5).

The first case represents a spider web of point-to-point interfaces which are "hard-coded" with specific languages, platforms, application and data formats. Applications maintain unique relationships between themselves.

In the second case, point-to-point links are replaced by the publication of common messages usually in a standard format which are sent to *Data Brokers*. The latters have the tables of subscribers for each type of the messages and forward the messages to subscribers.

The task was to evaluate the project with the emphasis on comparison of the two Publish-Subscribe models.

The constructed CSL model presents the project as a Communicating Structure which contains those and only those system features that influence the message traffic and are important for the system requirements were satisfied. The model helped to identify bottlenecks and the system sensitivity to changing parameters (the number of processing centers, bandwidth in local and global networks, message packaging principles, etc.).

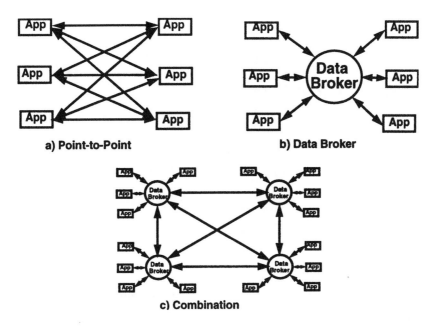

a) Point-to-Point   b) Data Broker

c) Combination

Figure 10.5: Publish-Subscribe Models

The sensitivity analysis included:

- system response on bursty workload;

- system scalability;

- Data Broker overhead;

- message packaging strategy.

Utilization analysis:

- utilization of Data Brokers as a function of workload;

- networks utilization.

The main result of the project validation was the reduction of the proposed three-level system architecture to two-level architecture. The CSL analysis of the traffic in the system has shown that if the functions of the second level are redistributed between the top level of Data Centers and the low level of the Operation Centers then the global traffic becomes less congested, response time is improving, basic requirements to the system are satisfied and the overall cost is, of course, dramatically reduced (see Figure 10.4).

10.6.2   Visualization

The huge analysis and design space of SoS requires a special instrumentation to deal with data collection, workload and test data generation, results collection and analysis, etc. Especially useful is visualization of the model behavior, visual analysis of results, visual

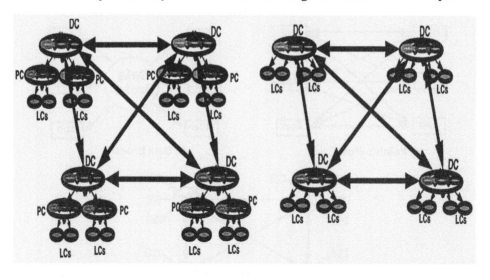

a) Tree-level architecture   **a) Two-level architecture**

Figure 10.6: Two-level versus three-level System Architectures

support of the model debugging and validation. Figure 10.7 shows a "hot spots" picture of a SoS model with traffic flowing between nodes of a hierarchical network of processing centers in a distributed enterprise computing environment.

Another visualization tool SIMON allows to see and verify the communication between concurrent processes (see Figure 10.7).

10.7   CONCLUSION

Communicating Structures reduces the complexity of the SoS modeling and analysis, in particular:

- simplify construction of SoS models of different levels of detail by using abstraction/refinement mechanisms;

- describe parallel processes and their interaction in an object-oriented way, speeding-up the model debugging and increasing the trustworthiness of the models;

- speed up the simulation of a large number of concurrent processes;

- accumulate and reuse prefabricated general-purpose and domain specific modules ("parts kit");

- generate and analyze a larger number of system configurations and behaviors;

- provide a friendly programming and modeling infrastructure (data generation, collection, analysis, visualization, etc.).

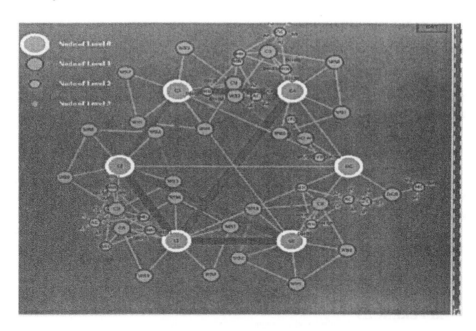

Figure 10.7: System Hot Spots

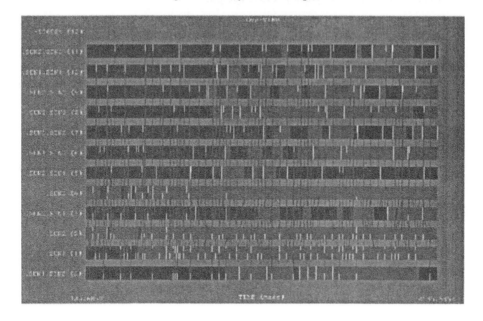

Figure 10.8: Communication between Processes

The current version of CSL has been mostly used for the simulation of SoS, because the analytical modeling methods were inapplicable to the SoS under consideration. However, the analytical methods, if they work for particular types of SoS, may complement simulations using the queuing analysis classes associated with the CSL nodes and a network of queues derived from the topology of a model.

The most interesting extension of CSL that we are going to build is related to the intelligent browsing of the huge solution spaces for SoS. The goal is not to miss good architectural solutions. This is a sort of system synthesis that relies on combining simulation, analytical methods, and formal methods.

10.8   ACKNOWLEDGMENT

Lucy Cherkasova and Tom Rokicki helped to shape the basic concepts of Communicating Structures. Tom helped to implement CSL by contributing his elegant code to the CSL BASE. Lucy was the first user of the first version of CSL and the feedback from her modeling efforts drove the CSL model at its most critical initial stage. The visualization tool SIMON was developed by Sekhar Sarukkai.

The author would like also to thank Denny Georg and Rajiv Gupta for sharing their ideas, encouraging discussions, and for their support.

10.9   REFERENCES

[1] UML Distilled. Addison-Wesley, 1997, 180 pp.

[2] D. Harel and E. Gery. Executable Object Modeling with Statecharts. In Computer, vol. 30, No. 7, pp. 31-42, July 1997.

[3] H. Schwetman. Object-oriented simulation modeling with C++/CSIM17. In Proceedings of the 1995 Winter Simulation Conference, Washington, D.C., ed. C. Alexopoulos, K. Kang, W. Lilegdon, and D. Goldsman, p. 529 - 533, Washington, D.C, 1995.

11

Suitability of CORBA as a Heterogeneous Distributed Platform

Amelia Platt

Communication Networks Research Group
De Montfort University
Leicester LE1 9BH
Tel 0116 2577586
Fax 0116 2578583
E-mail amp@dmu.ac.uk

Paul Mc Kee

BT Research Laboratories
Martlesham Heath IPSWICH
Suffolk IP5 7RE
Tel 01473 643933
Fax 01473 646885
E-mail paul.mckee@bt-sys.bt.co.uk

Abstract: CORBA has been proposed as a platform for distributed systems. A brief overview of the requirements of distributed systems is given in Section 11.1 and the background to CORBA together with an overview of the CORBA architecture is presented in Section 11.2. Essentially CORBA can be described as generic, object-based, middleware and initially was applied to client/server type applications. While there is a wealth of material already published about CORBA, much of the material relates to the conceptual ideas embodied in CORBA. This paper seeks to redress the balance by focusing on the more technical aspects. In particular a detailed critical analysis is presented with emphasis on the performance and implementations issues relating to CORBA. This is presented in the first part of Section 11.3. More recently proposals have been made to apply CORBA to more heterogeneous environments (at application, operating system and network levels). However it is argued in this paper that a number of other technical issues must be resolved first. The current deficiencies of CORBA are identified and potential interoperability problems with other software subsystems are noted. These are also discussed in Section 11.3. Finally, the benefits and weaknesses of CORBA for heterogeneous distributed systems are summarised in Section 11.4.

11.1 INTRODUCTION

The motivation for building a distributed system (as opposed to a centralised system) can vary greatly depending on the application area and the environment. One reason is to allow resource sharing; data, software and hardware. A striking characteristic of this type of distributed system is that the resource is (typically) located in a central (fixed) place, while access by the users is distributed. A typical application is a file server for a community of users over a LAN. This type of distributed system is used quite widely nowadays, even in small organisations and is typically implemented using the client/server paradigm. Another quite different reason for building a distributed system is to attempt to ensure high availability. In this instance, the resources will certainly be distributed and replicated, probably over a WAN. Many other reasons can also be cited. Whatever the reasons, it should be understood that if a standard universal platform for deploying distributed systems is adopted, then it must be able to support distributed systems with a diverse set of characteristics and requirements. In the recent past CORBA has been proposed as a standard universal platform for distributed systems. It has been favourably reviewed in the computing world and is considered by many to be the panacea for distributed computing in the 21st century. A brief overview of CORBA is given in Section 11.2. Essentially it can be described as generic, object-based middleware. The term middleware is seldom defined, but one possible definition is that it 'is software to correct mismatches between the requester and the server'. CORBA is designed to enhance distributed applications by automating common networking tasks such as parameter marshalling, object location and object activation. CORBA has been the subject of interest from the computing industry, and there is a wealth of material published about it. However, much of the material relates to the conceptual ideas embodied in CORBA and there is little published material relating to CORBA performance and implementation issues. However, if CORBA is to be used successfully in a more heterogeneous environment (at application, operating system and network levels) an understanding of performance and implementation issues is critical. Section 11.3 gives a critical analysis of CORBA, and its performance in a heterogeneous environment. The current deficiencies of CORBA are identified and potential interoperability problems with other system subsystems are noted. Finally, Section 11.4 summaries the benefits and weaknesses of CORBA for heterogeneous distributed systems.

11.2 CORBA

11.2.1 Background

Superficially, the CORBA model has strong similarities to the client/server model. This can be seen in Fig. 11.1. In this figure the client and associated client stub (Interface Definition Language (IDL) stub) are shown on the left and the server (object implementation) and associated server stub (IDL Skeleton) are shown on the right. The client and object implementation communicate via an invocation request issued by the client. The request is not made directly, but rather under the control of the Object Request Broker (ORB). In this way the ORB insulates (decouples) the client from the server. This insulation applies to the programming language, hardware/system software and location. The benefits of this approach are that changes in any of these characteristics, at either the client and/or server, are transparent.

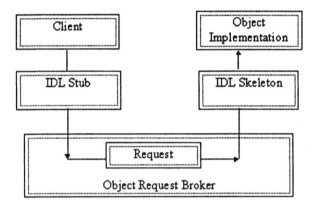

Figure 11.1: Client invoking request on object implementation, via the ORB

The insulation principle applied in CORBA is not new. It is similar to the technique used to achieve program/data independence in databases almost two decades ago. In this instance, the Data Base Management System (DBMS) was used to separate the applications' view of the data from the actual stored data. Similar benefits accrued.

11.2.2   Overview of object management architecture

It is not the purpose of this paper to give a detailed technical description of CORBA. Such descriptions are readily available elsewhere. However, a short technical discussion must be included so that the reader has an understanding of the CORBA architecture. There are four main elements of the architecture; these are shown in Figure 11.2 and are briefly described below. The architecture can be considered to be the software structure of distributed applications which run over CORBA.

Object request broker

This is sometimes referred to as the software bus. Its function is to accept requests from the client, deliver these to the server and return any results to the client. The key feature of the environment is the formal separation of the client and server, regardless of where these are located.

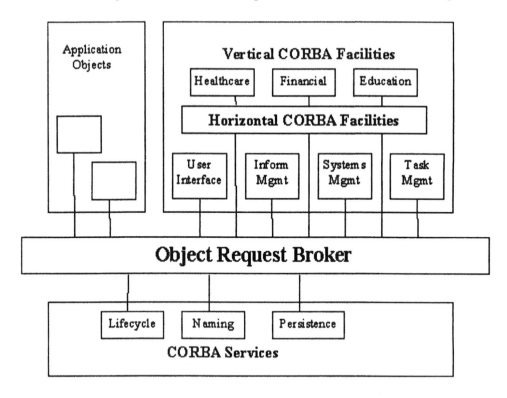

Figure 11.2: OMG's Object Management Architecture

Common object services

These are basic (quite low level) services which are provided as an integral part of many applications, and extend the functionality of the ORB. They can then be used to extend other objects. In Figure 11.2 they are shown as CORBA Services. For example an investment account object can be created and, using the object services, it can be extended to provide a concurrent, persistent and transactional version of the investment account. This is very much in keeping with the OO philosophy of software reusability. Altogether, there are sixteen basic object services.

Common facilities

There are two categories of common facilities - Horizontal and Vertical. Vertical facilities are those which relate to a particular market sector, for instance Education. The premise is that many applications in the Education sector will share common rules/constraints and these can be captured in a single high level application facility and reused many times by various applications. Horizontal facilities are those which are common to applications in many market sectors, for instance Graphical User Interfaces.

Application objects

These are the application objects, which are visible to the user.

Overview of the CORBA components

This section gives a brief overview of the various CORBA components and shows how they interact with the system software. The arrangement is shown in Fig. 11.3 below.

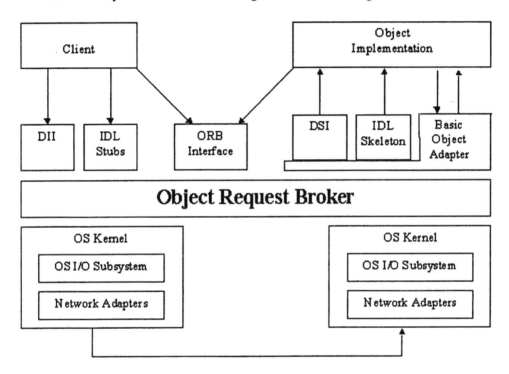

Figure 11.3: CORBA Components

Client Side   This comprises the Client component, the IDL stubs and the Dynamic Invocation Interface (DII). The client stubs are generated from an IDL interface and define precisely how the client can interface with the object. The client stubs are stored in an Interface Repository (not shown in Figure 11.3) and these are used by the client to invoke a request at compile time. The DII performs a similar function but in a dynamic way; essentially the invocation request is built at run time, rather than compile time. The code is generic and can be used to build any invocation request. It is transparent to the object implementation (server side) whether the invocation request has originated from an IDL stub or the DII.

ORB   The ORB's responsibilities are to accept an invocation request from the client, deliver it to the corresponding object implementation and return any result. Communication between clients and object implementations is based on the General Inter-ORB Protocol (GIOP).

ORB Interface   The ORB Interface defines an abstract interface through which the client and server sides communicate with the ORB. The major advantage of this arrangement is that it allows the clients and servers to be ported to any ORB which implements this interface. Note that the same advantage is gained by interfacing the Client and Object implementations with the IDL stubs and IDL Skeleton respectively; they can then be easily ported to any ORB implementation.

Server side   The IDL skeletons and Dynamic Skeleton Interface (DSI) essentially play the same roles at the server side as the DII and IDL Stubs play at the client side. The IDL skeleton provides a static interface and is generated by the IDL compiler, while the DSI provides a dynamic interface and is used by the object implementation at run time.

Basic Object Adapter   The Basic Object Adapter assists the ORB by demultiplexing the requests to the target object and calling the appropriate method on the object, according to the client request. A Basic Object Adapter (BOA) is defined which interacts with non persistent objects. Other Object Adapters can also be implemented. For example, it is envisaged that other adapters will be provided to deal with the various types of persistent objects which must first be 'restored' from persistent store to memory.

11.3   CRITICAL REVIEW OF CORBA

11.3.1   Introduction

Next generation distributed applications must be reliable, flexible, reusable and scaleable and an increasing number will have stringent Quality of Service (QoS) constraints. Some of them will require high bandwidth and hence must operate over broadband WAN networks. Reliability, flexibility and reusability will be needed to respond rapidly to changing requirements that span a wide range of media types and access patterns. Scalability will become an increasing problem as the number and extent of networked information sources increases. The move is away from batch oriented data processing applications to interactive (and real-time) process centred applications. These applications demand diverse and often conflicting QoS requirements. Hence if CORBA is to be deployed as the standard universal platform for distributed computing then it must satisfy all these demands. The purpose of this section is to consider how well CORBA meets the needs of all types of distributed application.

11.3.2   Throughput performance

It has been shown recently that CORBA does not perform well when used over high speed (gigabit) networks. Investigations carried out at Washington University indicate that

CORBA cannot deliver the required throughput for high bit rate applications running over high speed networks. In addition, the end-to-end delay is too long. Although it is outside the scope of this paper to consider the detailed results of this research, it is useful to summarise its findings. The investigation considered two CORBA implementations (ORBeline and Orbix). The performance of applications running over these was compared with the performance of the same applications running over C/C++ sockets and Remote Procedure Calls (RPCs). Sockets and RPCs can be described as low level communication mechanisms. The performance of both CORBA platforms was consistently poorer, for all types of data, compared to the low level communications mechanisms. In particular, the performance of the CORBA implementations was particularly bad when complex data types (structs) were involved. In this case, it was reported that for structs, the performance of the CORBA implementations was approximately 16% of the low level communication mechanisms. The conclusion was that CORBA introduces an excessive overhead. The extra overhead can be attributed to the generality of CORBA, which causes excessive processing to be carried out at the end points, and the inability of the implementation to consider the unique features of the underlying software subsystems. The result is that the end points cannot keep pace with the high speed network. Note that the performance mismatch is masked when CORBA runs over more conventional networks and at lower speeds. The investigators at Washington used a Unix system. Clearly the results would be different for other systems, depending on how they carried out tasks such as marshalling parameters, etc. However the same performance problem will exist. As a result of this research, there is concern that the need for efficient solutions to the problem of delivering distributed systems will force developers to choose low level communication mechanisms instead of CORBA. While this has the advantage of producing an efficient application at run time, it reduces the flexibility, portability and reliability at application development time.

11.3.3 Delay performance

Delay associated with any distributed application is the delay in the end systems combined with the network delay. Assuming the same network infrastructure, then the network delay will be exactly the same, regardless of whether a low level communication platform or a CORBA platform is used in the end system. Given the problems with CORBA implementations in the end systems identified above, it would be expected that the delay associated with the CORBA implementations would be greater compared to the low level communication mechanisms. The investigations carried out at Washington University confirm this. However, while the studies at Washington are useful in identifying problems with current implementations of CORBA, only very simple client requests (similar to conventional client/server applications) were modelled. It is expected that some CORBA client requests will be much more complex. For instance, activation (and possibly location) of objects may be required before invocations (client requests) can be processed. In particular, the client may store an object reference in a Naming Service, database or file, and retrieve it years later. The client may reasonably expect that an invocation using the retrieved object reference will work. The object implementation, the ORB and CORBA services (for example, Persistence) together, will give the client the illusion that the object has remained running - in reality this will seldom be the case. It is clear that this more complex request will require at the very least additional database accesses and processing and hence the delay will be greater. In addition to quantifying the absolute delay for a client request, it is just as important to consider the support given by the various subsystems, to allow applications to specify delay (and other QoS parameters) constraints; a discussion of this is given below.

11.3.4   Scalability

Scalability is the ability of the system to increase in size without any decrease in performance. With respect to CORBA, scalability must focus largely on the number of objects a server can support, the number of end systems which it can support, and the number of objects which the repositories can store and retrieve efficiently. The studies carried out in Washington indicate that the two CORBA implementations are not scaleable in terms of the number of objects which can be invoked simultaneously. Indeed, the study indicated that the scale of the experiments had to be reduced to prevent the ORBs crashing! In summary, neither CORBA implementation was scaleable when a large number of objects was involved. No studies have yet been carried out to measure the scalability of the distributed environment in terms of the total number of end systems. The repositories are merely databases and it would be easy to choose a structure for the database which could scale in terms of the number of entries which could be stored/retrieved efficiently. However, in choosing a database structure which could support a large number of entries, the choice is between a random access structure, which would give efficient retrieval at the cost of inefficient storage, and an indexed structure which would give efficient storage at the cost of inefficient retrieval. The inevitable choice would be a random structure, otherwise the increased latency will further exacerbate the delay performance problem. There is no published information on the design and implementation of these repositories, hence, before a large system could be deployed, a detailed technical performance analysis would be required.

11.3.5   Real-time considerations

Conventional client/server applications can be described as passive in the sense that they are all given exactly the same service by the various subsystems. Indeed, there is no means by which the application can communicate information about their specific service requirements to the subsystems. However, there is an increasing number of applications which have very stringent service requirements, for instance, real-time applications. Within the set of real-time applications, further subsets can be defined, for example, real-time entertainment applications and real-time process control applications. Even these two subsets have different service requirements. In general, it is accepted that future distributed applications will demand diverse and often conflicting service requirements from the underlying subsystems. Service requirements can impact on the Operating System (OS) SubSystem and/or the Communications SubSystem (and hence the subnet). The service requirements which must be considered by the Communications SubSystem can be separated into cell (packet) level and call level requirements. Cell, or packet level QoS requirements relate to end-to-end delay, delay jitter and cell loss. Call level QoS service requirements relate to traffic and are typically specified in terms of peak and average bit rates, call set-up delay, blocking probabilities and so on. To consider QoS in this hierarchical fashion has been recognised by the network community for some time and the results are the sophisticated protocol stacks which specify network architectures. The service requirements which impact on the OS SubSystem are the need to support timed operations and the ability to indicate the importance of the application (essentially priority). Timing constraints can be expressed in many ways, including for example, deadlines, earliest start times and execution time constraints. The delivery of these will necessitate the OS scheduling the various resources, such as processor and memory and allow it to allocate the necessary resources to high priority applications. A real-time SIG was formed by the OMG in January 1996 specifically to consider how CORBA could be extended to include real-time applications. A white paper which addressed three areas was published by the group. The specific areas of interest were:-

- Operating environment

- ORB architecture

- Object services and facilities

Hence, CORBA now incorporates support real-time applications. However, there are still a number of major issues still to be resolved:

- Allowing for real-time constraints in CORBA does not in itself guarantee the required level of performance to the application, because there are other subsystems involved in the execution of the application to which these constraints are not communicated.

- The most common implementation of GIOP is Internet Inter-ORB Protocol (IIOP). IIOP is TCP/IP based and TCP/IP was not designed to support real-time traffic. So, while CORBA may include real-time specifications, it is difficult to understand how these are currently be mapped to IP subnets.

- There are efforts being made by the Internet community (Real-time Transport Protocol (RTP), Multicast Backbone (MBone), Resource reSerVation Protocol (RSVP) etc) to allow IP subnets (specifically the Internet) to carry real-time traffic. However, given the unique nature of the Internet, it is unlikely that these will be deployed in any consistent or coherent way.

- Less attention has been given to CORBA over ATM, yet ATM is considered by many to be the only technology capable of delivering acceptable QoS to all types of traffic. Although the CORBA investigations at Washington University were ostensibly carried out over an ATM network, in reality the source and destination end points were merely two ports on an ATM switch. A more realistic network environment must be considered.

- No consideration has been given to mapping CORBA to the ATM protocol stack. For instance, ATM uses out-band signalling which means that, in the network, the signalling (for example, call set-up) is carried separately from the application information. Out-band signalling was adopted by the standards authorities for efficiency and security reasons. CORBA must address the out-band signalling issue.

From the above discussion it is clear that more research is needed to discover how to map CORBA to IP and ATM subnets. Additional work is also needed to consider how these disparate subnets can interoperate when running on a CORBA platform. Further, there is a growing requirement for sophisticated network connections such as multi-cast, multi-media calls. It is unclear how applications will map these call requirements to the subnet via CORBA.

11.4 SUMMARY AND CONCLUSIONS

CORBA is object based middleware. It is designed to make any changes in the software and hardware which supports applications transparent to the client and/or server. It has been demonstrated that CORBA performs well over conventional networks speeds (10Mbps). However, when run over high speed (gigabit) networks the processing overhead in the end points means CORBA cannot keep pace with the network. It has also been shown that current implementations of CORBA are not scaleable and, given the way in which it is forecast that CORBA systems will be deployed, the performance is likely to degrade further. The CORBA standard has recently been revised to include enhancements which make it a suitable platform for real-time distributed applications. There is no reported information on how successful these have been with real applications. In addition, this enhancement will add to the already large processing overhead. Finally, no allowance has yet been made for the requirements of more sophisticated distributed systems, for instance mission critical systems. In summary, there are benefits to be gained by using CORBA for small scale, conventional client/server applications, however there is still much work to be done before CORBA can be used for large scale, complex, distributed systems.

11.5 REFERENCES

[1] P. Carando. Selecting an Object Request Broker for Large-Enterprise, Distributed Computing, AT&T Solutions, July 1996,
http://members.aol.com/carando/SelectingORB.html.

[2] G. Coulouris, J. Dollimore and T. Kindberg. Distributed systems concepts and design, Addison-Wesley, 2nd Edition, 1994.

[3] L.C. DiPippo et al. Expressing and Enforcing Timing Constraints in a CORBA Environment, TR97-252, Dept of Computer Sc, University of Rhode Island.

[4] E. Fong and D Yang. Interoperability Experiments with CORBA and Persistent Object Based Systems, Sept 1995, http://speckle.ncsl.nist.gov/ yang/tmp_all.html.

[5] A.S. Gokhale and D.C. Schmidt. Measuring the Performance of Communication Middleware on High-Speed Networksa, Proceedings of the SIGCOMM Conference, Stanford University, Aug. 1996.

[6] A.S. Gokhale and D.C. Schmidt. The Performance of the CORBA Dynamic Invocation Interface and Dynamic Skeleton Interface over High-Speed ATM Networks, Proceeedings of the GLOBECOM Conference, London, Nov 1996.

[7] A.S. Gokhale and D.C. Schmidt. Evaluating CORBA Latency and Scalability Over High-Speed ATM Networks, Proceedings of the 17th International Conference on Distributed Systems, May 1997, Baltimore, USA.

[8] T. Harrison et al. The Design and Performance of a Real-time CORBA Object Event Service, Proceedings of OOPSLA 97 Conference, Atlanta, Georgia, Oct 1997.

[9] S. Maffeis. Adding group communication and fault-tolerance to CORBA, Proceedings of the USENIX Conference on Object-Oriented technologies, Monteray, California, June 1995.

[10] S. Maffeis and D.C. Schmidt. Constructing Reliable Distributed Communication Systems with CORBA, IEEE Communications Magazine, Vol 14, No. 2, February 1997.

[11] D.C. Schmidt, A. Gokhale, T. H. Harrison and G. Parulkar. A High-performance Endsystem for Real-time CORBA, IEEE Communications Magazine, Vol 14, No. 2, February 1997.

[12] J. Seigel. CORBA Fundamentals and Programming, John Wiley and Sons, 1996.

12

Using OO Design to Enhance Procedural Software

Mandy Chessell

IBM United Kingdom Ltd
MP 189, Hursley Park
Winchester - Hants
SO21 2JN
Tel: 01962 815985
Fax: 01962 842327
mandy_chessell@uk.ibm.com

Franco Civello

University of Brighton
Watts Building
Moulsecoobe
Brighton
Sussex
BN2 4GJ
Tel: 01273 600900
Fax: 01273 642405
F.R.Civello@bton.ac.uk

Abstract: This paper describes the experiences of a study where object-oriented (OO) techniques were used to make significant enhancements to an existing software product written in a procedural language where no OO model of the product existed. The source code was not converted to an OO language, but its design gradually evolved towards an OO form. This way the OO method was used for design and technical documentation purposes, without impinging on other aspects of the in-house methodology and documentation standards.

The paper covers the techniques used for describing procedural code in an OO design and describes how classes and objects can be implemented as part of existing procedural code. It also considers how this approach could be used by a development team to migrate existing software from a procedural design to an OO design, through its iterative application to successive versions of the product.

12.1 INTRODUCTION

Legacy software products need to evolve in order to remain competitive. Such evolution is a complex matter requiring skilled software engineers to make significant design changes to the system rather than the simple patches usually associated with code maintenance.

It would be desirable to exploit modern software design principles, such as object-oriented (OO) design, and their associated graphical tools in this work. However, it is not clear how these ideas and tools can be used when the software is written in a procedural language with a structure that is not based on objects and classes.

The problem is that even when brand new function is added to an existing software product it is not designed independently from the existing software as, in order to provide seamless integration, its affects often penetrate deeply into the old code. Thus, the structure and behaviour of the existing code constrains the design. Also, there are areas in the code that are almost always affected by new function (such as, administration and configuration). If one tried to restrict the OO development to new code these areas will never migrate to OO as they already exist.

One approach that has been suggested is to extract the complete design of the system, through various techniques, and build an OO model. This model is then used to rewrite the software in an OO style [8, 12, 3]. However, this is often too expensive [11, 9] and holds the product back, making it less competitive in the market. A less drastic approach is required in which only those parts of the system affected by enhancements are modelled using OO, and in which the system evolves gradually towards an OO structure.

This paper describes the results of a project aimed at discovering whether a gradual re-design approach was feasible within the given working environment. The project involved one developer for ten months and was supervised by University of Brighton staff. The software product in question is large (300,000 lines of C) and runs on six different operating systems (UNIX variants and NT). The developer had extensive knowledge of the existing software product, and limited knowledge of OO acquired mainly through attending intensive postgraduate level courses. There was a more specific objective of discovering whether and how the Booch method and the Rational Rose tool could be used during maintenance in association with the in-house method and documentation standards.

The remainder of this paper is structured as follows. Section 12.2 describes the approach that was taken in modelling the existing software and designing and implementing enhancements. Section 12.3 describes specific techniques that were found useful and some interesting features of the models produced. Section 12.4 considers issues that arose during the implementation of the enhancements. Finally, in section 12.5, we offer some conclusions on the benefits we derived from the project.

12.2 APPROACH TO MODELLING AND DESIGN

Since the existing software design constrains the design of new function, we found it was necessary to have some OO model of the current behaviour to build upon. This model had to be generated by hand as there were no tools available to the developer at that time to extract the design from the code automatically [1]. The schedule was short so the aim was to spend as little time on modelling existing code as possible.

The source code and its inline function descriptions were the only reliable form of documentation for the product. Not surprisingly, looking at the code gave little inspiration for producing the OO model as the level of detail was too great and the format unhelpful to "see" how it could appear in an OO model.

So, as a starting point, outline descriptions of the product's key functions were written and from these candidate classes and relationships were identified. This led to a model with about a dozen classes in it. Using the developer's experience of the product's function and internal design it was possible to determine how the resulting OO model mapped to some of the key software modules of the system.

Although the level of detail of this initial model was insufficient for the new design work it provided some context for the next phase where a new enhancement to the product is designed.

The requirements document for a planned enhancement identifies which part of the software was likely to change. More detailed descriptions of the product behaviour for these areas were generated and used to develop additional classes.

With a reasonable set of class diagrams in place, creating the design for an enhancement could begin.

- Object interaction diagrams and scenario diagrams were used to determine how objects of existing classes interacted with new objects.

- Classes were defined for the new objects and added to the appropriate places in the class diagrams.

- The internal processing of the new classes was described using state diagrams.

The processes of modelling existing functionality and creating new design were never completely separate. As use cases were identified from the requirements, each was modelled by blending together old and new functionality. We discovered and used some simple heuristic principles that helped us find good cohesive abstractions.

- If a class is too complex its state diagram becomes impossible to draw. A complex behaviour often hides more than one abstraction - introducing a new class may produce a more balanced design.

- Associations between classes define where objects interact - basically the dependencies between objects. The class diagram looks crowded if the classes are too tightly coupled. Dependencies can sometimes be simplified by redesigning a mechanism or introducing new classes.

- If an object interaction diagram/scenario diagram shows that two objects exchange many messages in order to perform a task, it suggests the sharing of responsibilities between these objects is poor. If too many objects are required to complete a scenario it can indicate a possible performance problem.

Once each view of the design looks reasonable, the structure is usually good. The ability to reposition objects/classes in a diagram provided by the OO design tool was important in this process as it helped identify symmetry in the design, common patterns and inconsistencies.

The structure of classes modelling existing function was extracted as much as possible from the code. (See section 12.3.) This avoided having to re-implement parts of the software that did not need reengineering and minimised the distance between the model and the code. In effect we considered the code as part of the problem domain that must be taken into account in building the model.

The level of detail used was different according to how much impact a new use case had on a particular area. New classes, or old classes that were affected by the new functionality, were modelled in great detail. Those that were involved but did not require modifications were only modelled at the level of their interfaces, without considering their internal behaviour or structure. Areas of function unaffected by the change were not modelled at all, or were represented by a high-level class which contained no detail. Thus, modelling effort was only spent where it was relevant and useful.

As the OO model was reused for subsequent enhancements (which occurred three times during the study) different areas of the product's function were affected and so were added to the OO model. This way, more and more of the product received the OO treatment. However, stable areas of the product were unaffected.

When the OO design of an enhancement was detailed enough, English descriptions were added to the standard internal design document usually produced. This was not strictly necessary but helpful for those in the team not used to the OO models.

In fact we found that the use of the design tool, and all the models and diagrams produced with it, did not require significant changes to the structure and contents of the in-house documentation produced during maintenance. It merely added a new level between the external and internal descriptions of the product, which helped to bridge the semantic gap between the two (see Fig. 12.1).

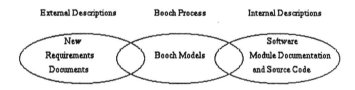

Figure 12.1: Booch models positioned between external and internal descriptions

Although the model was never truly free of the constraints of the existing design, working at a level of abstraction above the code made it easier to come up with better solutions and discover and exploit commonalities between different areas of the design. Section 12.3 describes the structure and content of this model in more detail.

12.3 MODELLING TECHNIQUES AND MODEL FEATURES

12.3.1 Model structure

Section 12.2 described how the initial structure of the model generated some high level classes that mapped to the key software modules of the product. Then using more detailed descriptions, further classes were developed.

Initially we thought of linking these new classes to the existing high-level classes in the initial OO model using a "contains" relationship (see Fig. 12.2).

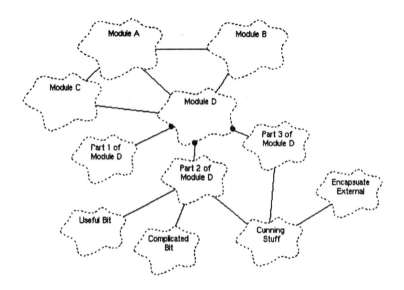

Figure 12.2: The high-level class (Module D) contains lower level classes

However, pretty soon we decided to eliminate the original high level classes as they tended to have fifty or more methods in their interface that did no more than call another method, making them cumbersome and inelegant.

Once these high level classes were removed (see Fig. 12.3), it was easier to see the real dependencies between areas of the code/model.

With this scheme, the number of classes increased rapidly and some order needed to be imposed. So class categories were used to organise the model into a hierarchy of sub-systems. The top-level class diagram uses one class category for the entire system, and a few other categories to include classes that represent other interfacing products (operating system software and other middleware products) which the developer is not able to modify.

Within the class category that represented the system, further class categories were added to group related classes. This achieved a clean separation of different areas of functionality of the product whilst retaining the flexibility of connecting classes from different

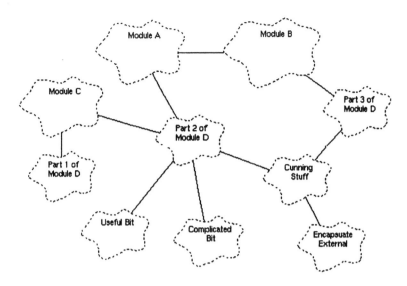

Figure 12.3: The high-level class (Module D) has been removed and the lower level classes have been associated with relevant high level classes

areas when needed.

As the design progressed, the classes were reorganised into class categories at frequent intervals to keep the structure clean. We also kept the number of classes on a single class diagram down so that a class diagram fitted comfortably on a sheet of A4 paper and ensured each class diagram represented a single theme. This prevented the diagrams from becoming overwhelming.

12.3.2 Encapsulating external dependencies

In addition to managing the huge amount of function in the product, the model also had to describe some fairly advanced programming features that the product made use of.

For example, the product runs on a number of operating systems. A software module, called the mapping layer, isolates the differences between the operating systems. Code that is common to all operating systems calls the mapping layer interface and is not aware of which operating system it is running on.

The mapping layer was described in the OO model as a number of abstract classes, that defined the interfaces used by the operating system independent parts of the system. Each abstract class had a number of concrete subclasses, each implementing the interface for a given operating system.

12.3.3 Breaking down large modules

Creating an OO model of many of the other parts of the product was in general not too difficult. The modules that made up the product were fairly well encapsulated but tended to support an external interface with over fifty functions in it. Rather than describe the module

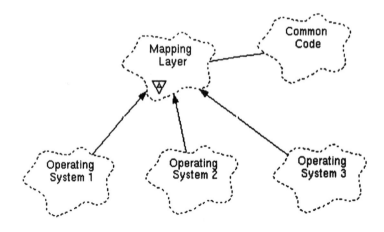

Figure 12.4: Modelling the mapping layer module

as a single class, it was often possible to subdivide its functions into related groups, each of which formed a new class in the OO model. In many cases the contents of the modules private data structures could be split along similar lines giving each new "class" its own state data. When a software module was split up in this way we defined a Booch module to represent it. The class specifications then pointed to these Booch modules to show where the behaviour was implemented.

12.3.4   Abandoning the code

Unfortunately, some C functions were impossible to model as a single method for an object because they were very long and/or made haphazard use of a variety of groups of data. The only way to approach this was to determine what the function did and add this behaviour to the model without following the structure of the code. It was necessary to document (in English) which part of the code was being described by this part of the model as it may not be obvious!

12.3.5   Using inheritance to identify similarities and differences

There were other cases in the code where generic functions were used for groups of similar objects. The data structure representing one of these objects had a field identifying the object's subtype. This is used to determine when special case processing is required. For example:

```
Function SendToUser(UserScreen\_t *UserScreen,
                    char          *Data)
BEGIN
    <perform standard tasks>
```

```
    IF UserScreen->Type == WINDOW
        <perform special task for this type of screen>
    ENDIF


    <perform more standard tasks>
END


Function ReceiveFromUser(UserScreen\_t *UserScreen,
                         char           *Buffer)
BEGIN
    IF UserScreen->Type == TEXT
        <perform task for text screen>
    ELSE
        <perform task all other screen types>
    ENDIF
END
```

One way to represent this style of code in an OO model is to use a super-class (for example, Screen) with a number of sub-classes (for example, Window and TextScreen).

This can be a powerful technique for modelling the similarities/differences of these types of objects. However, it has the disadvantage that the model is not so closely related to the real code.

12.3.6 Modelling multitasking

Multitasking concepts such as threads and processes are normally considered to be a physical design concern, and are not added in logical descriptions of behaviour. However in our system multitasking was a pervasive feature of the architecture, which we had to consider early on if we wanted our new models to fit nicely with the existing design. For example, mechanisms used for communication between different objects depend on whether the objects reside in the same thread, the same process, or different processes. We found that an effective way to model this was to create classes that represented the multitasking structure of the system.

This involved two classes: one representing the operating system interfaces for a process, the other representing the operating system interfaces for a thread. The Thread class interface enables threads within a process to communicate and the Process class interface allows a thread in one process to send a signal to another process. Thus, objects running in different threads can communicate. Each type of process in the system is represented by a subclass of Process, and each type of thread is represented a subclass of Thread.

The Process class has a "has" relationship between one or more instances of the Thread class (see Fig. 12.5). This captures the concept that a thread belongs to a process (and a process can have many threads). There is no association between threads in a process. Thread-to-thread communication actually goes via the Process class to ensure both threads are part of the same operating system process.

The classes that represent each type of process are joined using "has" relationships with the appropriate classes that represent the types of threads. This shows the threads

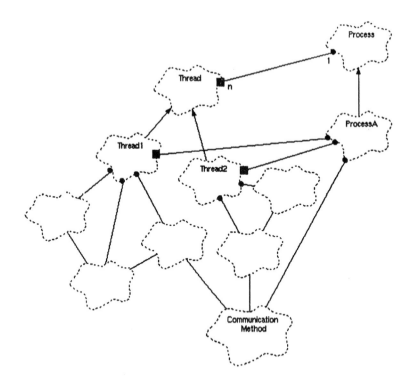

Figure 12.5: Representing processes and threads in the OO model

that each type of process contains. The classes that represent the threads own (though the "has" relationship) the objects that made up the behaviour of the thread. Some objects are shared between threads in a process. These are shown as owned by the particular class for the process. These types of objects are responsible for supporting any locking required to allow concurrent access.

Following our policy to model only parts of the existing software affected by new functionality, we did not model every single class in its multitasking context. Classes whose internal behaviour was not affected by new design could span threads/processes.

12.3.7   Reuse and Design Patterns

We found that the separation of concerns encouraged by the OO design process allowed us to identify and create reusable abstractions. This is because the classes in a good OO design can be divided into different roles:

- Classes that control the task being performed.

- Classes that encapsulate a data structure

- Classes that interface with external components/tasks. (Usually these classes are supplying work or passing on completed work.)

These classes communicate using method calls if they are running in the same operating system thread, or via other classes that encapsulate a communication mechanism if they are on different threads. (Such is shown in Fig. 12.5.) There were a number of examples of this in the OO model created for this project, where an operating system process required requests to be passed from thread to thread in an asynchronous fashion. This was done using queues. The design for each occurrence of this request passing mechanism had:

- A class that represents the request

- A class that adds the request to the queue

- A class that provides the queuing mechanism itself

- A class that retrieves the request from the queue.

The classes that add and remove the requests from the queue are very specific to the task being performed but the request class and the queuing mechanism class are generic, and can be used over and over again - thanks to the separation of responsibilities that object-oriented design brings. Unfortunately, code reuse is not always possible. A class may seem to have the required behaviour. However, it may use the wrong type of storage, use the wrong services for producing diagnostics or the wrong communication method to contact another object. Such classes can be made more generic by adding configuration parameters to the constructor (initialising) method. However, this makes it harder to use and more complex inside. It is sometimes better just to copy the design. For example, the process described above also receives administration requests from other processes via a queue. Because the request must travel between operating system processes it needs to be saved in a different type of storage to the request that is just being passed between threads in the same process. The cross-process queuing class also needs to use different locking mechanisms to be effective at controlling simultaneous access by multiple processes. It is possible to create a queuing mechanism to handle both cases. However, this would be larger than the sum of two, more specific, classes. The code would be more complex and would run less efficiently. So creating two classes is a better choice. However, in such circumstances, design reuse still occurs because the pattern of how the classes interact is the same. The ability to copy the pattern of a design should not be underestimated. It is true the classes still have to be coded, but this is much easier than starting from scratch because the logic and tricky special cases are all known. So the resulting code is likely to have less errors in it.

12.4 IMPLEMENTATION

If the project was to be judged a success, the implementation in C of the new design had to be driven by the OO model. So any mismatch between the OO and the procedural view had to be resolved. In areas where the new design conflicted with the existing implementation, the OO design generally won the day as it was considered to represent a more "problem-oriented" view of the solution. This involved a limited amount of re-implementation of existing code. A tight schedule kept this to a minimum. Fortunately, most of the relation-ships between classes in the design were of the "uses" or "has" type rather than the "is a" inheritance relationship. Where inheritance was used, it was mainly to show the conceptual structure of the existing code, or to represent common interfaces with varying implementations. Since any new concrete classes inherited only from abstract "interface" classes, a simple implementation scheme was used, making it easy to see the correspondence between code and model:

- A single C structure encapsulating the class's private data. The location of this structure was considered to be the location of the object.

- A C function for each operation.

- Messages were passed using C function calls.

The effect of even such a naive mapping was surprising, as the next section describes.

12.4.1   Improving encapsulation and reducing dependencies

In the code base used for the study, each C module has a flat data structure for its private data. Fields in this data structure are not accessible to functions outside the module. However, they may be accessed by any function in the module and this is via a well-known (global) pointer (see Fig. 12.6).

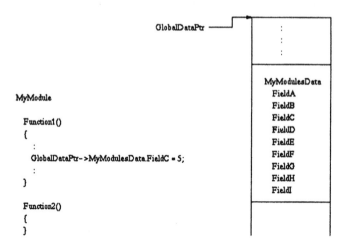

Figure 12.6: Standard module structure

The aim is to protect the callers of a module from its internal design. However, little attempt is made to protect one part of a module from the implementation details of another. In the larger modules it can get quite difficult to discover the lifetime and purpose of each field and its relationship with other fields.

The new modules with the OO design have functions that are grouped according to the class they belong to. Similarly, the module's data fields are grouped in a number of nested structures, one for each object (see Fig. 12.7).

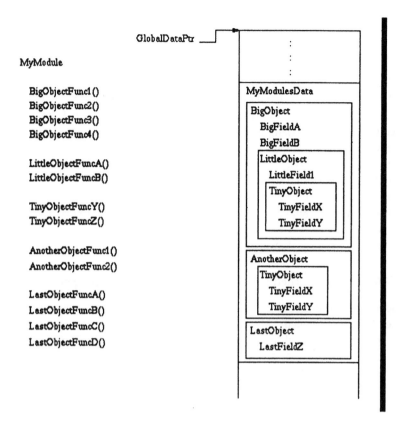

Figure 12.7: Structure of a module with an OO design

This improved the encapsulation within the module. By prefixing each function name and structure type with the name of the class, it was very easy to determine where each piece of the module's private data was used within the module.

The major problem with nested structures in C is that fields tend to be accessed as follows: GlobalDataPtr->MyModulesData.BigObject.LittleObject.LittleField1

To avoid this, each function was passed the address of their object's data structure in the first parameter. (Just as if it were the object's "handle".)

```
LittleObjectFuncA(LittleObject_t    *MyObject, ...)
{
  MyObject->LittleField1 = 5;
}
```

This made a critical difference because many of the functions within the module were no longer dependent on the global structures. For example, in Figure 12.7, functions TinyObjectFuncY and TinyObjectFuncZ do not need to know whether they are working with:

```
GlobalDataPtr->MyModulesData.BigObject.LittleObject.TinyObject.TinyFieldY
or GlobalDataPtr->MyModulesData.AnotherObject.TinyObject.TinyFieldY
```

because they will access either field as:

```
MyObject->TinyFieldY
```

Encapsulation is being applied both ways. Not only is the caller protected from the internal design of the called function, but the called function is also protected from the environment of the caller. This means the life-time and occurrences of the objects from a class can be controlled by the caller, making it possible to apply them to different situations. The fact that the class often encapsulates a useful concept increases the desire and opportunity to reuse it in different contexts.

In addition, the external dependencies of an object tend to be less that those of the module as a whole. Significantly for this piece of work, if an object's implementation is not dependent on an operating system call, the class does not have to reside in the mapping layer. This allows code that would normally reside in the mapping layer to be located in the common code, making it available on all operating systems.

12.4.2   Effects of new structure on program and programmer's performance

The disadvantages of this coding style are twofold and are basically down to the increased number of functions created. More functions add to the workload of the programmer, who must provide additional function prototypes and documentation. On the other hand, smaller functions and smaller abstractions improve understandability. Function calls also add to the workload of the machine. In performance critical sections of the code, this must be a consideration. However, it must be said that it will always be easier to add performance improvements to well structured code rather than to great monolithic monstrosities because:

- Critical parts of a process/algorithm can be defined in a single place and encapsulated within a well-defined abstraction, making it easier to improve the algorithm.

- It is easier to understand the behaviour and spot shortcuts. In fact one of the enhancements designed added a new object to the design, which was called during main line processing. However, it resulted in a 13% improvement in throughput by enabling a critical process to switch to more efficient algorithms under certain circumstances.

12.4.3   Is this real object-oriented programming?

The coding style described above brings obvious benefits. However, a discipline is required to code in this way as the encapsulation by the objects is not enforced by the C language. Initialisation and termination of objects is also an issue as there is no automatic calling of the constructor and destructor functions. So an object is dependent on its caller to give it the opportunity to acquire, initialise and free any storage it uses. Finally, the C language does not support inheritance and polymorphism.

According to Grady Booch ([4], Page 38) inheritance is an integral part of object-oriented programming.

Object-oriented programming is a method of implementation in which programs are organized as cooperative collections of objects, each of which represents an instance of some class, and whose classes are all members of a hierarchy of classes united via inheritance relationships. And goes on to say ... programming without inheritance is distinctly not object-oriented; we call it programming with abstract data types.

In the implementation of our application, inheritance is not used and the classes certainly do not all link up into an inheritance hierarchy.

Even with these limitations, a better structured implementation is a big step forward especially if this improved structure migrates the design to an OO style.

In the longer term, as the OO skills of the developers increase, this simple coding style may become too restrictive as they become more comfortable with mechanism such as inheritance and polymorphism.

When it turns out that inheritance and polymorphism are really needed in a design it is probably time to question the use of the C language. Of course, technically, it is perfectly possible to simulate these constructs in C. However, each developer must be aware of how these mechanisms have been implemented. If used extensively, these mechanisms are likely to be slightly different in each case, depending on the developer and the specific class. They may have errors in them, or may be "broken" by maintenance changes. The idea of recreating/debugging these mechanisms over and over again is so against the philosophy of object-oriented programming where code is supposed to be written once and then reused. If we need/want to make extensive use of inheritance and polymorphism we should use an object-oriented programming language where standard mechanisms are available. In which case, C++ would be a good choice because of its compatibility with the C language, allowing the existing code to run unchanged along-side the new.

12.5   CONCLUSIONS

Our experience indicates that it was possible and beneficial to use OO design to enhance the functionality of our legacy system. Even with the additional task of creating the OO model, the development work undertaken on this project was completed within the schedule expected if the usual method had been employed. We believe this was possible partly because the product itself was broadly designed around the idea of large data abstractions. In addition, as others have found, developers involved in any such reengineering work need a good knowledge of the existing software if this work is to be complete in a timely fashion [2] as it is very important to use knowledge of the domain when building OO models of existing software [5, 7, 6, 10].

Using the approach on a wider scale would require careful management. The developers involved in maintaining the products would need education and training in OO and there is a need for a senior OO architect to manage the emerging OO design. This is because the level of detail across the model was not constant. The detail evolves as required. So a developer working on a different area of the product would not find our model very useful because it would contain next to no information about their functional area. If this developer created her own model, the chances are it would bear little resemblance to our model because the emphasis would be different. Nor is it likely that it would be possible to join the two models together as there is no "correct" way to encapsulate function. This means that unless we worked together, our models would describe the central functions of the software using different classes. The OO architect is therefore required to provide some coordination between the developers creating the model, even if they are modelling different aspects of the system. (An alternative approach would be to allow each developer to use their own model. The individual developers may find their own model easier to work with because it is biased towards their view of the code. However, design reviews are likely to be less effective as the reviewer will have to invest time understanding the basic model as well as the new design, and opportunities to reuse classes and design patterns could be lost.)

So in summary, we consider the main benefits of this approach to be:

- A way to move to OO without revolution

- Better software structure and more opportunity for reuse of code and designs

- Models can be used for planning, future designs and for training new project members

Finally, as this method is applied over time, not only is the software moving from procedural to object-oriented, but so are the skills of the developers responsible for the maintenance of the code.

12.6 REFERENCES

[1] B. L. Achee and D. L. Carver. Identification and extraction of objects from legacy code, IEEE Aerospace Applications Conference Proceedings, vol 2, Los Alamitos, CA, USA, 95TH8043, 1995, pp. 181–190.

[2] W. S. Adolph. Cash Cow in the Tar Pit: Reengineering a Legacy System, IEEE Software vol. 13. no. 3, May 1996, pp. 41–47.

[3] J. B. Arseneau and T. Spracklen. An artificial neural network based software reengineering tool for extracting objects, IEEE International Conference on Neural Networks. IEEE World Congress on Computational Intelligence (Cat. No.94CH3429-8), P3888-93 vol.6, 1994.

[4] G. Booch. Object Oriented Analysis and Design with Applications (2nd Ed), Benjamin/Cummings, 1994, ISBN 0-8053-5340-2.

[5] J.-M. DeBaud and S. Rugaber. Software re-engineering method using domain models, Proceedings of the IEEE International Conference on Software Maintenance, Piscataway, NJ, USA, 95CB35845, 1995, pp. 204–213.

[6] H. Gall, R. Klosch and R. Mittermeir. Object oriented re-architecturing, Proceedings of the 5th European Software Engineering Conference, Springer Verlag, 1995, pp. 499–519.

[7] H. C. Gall, R. R. Klosch and R. T. Mittermeir. Using domain knowledge to improve reverse engineering, International Journal of Software Engineering and Knowledge Engineering (Singapore) Vol 6, No 3, World Scientific Publishing Co., September 1996, pp 477–505.

[8] G. C. Gannod and B. H. C. Cheng. Using informal and formal techniques for the reverse engineering of C programs, Reverse Engineering - Working Conference Proceedings, IEEE, Los Alamitos, CA, USA, 96TB100093, 1996, pp. 249–258.

[9] J. M. Neighbors. Finding reusable software components in large systems, Reverse Engineering - Working Conference Proceedings, IEEE, Los Alamitos, CA, USA, 96TB100093, 1996, pp. 2–10.

[10] R. T. Mittermeir, R. R. Klosch and H. C. Gall. Object recovery from procedural systems for changing the architecture of applications, Proceedings of the Third International Conference on Systems Integration, vol. 1, 1994, pp. 148–57.

[11] A. O'Callaghan. Object technology migration is not (just) reverse engineering, Object Expert (UK), SIGS Vol.2, No.2, Jan. Feb. 1997, pp. 16,18–19.

[12] H. M. Sneed and E. Nyary. Extracting object oriented specification from procedurally oriented programs, Proc. Second Working Conference on Reverse Engineering (Cat. No.95TB8101), 1995, pp. 217–226.

13

Reengineering Procedural Software to Object-Oriented Software Using Design Transformations and Resource Usage Matrix

Sagar Pidaparthi, Paul Luker and Hussein Zedan

School of Computing Sciences
De Montfort University
Leicester,
UK
e-mail: {sp,zedan,luker}@dmu.ac.uk

Abstract: The movement from algorithmic decomposition, structured design and procedural implementation towards object-oriented design and programming has resulted in a growing need to restructure/re-engineer old programs which have a poor architecture in order to reap the benefits of this new technology. It is more economic to restructure existing software into an object-oriented topology by identifying objects within the subject system rather than to redesign the software starting from the requirements. Such object identification relies upon program analysis and a study of inter-component relationships and dependencies. This paper initially provides a conceptual foundation for migration from a procedural to object-oriented software architecture for legacy software. It relies upon a view of the software life cycle, in which all software development is considered to be an evolutionary activity with re-engineering/restructuring as an important process applied repeatedly on the artefacts of development at various stages in this evolution. We then introduce a novel approach of viewing a procedural program from an object-oriented perspective in which there is single "god" class, which has a large number of global variables and methods, supported by several user defined classes which have no behaviour, only data definitions. This view, coupled with repeated restructuring, enables a seamless migration of behaviour from the god class to other classes using design transformation methods. There is a distinction between the processes of translation and transformation, processes that we contend are orthogonal to each other, which thereby enables us to concentrate on behaviour-preserving design transformations in order to migrate from one design to another, leaving the language issues to be handled by translators. This paper describes some basic design transformations that preserve system behaviour over the partitioning of classes. Finally, this paper presents one of the case studies undertaken with the help of a CASE tool 'RESTRUCT' based on the ideas presented in this paper.

13.1 INTRODUCTION

Software design and development is inherently evolutionary, which is true across the life cycle and within phases of the life cycle. The structured methodologies of the 1970s and 1980s supported linear design processes, which do not lend themselves well to evolutionary development. It is now commonly accepted that software design and development requires cyclic or iterative approaches in order to control evolution. Booch [3] proposes a life cycle in which there are two kinds of processes for software design, the macro design process and the micro design process. Each phase in the macro design process encompasses a complete iteration of micro design processes. From this and other contemporary evolutionary life cycles, it is possible for us to infer that artefacts of design are repeatedly subjected to review/restructuring.

Artefacts of early analysis and design lack detail such that they may be viewed as being black box representations. As the design cycle progresses, detail or transparency is added to the system until, ultimately, a glass box representation is realised. The main artefact of this process is **design** which is refined using transformations and embellished by adding detail to produce a program. To understand the evolution, we need to define: design; black box representation; glass box representation; black box (design) transformation and glass box transformation.

The **design** of a software system can be viewed as the organisation of software components in a program, or, more specifically, as a hierarchically structured and component-wise specified software system [6, 5, 2] wherein each component has a specification and an optional implementation. Usually there is one component called the system, which controls the execution of the system. Components in a software system are: classes, procedures, functions, types, and variables. Design can be developed using design languages, which can be graphical such as OMT [17], UML [20], or Booch [3], or by using languages like Language for Object Oriented Modelling (LOOM) [1]. Alternatively they can be specified using formal languages like COLD-K [6, 5, 2] as in the Meteor Project. The authors of OMT, UML, and LOOM concentrated on design representation and do not discuss design transformations, whereas the Meteor [6, 5, 2] project works on design transformation using formal languages and provides formal proofs for behavioural equivalence in design transformation. However, it is important to note that the design transformations discussed by Feijs [5], are at a very high level of abstraction and are not suitable for our purpose of migrating from procedural to object-oriented programs. COLD-K is used to specify the designs of software systems, for which it introduces the concepts of black box descriptions and glass box descriptions of software systems.

A **black box representation** or description makes available only an interface specification, whereas the **glass box representation** (description) provides all the details of a system component. Certain components are primitives which do not therefore have glass box descriptions. It now becomes possible to extend this distinction to enable us to define two notions of correctness for design, namely **black box design correctness** and **glass box design correctness**. Black box correctness is based on the principle that no details of the implementation module need be known when using the modules, i.e. the user must rely entirely on interface specifications, that is to say the black box description.(This is the principle behind the abstract data type, or ADT.) It is essential that the user of an interface should not have to know anything about the details of implementation. In particular, the fact that this interface may be presented by a single body or a set of several bodies should not make any difference. Black box descriptions have been formalised using mathematical logic in the Meteor project, therefore, when a design is built up from components, the correctness of a complete design follows from the correctness of its components. When modifying one component, the correctness of the resulting design follows from the correctness of the modified component.

Software transformation can take place at least at or between the two extremes of black box level and glass box level, while preserving the semantics of a system. When a component retains its black box semantics but is modified at the glass box level, then it is sufficient to ensure local correctness of the component to prove the semantic equivalence of the initial and modified systems. When a design (black box transformation) is performed it is sufficient to prove the equivalence at the black box level.

There remain some important issues to address, which are not adequately covered by the reported literature on migration. Some important questions include:

1. What is the relationship between design transformation and program translation?

2. How is the paradigm shift from procedural programming to object-oriented programming addressed for the migration of a system from a procedural structure to an object-oriented structure?

3. What are the basic transforms required for migration from a procedural design to an object-oriented design?

4. How good are the object identification algorithms reported in the literature?

5. What is the quality of an object-oriented system obtained by design transformation? How does it compare with that of a system designed starting from requirements using object-oriented analysis techniques?

The main contribution of this paper is to provide answers to the first three of these questions. We aim to provide the answers to the remaining questions in the near future. Section 13.2 describes the distinction between translation and transformation, which is followed by section 13.3 in which an object-oriented perspective of a procedural program is provided. Section 13.4 provides some basic transformations, which are followed by section 13.5 with a discussion on other approaches to the migration process and the process of transformation.

13.2 DISTINCTION BETWEEN TRANSLATION AND TRANSFORMATION

To transform a procedural program written in a language like 'C' into an object-oriented program written in a language like Java, we need two processes, the first of which is **translation,** the second of which is (design) **transformation.** This paper argues that these two processes are orthogonal to each other, so that the order in which they are carried out does not affect the migration process.

A translator translates a program from one language to another while retaining the software architecture of the system. During the **translation,** the artefacts of one language will be replaced by the artefacts of another language, without effecting any significant changes to the architecture but for a few exceptions, such as might occur when a procedural language like Pascal supports a nested procedural definition and a target object-oriented language like Java does not support such definitions. However, it is possible to translate a Pascal program with nested procedures to a flat structure like that of C before migration to an object-oriented structure, while preserving the semantics of the program.

This paper defines a **design transformation** to be one in which the organisation of components of the system is modified, based on inter-component relationships. This is distinctly different from a translation process. From the above definitions, we observe that both of these notions are orthogonal to each other. The concepts of translation and transformation alone are not sufficient to explain the migration process completely. In order to explain this migration process in a coherent fashion we study a procedural program from the perspective of the object-oriented paradigm.

13.3 OBJECT-ORIENTED PERSPECTIVE OF A PROCEDURAL PROGRAM

It is possible to translate a procedural program into an object-oriented programming language without making any structural changes to the program. (The resulting program is not yet an object-oriented one.) In such a translation, it is possible to correlate components from procedural programs with those in an object-oriented language after the translation. The translated version of the program will have a large number of global variables and methods encapsulated by the major (system) class of the system called the "god" class [16], while there will be several small classes, which represent the user-defined types of the procedural subject program. In effect, we can state that a procedural program is a badly designed object-oriented program with a single large god class in which all the program behaviour is centralised. From this point onwards improvement of the topology of the object-oriented program can be considered as the distribution of behaviour (and associated data) from this god class to smaller classes which can be obtained by inter-component analysis and the use of metrics and heuristics.

Having presented the need for design transformations and how they can be used in the transformation of software from a procedural to an object-oriented architecture, it is now necessary to provide a suitable format for the communication of design transformations. A common format accepted by a large number of researchers will ensure that the design transformations can be understood more easily by all concerned, as has been achieved by researchers in design pattern specification, who have adopted a common format for the communication of design patterns. There are several common features in the presentation of design transforms and design patterns, which enable us to adapt the template being used for the design pattern specification for the communication of a design transformation.

13.4   BASIC DESIGN TRANSFORMATIONS

This section discusses some **behaviorally equivalent** basic design transforms which can be used repeatedly to migrate from a procedural program to an object-oriented program. We take the following formal meaning to define behaviorally equivalent designs:

Let D_1 and D_2 represent two designs, for a program with requirements R then

$$wp(D_1, R) = wp(D_2, R) \qquad (13.1)$$

where wp represents the weakest pre-condition semantics of D_i, for i = 1,2.

We begin by assuming that the architecture of a procedural program is not dissimilar from that of an object-oriented program with a single class, which can be justified and achieved by translation techniques. We make this assumption so that we may work in the same programming language from the beginning to the end of the design transformation. The user defined types of a procedural program are converted to classes, which do not have any behaviour attached and so are not considered as true classes until it is possible to attach behaviour during the processes of transformation. From this point onwards we should ensure that the design transforms that we perform to partition this object-oriented program preserve the behaviour of the program. In presenting the design transformations given below, we assume that the subject system has a large number of small procedures as against a small number of large procedures. If the subject system has a small number of large procedures, then the subject system should go through a process of slicing in which large procedures are sliced into small procedures before attempting the design transformations given below. The design transforms presented below provide only a short description of the transform. In order to communicate the full impact of a design transform, we need a formal template [15], which specifies all the changes that result from a given transform. In the design diagrams presented below, we adopt OMT notation for design description. Given below are some basic transformations:

Simple Partition: Figure 13.1 describes two behaviourally equivalent designs, before and after the partition. The design before partition represents a god class, which requires partitioning due to the non-cohesive nature of this class. This partitioning is useful in order to move out a set of variables and methods which can be placed in a component class. Such variables are usually modified by a group of methods and are unrelated to other sets of methods within the same class, which indicates that these sets of methods and variables define a common behavior and can be classified in a separate class. This kind of partitioning helps in encapsulation of variables and can protect them from inadvertent modification in addition to providing a cohesive class. The example given below only uses one variable and two methods to represent this kind of candidate class. After the transformation, the main class will now have a reference to an object of this new class in the god class which was partitioned. The methods which have been moved out should be called using the appropriate receiver as shown in the usage section in the figure.

Pre-conditions for the application of the transformation

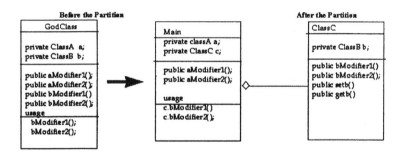

Figure 13.1: Simple Partition

- Instance variable *b* is modified by methods: *bModifier*1(); and *bModifier*2().

- Instance variable *a* is not modified or accessed by *bModifier*1(); and *bModifier*2().

- Methods *aModifier*1 and *aModifier*2 may call methods *bModifier*1() and *bModifier*2().

Partition with Parameterised Methods: Figure 13.2 describes two behaviourally equivalent designs, before and after the partition. The design before partition represents a god class, which requires partitioning due to the non-cohesive nature of this class. It is not always possible to have a very clean separation of concerns as required in the conditions of the first design transformation. The methods in the set to be moved out may access some of the variables of the class to be partitioned. However, the design heuristics suggest that these methods should be ideally located in a class to be defined after a partition, which can be achieved by passing the variables accessed by the methods to be partitioned as parameters. The parameters should be passed by value if the variables are referred to and by reference if the variables are modified. In a pure object-oriented language there is no concept of passing by value, in which case parameters will be passed by reference.

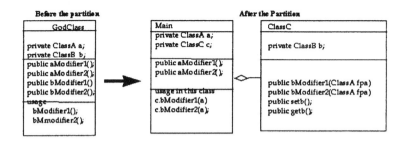

Figure 13.2: Partition with parameterised methods

Pre-conditions for the application of the transformation:

- Instance variable *b* is modified by methods: *bModifier*1(); and *bModifier*2().

- Instance variable *a* is accessed by *bModifier*1() and *bModifier*2().

- Methods *aModifier*1() and *aModifier*2() may call methods $b_m odifier$1(); and $b_m odifier$2().

Partition with Inheritance: Figure 13.3 describes two behaviourally equivalent designs, one before a partition and the other after. Transformations one and two can be applied to obtain aggregation relationships in a system. In a program which starts as a procedural creation aggregation relationships are more probable than inheritance hierarchies. However, it is also possible to discover inheritance hierarchies in many cases where it is a more natural relationship between classes. This transformation provides one such example of obtaining an inheritance hierarchy from existing god class. We would like to point out that the relationship that exists between ClassC and ClassD below could also be modelled (though with different "meaning") using aggregation. The choice between aggregation and inheritance should be made using design heuristics and modelling intuition.

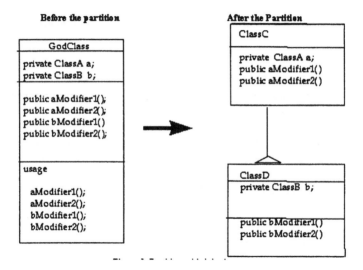

Figure 13.3: Partition with inheritance

Pre-conditions for the application of the transformation

- Instance variable *a* is modified by methods: *aModifier*1(); and *aModifier*2().

- Instance variable *b* is modified by methods: *bModifier*1() and *bModifier*2().

- Methods *bModifier*1() and *bModifier*2() may call methods *aModifier*1() and *aModifier*2().

Extracting the Re-usable Static Class Libraries: Figure 13.4 describes two behaviourally equivalent designs. Most programs contain several utility methods which are required by a large number of classes and which cannot be included in any of the classes. Such methods can all be clustered into a library class, which is declared as public and static indicating that there is no instantiation of this class object. The diagram below explains the design transformation, in which the usage section shows us clearly how these utility classes can be used. It is possible to further partition the utility classes into smaller classes by using design heuristics.

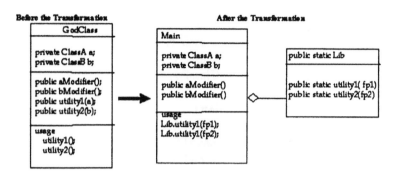

Figure 13.4: Allocation of methods to Static Class libraries

Partition with a reusable static super class: This design transformation partitions a non-cohesive "god" class which is coupled mainly by method calls. It is possible for some methods in a god class to be very closely associated with a sub-set of variables defined in the god class. In such a case it is possible to use a simple partition to spawn off a new class with this set of variables and methods which are closely related to each other. However, the main problem lies in the fact that this set of methods uses some methods from some other set of god-class methods, which are candidates for another class. This can cause a problem owing to the scope rules of strongly-typed object-oriented languages as these two sets of methods will not lie in the same scope after the design transformation. In order to solve this problem, we can use the called methods and their associated variables as super class members and inherit the components into the class containing the calling methods. However, there is a second problem that arises if there are to be two sub-classes in such a situation i.e. the instantiation of two instance variables after the transformation while there was only one variable before the transformation. The solution given below uses the variables of the super class as static variables, thereby creating a single instance of the variables of the super class. It is important to ensure that there is only a single instance of the variables defined by the super class as the god class originally had only a single instance of these global variables, accessible to all the members of the class. The proposed solution incorporates the singleton [8] design pattern.

Structure before transformation: Refer to figure 13.5.

Pre-conditions for the application of the transformation:

- Variables a and b are modified only by *abModifier1*() and *abModifier2*().

- Variables c and d are modified only by *cdModifier1*() and *cdModifier2*() and are not referred to or accessed by *abModifier1*(), *abModifier2*(), *efModifier1*() and *efModifier2*().

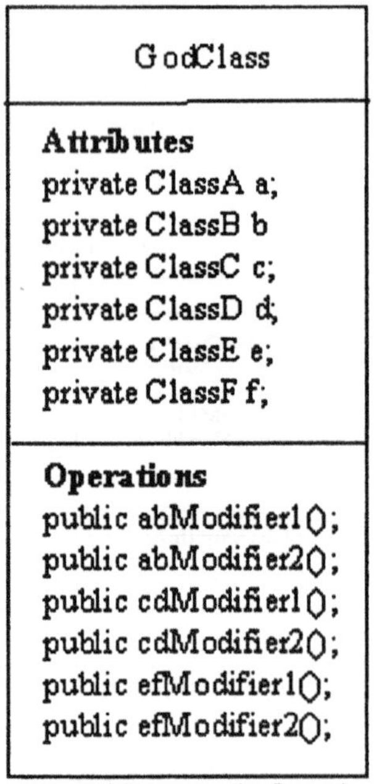

```
┌─────────────────────────────┐
│          GodClass           │
├─────────────────────────────┤
│ Attributes                  │
│ private ClassA a;           │
│ private ClassB b            │
│ private ClassC c;           │
│ private ClassD d;           │
│ private ClassE e;           │
│ private ClassF f;           │
├─────────────────────────────┤
│ Operations                  │
│ public abModifier1();       │
│ public abModifier2();       │
│ public cdModifier1();       │
│ public cdModifier2();       │
│ public efModifier1();       │
│ public efModifier2();       │
└─────────────────────────────┘
```

Figure 13.5: Software architecture before the transformation

- Variables e and f are modified only by *efModifer1()* and *efModifier2()* and are not referred to or accessed by *abModifier1()*, *abModifier2()*, *cdModifier1()* and *cdModifier2()*.

- Method *cdModifier1()* or *cdModifier2()* calls either *abModifier1()* or *abModifier2()*;

- Method *efModifier1()* or *efModifier2()* calls either *abModifier1()* or *abModifier2()*;

- there is a need to have only one instance of variables a and b, which are accessed by all the other methods in the class. Effectively variables a and b act within the class like global variables, which are the conduit for communication between the rest of the system.

Structure after the transformation: Refer to figure 13.6.

13.5 DESIGN TRANSFORMATION PROCESS

13.5.1 Reported techniques for object identification

The reported literature [11, 18, 10, 4, 19, 7, 9] on migration from a procedural architecture to an object-oriented architecture concentrates upon finding and extracting objects and classes using program analysis, by clustering related procedures and data. Algorithms described by Livadas and Roy [11], Liu and Wilde [10] analyse calling and functional dependencies between program components and then identify classes in a subject program.

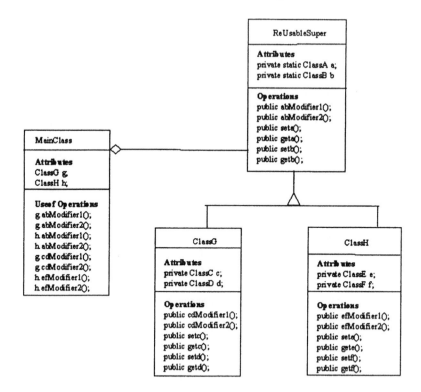

Figure 13.6: Structure of the system after the transformation

The calling dependencies exist where one function calls another, while the functional dependency is defined as the relationship between a function and a variable used within that function.

Global based object identifier (gboi) defines a candidate objects to be a pair (F,x) where F is a set of routines and x is a variable that is referred i.e. accessed or modified by each element of F.

The second algorithm, is type based object identifier (tboi) [11, 10] which clusters together types defined by programmer with functions which use these types for formal parameters or return values. It defines a candidate object in two steps, the first of which clusters a routine with the union of the set of types of all its formal parameters and type of its return value. The second step is based on the intuition that if a routine must be clustered with one of its parameter types, it should be clustered with the most complex of these types [10].

The third algorithm, is a receiver based object identifier (rboi) [11] which clusters together types and functions which modify variables of these types. Receiver based object identifier (rboi) algorithm defines a candidate object as a pair (F,T), where F is a set of routines that modify variables of type T. Receivers are types of variables that are represented either by global variables or pass-by-reference parameters.

These algorithms have been improved upon by Conflora et.al. [4] and Jarzabeck and Woon [9]. While we adopt similar search and clustering processes in identifying objects,

we differ in the fact that we identify basic provable design transforms first and then try
to search for dependencies that satisfy the pre-conditions of the design transforms in the
procedural software. We believe that our approach enables us to prove the equivalence
between a subject system and its transformed equivalent in an easier manner than those
reported in the literature. This approach also ensures that we take into account the scope
rules that govern the communication of information between one class and another.

It enables us to take into account the modern techniques for object-oriented design like
the design patterns. It is possible to identify at least one design transformation for each of
the design patterns described by Gamma.et.al., and apply them on the design of the legacy
code to migrate from a poor structure to a better structure.

These differences can be observed in the transformation Partition with **a reusable static
super class**, in which a design pattern is used, the relationships between the classes are defined, and the scope or visibility of a variable in the other components is decided by declar-
ing a variable to be static/public/private etc. Such design decisions can not be inferred
from the other reported techniques. We believe that migration from procedural architecture
to object-oriented architecture is best addressed by a transformational approach such as
ours, which addresses all the issues connected with a transformation including the usage
aspects of the transformed components. This approach is similar to the approach taken by
Opdyke [12], who concentrates on the refactoring of object oriented systems. We extend
this to procedural software with the help of the assumption we make about the procedural program. This paper provides some of the basic design transformations necessary for
partitioning a large procedural system which can be represented as a single class. We are
working on designing a canonical set of design transforms and a template [15] for reporting
design transforms in an unambiguous manner.

13.5.2   The transformation process

The next question that needs to be addressed is, how are these design transforms chosen
for application and in what order? The answer to this question depends on the relationship
between the transforms and the complexity of the inter-component dependencies considered for a transform. If two transforms are not related to each other, i.e. do not consider the
same inter-component dependencies, then the order in which they are applied should not
affect the resulting design. However, when two transforms take into account the dependencies which are related to each other, then the application of one of the transforms changes
the dependencies and may not permit the application of a second related transform. So we
recommend the application of the transform with the most complex set of inter-component
dependencies first, followed by transforms with less complex inter-component relationships. Based on this argument, we recommend the following application order of design
transforms:

- Extracting the reusable static class libraries,

- Partition with a reusable super class,

- partition with parameterised methods,

- partition with inheritance,

- simple partition.

We have conducted several case studies in re-engineering of software from procedural paradigm to object oriented paradigm and have also reported one such case study [14]. We are reporting one more case study in this paper, but before we do that we describe an interesting observation about object oriented systems and use that in the presentation of this case study.

13.5.3   Resource usage matrix and mbject visualisation

This is an approach for object visualisation which uses two-dimensional view of resource utilisation within a given system. In this analysis, instance variables within a class were represented as columns and the methods within a class as rows in a matrix. If a variable was modified within a method we colour the corresponding cell with blue and if a variable was referred within a method it is coloured green. We observe that the resulting matrix can be classified as a sparse matrix because of localised access due to encapsulation of methods and variables within classes. Such a sparse matrix can be sorted to obtain a diagonal matrix in which all classes are organised along a diagonal. It is now possible to further sort the elements within non-cohesive classes within this diagonal, to ensure that we cluster related methods and variables within a single class. The process of further sorting facilitates class partitioning with the help of design transformations, when there are large non-cohesive classes within an object-oriented system. This approach can be used manually when the classes to be partitioned are not extremely large, but can provide a useful visual feedback in automated systems for large classes such as the 'god' class in a large procedural program.

To transform a procedural program to an object oriented program we start by representing the variables in a system as columns and functions/methods as rows. We also include member fields within types as variables as some of the methods can be associated with these variables only and should be clustered with these variables as such. If a variable is modified by a method we colour the corresponding location in the matrix. The resulting sparse matrix is sorted, to obtain a diagonal matrix and disjoint areas are encapsulated and design transforms applied on the resulting encapsulated areas. It is possible for a variable accessed by a large number of functions or a function which accesses a large number of variables to strongly affect the object identification algorithms. However, because of the visual feedback available from the system it is possible to block out such variables or functions, before reapplying partitioning algorithms, enabling improved object identification. The availability of visual feedback and the option of reapplying partitioning algorithms on selected classes makes this approach an interesting alternative to those reported in the literature. It can be used both in forward and reengineering in order to obtain cohesive small classes from large god classes. Since this technique is used in conjunction with basic design transforms, which preserve the behaviour, we state that we can migrate from a procedural program to an object oriented program while preserving the behaviour of a system. This technique can be used in providing a visual feedback in automated re-engineering systems, but can be used as the starting point in partitioning in a manual restructuring process.

13.6 TRANSFORMATION OF EVENT PROCESSOR SIMULATOR DESIGN

13.6.1 Subject system

Event processor simulator was taken as an example for design extraction and transformation using RESTRUCT. It was originally written in Pascal in a single file totalling over 2500 lines, with 90 procedures, over 100 global variables and 10 user defined types. This program was difficult to comprehend as there was little documentation of its design or comments within the program. It is difficult to maintain such program, let alone modify its structure to migrate to an improved structure. The program components were first loaded into the design database, this was followed by application of design transformation methods. After the transformations the identified objects had a strong relationship to the application domain, so maintainer could understand program better and improve the system structure.

13.6.2 Objects identified using resource usage matrix

Figure 13.7 provides the diagonal sparse matrix after the execution of object identification algorithms on Event Processor Simulator and figure 13.8 provides its OMT representation. One can observe that the classes identified have a strong relationship with domain entities. A processor has registers, memory, stack, alu, cache, busses, IOProcessor and synchronisation mechanism, which are obtained by restructuring processes. Some of the identified classes have very little behaviour other than get and set methods. However, the other classes have a very good behaviour indicating a decentralisation of control among newly identified classes. The only way to know how good our heuristics are in identifying good classes can be measured by metric tools. We are currently implementing one such suite of metrics within the RESTRUCT CASE tool. Eventually it would be possible for a programmer to interactively select a few classes and apply design transformations and then measure the quality of the resulting architecture. Future developments of this CASE tool will provide capabilities to perform design transforms based on the help derived from metrics. We observe in this particular case study there are a large group of utility methods which are used from a large number of other methods within the system. These methods have been placed in a library class which is declared as public and static to ensure that they are available to all the class objects which use them.

13.7 CONCLUSIONS

This paper describes some important concepts that are useful for the migration from a procedural to an object-oriented software architecture. It considers that software development is an evolutionary activity with re-engineering/restructuring as an important process applied repeatedly. It also introduces a novel approach of viewing a procedural program from an object-oriented perspective in which there is single god class which has a large number of global variables and methods, supported by several user-defined classes which have no behaviour but data definitions. This view, coupled with repeated restructuring, enables a seamless migration of behaviour from the god class to other classes using design transformation methods. It distinguishes between the processes of translation and transformation

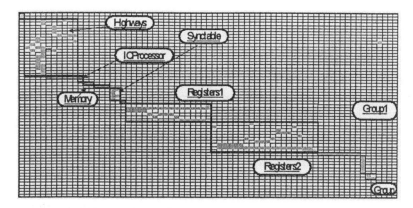

Figure 13.7: Diagonal sparse matrix after the execution of object identification algorithm. The columns represent the global variables and the member fields within the user defined types and the rows represent the functions. The coloured areas indicate that the functions modify the corresponding variable. The enclosed areas are the encapsulated classes.

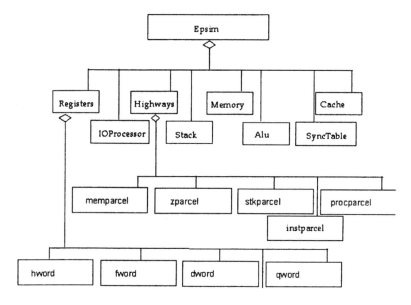

Figure 13.8: Transformed design of Event Processor Simulator

and states that these two are orthogonal to each other, thus enabling us to concentrate on design transformations to migrate from one design to another, leaving the language issues to be handled by translators. Some basic design transformations, which permit partitioning of classes while preserving the system behaviour are described, enabling a series of heuristics to be used in conjunction with design transforms to migrate to a better architecture. These transformations have a foundation based on a modified version of weakest precondition semantics. In this version we define a wp calculus in order to cope with type inheritance, which will be reported soon.

We have also emphasised the distinction between a design specification of a system and a functional specification of a system. Design specification concentrates on the structural design, which defines the organisation of components within a system. Functional specification concentrates on what each component is capable of performing and what a combination of components are capable of performing together in a given design. In order to improve the structure of legacy software, the design of a program should change while retaining its functional capability, which can be achieved by restructuring. Reverse engineering and the subsequent restructuring of software enables migration from poorly structured programs to systems with an object-oriented topological structure. This kind of migration enables a maintainer of software to obtain the full benefits of a modern methodology, while ensuring the continued availability of software during the restructuring processes. We have used these ideas in the design of a CASE tool called RESTRUCT for re-engineering software systems. We have also conducted three case studies with programs greater than 2500 lines in length, with encouraging results. The main conclusion we draw from our discussion is the need to identify a canonical set of design transforms and the order in which these can be applied on the structure of existing software architecture to improve the same.

13.8 REFERENCES

[1] K. Barclay and J. Savage. Language for object Oriented modelling taken from Object Oriented Design with C++, Prentice Hall Publishers, 1996, pp. 35–75.

[2] J.A. Bergstra, J. Heering and P. Klint. Module Algebra, JACM Vol. 37, No 2, 1990, pp. 335–372.

[3] G. Booch. Object-Oriented Design with Applications, The Benjamin/Cummings Publishing Company, 1991.

[4] G. Confora, A. Cimitile, M. Munro and Tortorella. A precise method for Identifying Reusable Abstract data Types in Code. Proc. Conference on Software Maintenance, British Colombia, 1994, pp. 404–413.

[5] L. Feijs and H.B.M. Jonkers. METEOR and beyond: industrialising formal methods, In: K.H. Bennet (ED.) Software Engineering Environments: Research and Practice, Ellis Horwood Limited, 1989, pp. 255–274.

[6] L. Feijs. Formalisation of Design Methods, Ellis Horwood Series in Computers and their Applications, 1993.

[7] H. Gall and R. Klosch. Finding Objects in Procedural programs. An Alternative approach. Proc. 2nd Working Conference on Reverse Engineering, WCRE95, Toronto, 1995, pp. 208–216.

[8] E. Gamma, R. Helm, R. Johnson and Vlissides. Design Patterns, Addison-Wesley Professional Computing Series, 1994.

[9] S. Jarzabeck and I. Woon. Toward a Precise Description of Reverse Engineering Methods and Tools, Proceedings of First Euromicro Conference on Software Maintenance and Reengineering, Berlin, 1997, pp. 3–10.

[10] S.S. Liu and N. Wilde. Identifying Objects in a Conventional Procedural Language: An Example of Data Design Recovery, Proc. of the Conference on Software Maintenance, 1990.

[11] P.E. Livadas, and P.K. Roy. Program dependence analysis, IEEE Conference on Software Maintenance, 1992.

[12] W.F. Opdyke. Refactoring Object Oriented Frameworks, Ph.D Thesis, Submitted to University of Illinois at Urban-Champagne, 1992.

[13] S. Pidaparthi and G. Cysewski. Migration to Object Oriented System Structure Using Design Transformation Methods, Proceedings of The Fifth International Conference Information Systems Development, 1996, pp. 555–571.

[14] S. Pidaparthi and G. Cysewski. Case Study in Migration to Object-Oriented System Structure Using Design Transformation Methods, Proceedings of First Euro-Micro Working Conference on Software Maintenance and Re-engineering, 17-19 March, 1997, pp. 128–135.

[15] S. Pidaparthi, P. Luker and H. Zedan. A Template for Design Transform Specification, 1998, http://www.cms.dmu.ac.uk/~sp/postscripts/ICSE98.ps

[16] A.J. Riel. Object-Oriented Design Heuristics. Addison-Wesley Professional Computing Series, 1997.

[17] J. Rumbaugh, M. Blaha, W. Premerlani, F. Eddy and W. Lorensen. Object-Oriented Modeling and Design, Prentice-Hall, 1991.

[18] H.M. Sneed. Migration of Procedurally Oriented COBOL Programs in an Object-Oriented Architecture, Proc. IEEE Conference on Software Maintenance, San Deigo, 1992, pp. 266–271.

[19] H.M. Sneed and E. Nyary. Extracting Object Oriented Specification from Procedurally Oriented Programs, Proc 2nd Working Conference on Reverse Engineering, WCRE95, Toronto, 1995, pp. 217–226.

[20] Unified Modelling Language, Available at http://www.rational.com/

DIGITAL SIGNAL PROCESSING: Software Solutions and Applications
J.M. BLACKLEDGE and **M.J. TURNER**, Department of Mathematical Sciences, Faculty of Computing Science and Engineering, De Montfort University, Leicester

ISBN: 1-898563-48-9   200 pages   1998

Complete with CD-ROM, this book delivers the necessary mathematical and computational background and some processing techniques used for Digital Signal Processing (DSP). Emphasises software solutions for which source code is provided.

Contents: PART I: MATHEMATICAL BACKGROUND - Fourier series and Fourier integrals; Convolution integrals; Analytical signals and the Hilbert transform; The sampling theorem; PART II: COMPUTATIONAL BACKGROUND - Sampling and aliasing; The convolution sum; The discrete Fourier transform; The fast Fourier transform; Computing with FFT's; Leakage and windowing; Digital filters; The FIR and IIR filter; PART III: PROCESSING TECHNIQUES - Inverse filters; The Wiener filter; Constrained deconvolution; The matched filter; Bayesian estimation; Maximum entropy filters; Non-stationary deconvolution; Super resolution techniques; Statistical filters; Singular value decomposition; The Kalman filter; Dynamic programming techniques; Fractal analysis of statistically self-affine signals; Wavelets.

IMAGE PROCESSING RESEARCH: Mathematical Methods, Algorithms, Applications
J.M. BLACKLEDGE, Department of Mathematical Sciences, Faculty of Computing Science and Engineering, De Montfort University, Leicester

ISBN: 1-898563-61-6   *ca.* 300 pages   1999

An up-to-date record of international research on image restoration on the interaction of image processing as it relates to mathematical modelling. It covers in great detail its reconstruction and restoration, image comprehension, fractals and wavelets, pattern recognition and image understanding. It is published for The Institute of Mathematics and Applications (IMA, UK), from the 1988 Imaging and Digital Imaging Conference, co-sponsored with The Institute of Physics. The level is appropriate for advanced study and advanced research for applied mathematicians, computer scientists, electrical and electro-mechanical engineers, and scientists working in IT, remote sensing, medical.imaging, vision systems, spectroscopy, virtual reality, military technology, electro-optics, biochemistry and cartigraphy.

Printed and bound by CPI Group (UK) Ltd, Croydon, CR0 4YY

03/10/2024

01040339-0012